CURRENT PERSPECTIVES ON LEARNING DISABILITIES

ADVANCES IN SPECIAL EDUCATION

Series Editor: Anthony F. Rotatori

ADVANCES IN SPECIAL EDUCATION   VOLUME 16

CURRENT PERSPECTIVES ON LEARNING DISABILITIES

EDITED BY

SANDRA BURKHARDT
St. Xavier University, USA

FESTUS E. OBIAKOR
University of Wisconsin-Milwaukee, USA

ANTHONY F. ROTATORI
St. Xavier University, USA

2004

ELSEVIER

JAI

Amsterdam – Boston – Heidelberg – London – New York – Oxford
Paris – San Diego – San Francisco – Singapore – Sydney – Tokyo

ELSEVIER B.V.
Sara Burgerhartstraat 25
P.O. Box 211
1000 AE Amsterdam
The Netherlands

ELSEVIER Inc.
525 B Street, Suite 1900
San Diego
CA 92101-4495
USA

ELSEVIER Ltd
The Boulevard, Langford
Lane, Kidlington
Oxford OX5 1GB
UK

ELSEVIER Ltd
84 Theobalds Road
London
WC1X 8RR
UK

First edition 2004

British Library Cataloguing in Publication Data
A catalogue record is available from the British Library.

ISBN: 0-7623-1130-4
ISSN: 0270-4013

⊗ The paper used in this publication meets the requirements of ANSI/NISO Z39.48-1992 (Permanence of Paper). Printed in The Netherlands.

CONTENTS

v

LIST OF CONTRIBUTORS

Candace Baker	School of Education, St. Xavier University, Chicago, IL, USA
Jeffrey P. Bakken	Department of Special Education, Illinois State University, Normal, IL, USA
Richael Barger-Anderson	Department of Special Education, Slippery Rock University of Pennsylvania, Slippery Rock, PA, USA
Sandra Burkhardt	Department of Psychology, St. Xavier University, Chicago, IL, USA
Meg Carroll	School of Education, St. Xavier University, Chicago, IL, USA
Pamela Castellanos	School of Education, St. Xavier University, Chicago, IL, USA
Julie A. Deisinger	Department of Psychology, St. Xavier University, Chicago, IL, USA
Elizabeth Dooley	Department of Educational Theory and Practice, West Virginia University, Morgantown, WV, USA
Patrice A. Fulcher	Attorney-At-Law, The Fulcher Law Group, Inc. Atlanta, GA, USA
Patrick A. Grant	Department of Special Education, Slippery Rock University of Pennsylvania, Slippery Rock, PA, USA
Beverly Gulley	School of Education, St. Xavier University, Chicago, IL, USA

Dani La Porte	Co-Founder and Co-Director, Wings Academy, Milwaukee, WI, USA
Nicola Leather	Co-Founder and Co-Director, Wings Academy, Milwaukee, WI, USA
Sunday O. Obi	Department of Education and Human Services, Kentucky State University, Frankport, KY, USA
Festus E. Obiakor	Department of Exceptional Education, University of Wisconsin-Milwaukee, Milwaukee, WI, USA
Ann Richards	Department of Educational Theory and Practice, West Virginia University, Morgantown, WV, USA
Anthony F. Rotatori	Department of Psychology, St. Xavier University, Chicago, IL, USA
Dale Septeowski	Department of Psychology, Concordia University, River Forest, IL, USA
Roger Stefani	Clinical Psychologist, Private Practice, Orland Park, IL, USA
Cheryl A. Utley	Juniper Gardens Children's Project, University of Kansas, Kansas City, KS, USA
Tim Wahlberg	Clinical Psychologist, Private Practice, Geneva, IL, USA
Brian W. Wojcik	Department of Special Education, Illinois State University, Normal, IL, USA

PREFACE

Students with learning disabilities constitute the single largest category of special education need. Early identification and intervention of learning disabilities can positively impact a child's academic performance by making achievement possible. Undetected learning disability may lead even an adult student to struggle with poor grades, low self-esteem, loss of interest in higher education, and reduced employment opportunities. Thus, learning disabilities, though considered both high-incidence and often mild in the continuum of disabling conditions, have a significant long-term impact on education, social adjustment and career achievement.

This volume reports current trends in the field of learning disabilities and related areas that impact learning disabilities. There are forces outside of the schoolhouse that impact the field of learning disabilities, including advances in evaluation and testing as well as diagnostic imaging of the functioning brain. There are evolving ways of conceptualizing learning differences that include multicultural perspectives and challenges to conventional views of intelligence. There are new federal laws that place performance demands upon schools.

Testing occupies a prominent role in the field of learning disabilities, both in terms of establishing eligibility for special education services as well as marking academic achievement. Standardized testing by federal mandate specifically requires that the test scores of students with disabilities be reported as a subgroup of a school's overall test results, and deficiencies in the progress of this subgroup may result in sanctions for the school. In the classroom teachers are subject to an increasing emphasis on general education as the venue of choice for the instruction of all students, including those with learning disabilities. The external pressures have never been greater than now for both special and general educators to demonstrate that children with learning disabilities are benefiting from curricular modifications.

The future of education for students with learning disabilities appears bright. New technology is expanding the possibilities for instruction for all students, including those students with learning disabilities. Model programs that provide innovative approaches to instruction within charter schools are in the forefront in the effort to establish best practices that provide measurable results. Teacher preparation programs are leading the way in producing educators who are ready to teach children with learning disabilities. The challenge of instructing students with disabilities in the general education setting brings increased opportunity for collaboration between general and special educators, with general educators offering more instruction to students with special needs, and special educators becoming highly qualified in the general education curriculum.

School counselors encounter students with learning disabilities who are planning for college and careers in a climate of societal expectation that promotes a college education as an obtainable goal for all students. Helping students with learning disabilities turn dreams into plans requires school and career counselors to have a working understanding of the academic, social and behavioral characteristics of learning disabilities across the lifespan. Similarly, counselors can advocate for students with disabilities, and help students learn to advocate for themselves, when they are informed regarding the impact of laws that establish the rights of persons with disabilities.

The book is composed of 13 chapters that address prominent trends in learning disabilities. The book should prove valuable to general and special education teachers, school psychologists, teacher educators, and school and career counselors. A secondary audience is graduate students enrolled in special education and counseling graduate programs.

Sandra Burkhardt
Festus E. Obiakor
Anthony F. Rotatori
Editors

CONCEPTUALIZATIONS OF LEARNING DISABILITIES: BEYOND THE ABILITY-ACHIEVEMENT DISCREPANCY

Julie A. Deisinger

The term *learning disability* (LD) refers to difficulties with academic abilities such as reading, writing, spelling, and mathematics (American Psychiatric Association, 2000; Sarkees-Wircenski & Scott, 2003). Estimates concerning the prevalence of this disorder vary, depending on the definition of LD that is used. As many as one in seven Americans, or about 15% of the United States population, has some form of LD (Sarkees-Wircenski & Scott, 2003). An even greater percentage of children may be affected, with prevalence rates ranging as high as 30% (Sarkees-Wircenski & Scott, 2003). Children with LD comprise the largest category of students who receive special education services (Beitchman, 1998; Coutinho et al., 2002; Spear-Swerling & Sternberg, 1998).

In the 1960s LD was called "minimal brain dysfunction" (Silver & Hagin, 2002, p. 99), suggesting that it is associated with problems in the central nervous system. However, this term was eventually abandoned because it lacked clarity. Too many disparate conditions with differing etiologies were included in this category, making it hard for educators to identify them (Silver & Hagin, 2002). Another limitation of conceptualizing LD as minimal brain dysfuction was that it provided no meaningful guidance for treatment planning (Hallahan & Kauffman, 1997).

Current Perspectives on Learning Disabilities
Advances in Special Education, Volume 16, 1–20
Copyright © 2004 by Elsevier Ltd.
All rights of reproduction in any form reserved
ISSN: 0270-4013/doi:10.1016/S0270-4013(04)16001-7

Currently, the most widely used definition of LD can be found in the Individuals with Disabilities Education Act (IDEA; cited in Kavale & Forness, 2000). This definition describes LD as

> a disorder in one or more of the basic psychological processes involved in understanding or in using language, spoken or written, in which the disorder may manifest itself in an imperfect ability to listen, think, speak, read, write, spell, or to do mathematical calculations (U.S. Office of Education, 1977, cited in Wicks-Nelson & Israel, 2003, p. 265).

The IDEA definition of LD stipulates that the aforementioned academic difficulties are not due to sensory, motor, emotional, or intellectual deficits, or to a lack of educational opportunity (Wicks-Nelson & Israel, 2003). However, it has been criticized for its vagueness and undue emphasis on exclusionary criteria (Kavale & Forness, 2000; Sorrell, 2000; Sternberg & Grigorenko, 2001; Wicks-Nelson & Israel, 2003). Therefore, other definitions have been suggested as alternative ways to conceptualize LD and to guide practice concerning LD assessment. One of these alternatives involves the notion of discrepancy (Bigler et al., 1998; Hallahan & Kauffman, 1997; Kavale & Forness, 2000).

In 1977, the United States Office of Education issued an operational definition of LD to guide the process for identification of learning disabilities. This definition called for the presence of "a severe discrepancy between achievement and intellectual ability" (U.S. Office of Education, 1977, cited in Sorrell, 2000, p. 57) in one or more academically related skills such as reading comprehension, written expression, and mathematics reasoning (Sorrell, 2000). Another aspect of this definition is that LD manifests as unexpected academic underachievement (Fuchs et al., 2002; Scruggs & Mastropieri, 2002). Underachievement may be determined in relation to age, grade, or level of intellectual functioning (American Psychiatric Association, 2000; Beitchman, 1998; Wicks-Nelson & Israel, 2003).

Since the federal government released its operational definition of LD, the concept of discrepancy has served as the primary criterion for identification of learning disorders (Kavale, 2001). Various formulas have been used to calculate discrepancies indicative of LD (Van den Broeck, 2002). The purposes of this chapter are to discuss the use of these formulas, to describe their merits and limitations, and to consider alternative methods of defining and identifying LD.

CURRENT FORMS OF ABILITY-ACHIEVEMENT DISCREPANCY

Four types of calculations are currently being used to identify discrepancies between intellectual ability and achievement. These include deviation from grade level, expectancy formulas, simple standard score differences, and regression-based differences (Fletcher et al., 1994; Gresham, 2001; Sattler, 1992; Van den Broeck, 2002).

Calculations involving deviation from grade level are the simplest way to define underachievement (Sattler, 1992). For example, if a child obtains a grade-equivalent score on an achievement test that is two or more years below his or her current grade placement, this difference could be considered a discrepancy (Hallahan & Kauffman, 1997).

Expectancy formulas calculate discrepancies by including measures of mental age (MA) and chronological age (CA), and by using expected grade placement instead of actual placement. Sattler (1992, p. 607) gave the following example:

$$\text{Expected Grade Equivalent} = \left[\frac{2\text{MA} + \text{CA}}{3} \right] - 5$$

The MA used in this formula is obtained from an ability test such as a standardized intelligence test. Upon completion of this calculation, the expected grade equivalent would be compared against actual grade placement to determine whether a discrepancy exists.

According to Van den Broeck (2002), the most widely used method for calculating discrepancies relies on simple standard score differences. Standard scores on tests of intellectual ability and academic achievement can be compared to see if they are significantly different, e.g. one or more standard deviations apart (Sattler, 1992; Van den Broeck, 2002).

Regression-based formulas often are recommended as the best approach for calculating a discrepancy (Fletcher et al., 1994; Morgan et al., 2000; Silver & Hagin, 2002; Tomasi & Weinberg, 1999). These formulas recognize that when there is an imperfect correlation between intelligence quotient (IQ) scores and achievement test scores, the statistical phenomenon of *regression toward the mean* may occur on at least one of these scores (Sattler, 1992; Van den Broeck, 2002). For example, someone who obtains a high score on an IQ test is likely to receive a somewhat lower score on an achievement test. Similarly, a person who receives a low score on an IQ test may obtain a higher score on an achievement test. In both cases, the discrepancies between test scores would be due to regression toward the mean, rather than LD. These differences in scores would cause over-identification of LD in individuals with high IQ scores and under-identification of LD in those with low IQ scores (Van den Broeck, 2002). To correct for regression toward the mean, a regression formula is employed to calculate a difference between actual and predicted achievement, using a predicted achievement score derived on the basis of the IQ score. If the difference between predicted and actual achievement exceeds a specified criterion, such as

1.5 to 2 standard deviations, then it is believed to represent a significant discrepancy (Van den Broeck, 2002).

SUPPORT FOR DISCREPANCY MODELS

Some support for the ongoing use of discrepancy models can be found. Researcher Kenneth Kavale, whose work has been published extensively in the educational literature, wrote that "discrepancy is an important and legitimate concept associated with LD" (Kavale, 2001, p. 7). The American Psychiatric Association's (2000) description of learning disorders specifies the need for a discrepancy of one to two or more standard deviations between achievement and IQ. Additionally, in summarizing the practice parameters adopted by the American Academy of Child and Adolescent Psychiatry for the assessment of LD, Beitchman (1998) noted that the diagnosis of LD depends upon the existence of a discrepancy between potential ability and actual academic performance.

One valuable aspect of discrepancy formulas is that they provide an objective measure of LD. Scruggs and Mastropieri (2002) feared that discontinuing their use would lead to over-identification of LD. More importantly, current legal definitions of LD are based on discrepancy models (cf. Gunderson & Siegel, 2001; Sorrell, 2000; Wicks-Nelson & Israel, 2003). According to Willson and Reynolds (2002),

> researchers are free to advance many alternative models for learning disabilities, and in fact they have done so continuously, but in the reality of the therapeutic situation, practitioners must use data based on the legal definition of a discrepancy between intellectual functioning and academic achievement (p. 205).

Results of a recent survey examining the educational practices of 40 states found that most states use a definition of LD that is virtually identical to the federal definition (Kidder-Ashley et al., 2000). Similarly, most school districts employ discrepancy formulas to classify children with LD (O'Malley et al., 2002; Silver & Hagin, 2002; Swanson, 2000).

Further support for the utility of discrepancy models may be found when comparing children with and without LD. Scruggs and Mastropieri (2002) cited a 1990 study of over 1700 students in Indiana, indicating that students identified as having LD differed significantly from students who were referred for evaluation but not found to have LD. These authors also cited a 1991 study conducted in Iowa, involving a survey of over 500 teachers who instructed students with LD. Over 80% of these teachers reportedly agreed that LD is associated with a discrepancy between ability and achievement.

A final point in favor of discrepancy models is that they allow for the possibility of significant learning difficulties even in the absence of below-average intellectual abilities. Children of average or above-average intelligence who exhibit learning problems are eligible for intervention according to discrepancy-based definitions of LD (Silver & Hagin, 2002).

CRITICISMS OF THE DISCREPANCY APPROACH

Despite these findings, in recent years there has been growing concern over the use of discrepancy formulas (Berninger, 2001; Dean & Burns, 2002; Kavale & Forness, 2000; Spear-Swerling & Sternberg, 1998; Stanovich, 1999; Torgesen, 2001a, b; Vaughn et al., 2003; Zera & Lucian, 2001). One problem associated with discrepancy models is the lack of consensus regarding which model is most appropriate for LD identification (Fuchs et al., 2002; Gresham, 2001; Morgan et al., 2000; Silver & Hagin, 2000; Stanovich, 1999; Van den Broeck, 2002; Willson & Reynolds, 2002). A 1992 study cited by Scruggs and Mastropieri (2002) found that "seven of the lowest 10 states in rates of identification employed a specific method of assessing a discrepancy, while only 2 of the highest 10 states employed such a requirement" (p. 156).

According to Van den Broeck (2002), models based on either deviation from grade level or expectancy formulas are statistically flawed. As Fletcher et al. (1994) explained, the problem with these two methods is that they "incorporate uneven metrics across ages, such that disability at one age is not comparable with disability at another age" (p. 7). Silver and Hagin (2002) also noted that discrepancies based on deviation from grade level might under-identify LD in children with higher IQ scores and over-identify LD in those with lower IQ scores.

The use of simple standard difference scores or regression-based discrepancies may be problematic as well, due to their tendency to yield different results. Willson and Reynolds (2002) noted that standard difference scores are more likely than regression-based discrepancy scores to identify LD cases when the IQ score is above average than when the IQ score is below average. In contrast, Van den Broeck (2002) claimed that regression formulas too often identify underachievement among persons with low IQ scores while failing to identify underachievers among persons with high IQ scores. Such conflicting reports promote confusion about the best approach to use for the identification of LD.

Another set of criticisms regarding the use of discrepancy models involves the use of intelligence tests in the assessment of LD. As highlighted by Spear-Swerling and Sternberg (1998), an erroneous assumption underlying the use of IQ in discrepancy calculations is that an IQ score can serve as a perfect predictor of achievement. However, Tanner (2001) noted that ability and achievement are not always closely correlated. Therefore, the assumption that they are correlated raises questions about whether regression-based discrepancies can accurately identify LD.

A second flaw regarding the use of IQ scores in discrepancy formulas is the supposition that intelligence and achievement are independent constructs (Wicks-Nelson & Israel, 2003). This assumption overlooks the possibility that poor academic achievement may adversely affect performance on an intelligence test and lead to a lowered IQ score (Hallahan & Kauffman, 1997; Scruggs & Mastropieri, 2002; Wicks-Nelson & Israel, 2003; Zera & Lucian, 2001). For example, someone who is a poor reader consequently may have deficient knowledge of vocabulary and other information. These deficits would hinder performance on an IQ test and decrease the likelihood of obtaining a significant discrepancy between IQ and achievement (Hallahan & Kauffman, 1997; Periera-Laird et al., 1999; Silver & Hagin, 2002). Similarly, Gunderson and Siegel (2001) stated that persons with LD might have difficulties with skills that affect performance on an IQ test, such as memory, language, or fine-motor abilities. Problems in these areas might lead to underestimates of intellectual functioning and thereby reduce the likelihood of detecting significant discrepancies.

A third objection that has been raised about the use of IQ tests to determine discrepancies is that intelligence may not be relevant to LD (Badian, 1999; Kavale, 2001; Vaughn et al., 2003). For example, Stanovich (1999) and Gunderson and Siegel (2001) have argued that IQ scores do not shed light on the nature of reading disorder. These authors cited empirical evidence indicating that poor readers with high IQ scores do not differ from poor readers with low IQ scores in the processing mechanism that contributes to word recognition problems (Stanovich, 1999) and in scores on reading tests (Siegel, 1988, cited in Gunderson & Siegel, 2001).

A fourth criticism concerning the inclusion of IQ tests in LD evaluations is that IQ tests are culturally and linguistically biased (Gunderson & Siegel, 2001). Culture, language, and socioeconomic status (SES) are factors that may confound performance on an IQ test (Gunderson & Siegel, 2001). Therefore, persons from minority groups, those who are being tested with instruments in a language other than their language of origin, and those from low SES backgrounds may not obtain IQ scores that are truly representative of their intellectual abilities. This error would be expected to result in lack of access to educational assistance due to a failure to meet the discrepancy criterion for identification of LD (Gunderson & Siegel, 2001). Coutinho et al. (2002) reported that in 10 of 15 cities surveyed in 1994, students of Hispanic descent were underrepresented among LD student populations. Two other studies (Colarusso, 2001; Warner et al., 2002) mentioned that African American students typically were underrepresented among those identified as having LD.

However, Coutinho et al. (2002) noted that as poverty increases, so does the likelihood that African-American and Hispanic students, as well as male

Asian students, will be identified as learning disabled. This information supports Gunderson and Siegel's (2001) contention that SES affects the use of IQ tests in LD evaluations.

Identification of LD in minority populations also is negatively affected by psychometric problems when using regression-based discrepancy formulas. Warner et al. (2002) stated that regression equations should include reliability measurements for tests used in an LD evaluation. However, such reliabilities are derived from normative samples that consist mainly of European American individuals; therefore, these measurements may not apply equally to other ethnic groups. Furthermore, regression lines that are used to predict achievement on the basis of IQ are not the same for all ethnic groups. Warner et al. indicated that regression lines derived from normative samples of European Americans tend to inflate predicted achievement scores for children from ethnic minorities, thus making it more likely that they will be identified as having LD.

In addition to culture and ethnicity, age may be a variable that confounds the use of discrepancy formulas (Gunderson & Siegel, 2001; Periera-Laird et al., 1999). Some authors (e.g. Badian, 1999; Kavale, 2001; Silver et al., 1999; Vaughn et al., 2003) have indicated that discrepancy scores may not be stable over time. Therefore, children's discrepancy scores may change as the children grow older (cf. Badian, 1999). Large discrepancies are believed to indicate more serious problems for younger children than for older children (Wicks-Nelson & Israel, 2003). Yet some authors (e.g. Dean & Burns, 2002; Hallahan & Kauffman, 1997) have contended that discrepancies between predicted and actual achievement would be hard to identify in children younger than 10 years of age because such children would not be expected to have attained high levels of academic achievement. Additionally, children might have to be older (e.g. having already completed first grade) in order to exceed the floor level of achievement tests (Stuebing et al., 2002; Vaughn et al., 2003).

Age is a factor that affects LD identification not only for young children but also for adults. Gregg et al. (1999) remarked that the construct of discrepancy has not been well defined in relation to adults. As a result, adults' eligibility for LD services in higher education or vocational rehabilitation settings may differ across states. Furthermore, Gregg et al. stated that the use of discrepancy models might fail to identify LD in adults with moderate to severe learning disabilities.

Additional criticism of discrepancy models relates to their inability to distinguish LD from low achievement (Badian, 1999; Elksnin et al., 2001; Fletcher et al., 1994, 2001; Kavale, 2001; Scruggs & Mastropieri, 2002). Much of the professional literature concerning this topic compares poor readers who have been diagnosed with LD on the basis of discrepancy criteria versus poor readers without LD. Scruggs and Mastropieri (2002) reported that poor readers with IQ-achievement discrepancies did not differ from poor readers with lower aptitude scores on tests of reading, spelling, and language. Other studies have reported similar patterns regarding mathematics disabilities and speech-language disorders (Fletcher et al., 2001; Jimenez Gonzalez & Garcia Espinel, 1999). "Children who meet discrepancy definitions just do not show major differences relative to children whose poor achievement is consistent with IQ" (Fletcher et al., 2001, p. 3).

Yet another problem associated with the use of discrepancy formulas is the possibility that gifted students with LD may not be diagnosed. Approximately 2–10% of children enrolled in gifted education programs have a learning disability, but an estimated 41% of gifted students with LD are not diagnosed as such until they reach college (McEachern & Bornot, 2001). Failure to properly identify LD in gifted students may be due to the type of discrepancy formula used. For example, gifted students with LD whose academic performance is consistent with grade level would not meet the discrepancy criterion when deviation from grade level is the formula used to determine eligibility (cf. Little, 2001). Also, as noted earlier, regression-based discrepancies are less likely to identify LD in persons with high IQ scores (Van den Broeck, 2002). As a result of such errors, gifted students with undiagnosed LD may struggle to maintain average academic performance (Little, 2001) and may be excluded from specialized instruction (McEachern & Bornot, 2001). On the other hand, formulas that do not correct for regression may over-identify children with high IQ scores as having LD (Spear-Swerling & Sternberg, 1998; Stanovich, 1999).

Discrepancy formulas to identify LD also have been criticized as difficult to implement. The use of regression-based formulas requires not only standardized achievement scores but also validity and reliability coefficients for IQ and achievement tests. However, these coefficients frequently are unavailable (Tomasi & Weinberg, 1999). Correlations between IQ and achievement tests, which also are required for regression analyses, may be unknown as well (Spear-Swerling & Sternberg, 1998). Thus, clinicians are more likely to employ less psycho-metrically acceptable methods such as deviation from grade level (Tomasi & Weinberg, 1999).

Furthermore, not all states use discrepancy formulas involving the same standardized scores. For example, Coffey and Obringer (2000) noted that most states employ discrepancy formulas in which achievement scores are compared with only the Full Scale IQ score. However, in Mississippi, discrepancy scores may be calculated using any of the three IQ scores obtained from the third edition of the Wechsler Intelligence Scale for Children, i.e. Verbal IQ, Performance IQ, or Full Scale IQ. Coffey and Obringer anticipated that this practice would most likely result in the over-identification of LD among at-risk students in rural settings.

Another concern raised about the use of discrepancy formulas is that some children who may have legitimate learning disabilities but who do not obtain a significant IQ-achievement discrepancy may be excluded from receiving academic help (Gunderson & Siegel, 2001; Wicks-Nelson & Israel, 2003; Zera & Lucian, 2001). One reason for not obtaining a significant discrepancy might pertain to poor performance on an IQ test (Wicks-Nelson & Israel, 2003). Gunderson and Siegel (2001) cited a 1998 study by Berninger in which only 44% of students with poor reading achievement demonstrated a significant discrepancy between IQ and achievement. Therefore, 56% of children who need help for reading problems do not receive it due to having low IQ scores.

An alternative explanation for failing to obtain a significant discrepancy might be adequate performance on achievement tests despite ongoing difficulties with daily classwork. An investigation by Morgan et al. (2000) found that 65% of children who demonstrated information processing difficulties in classroom settings but who obtained adequate scores on standardized achievement tests would not receive an LD diagnosis on the basis of discrepancy criteria.

Finally, the use of discrepancy scores to identify LD may be inappropriate because it gives educators "a false sense of precision" (Hallahan & Kauffman, 1997, p. 165). Defining LD in terms of a single score fails to convey its complexity and heterogeneity (Berninger, 2001; Hallahan & Kauffman, 1997; Sternberg & Grigorenko, 2001). Assessment procedures to identify discrepancies do not provide information about the types of learning difficulties that a person may be experiencing (cf. Berninger, 2001; Fletcher et al., 2001; Kavale & Forness, 2000) nor do they indicate the types of interventions that might be most helpful in remediating such difficulties (Gresham, 2001; Kavale & Forness, 2000; Spear-Swerling & Sternberg, 1998).

PROPOSED ALTERNATIVE CONCEPTUALIZATIONS OF LD

As noted by Kavale (2001), "The deification and reification of discrepancy have obscured some fundamental considerations" (p. 6) such as those already described. Educational researchers and clinicians are seeking more empirically supported and practically applicable conceptualizations of LD.

Several authors (e.g. Fletcher et al., 2001; Torgesen, 2001a, b; Swanson, 2000) have suggested that LD might be most appropriately conceptualized as intrinsic deficits in information processing. Torgesen (2001b) defined intrinsic processing as "domain-specific processing capabilities that arise relatively early in development and are usually executed automatically" (p. 3). However, this same author (2001a) cited research by Swanson and Siegel implying that these deficits are general rather than domain-specific and that they involve impairment in sustained attention, resulting in problems on tasks that demand simultaneous information processing and storage.

The advantages of an intrinsic processing deficit model of LD are its focus on the assessment of cognitive processes specifically related to learning difficulties and its potential for earlier identification of children with LD (Torgesen, 2001b). Torgesen (2001a, b) claimed that the current emphasis on the discrepancy construct creates a situation in which children must first experience academic failures before they are identified with learning difficulties. He believed that direct diagnosis of learning processes might identify students at risk for LD before they begin receiving formal academic instruction. Torgesen (2001b) also stated that "direct assessment of processing weaknesses would allow instruction to be targeted on all children who have common learning problems, not just on those who satisfy an arbitrary discrepancy criterion" (p. 4).

In contrast to the idea of general deficits in intrinsic cognitive processing, Stanovich (1998, cited in Scruggs & Mastropieri, 2002) proposed a processing deficit model with specific relevance for reading disorder. Stanovich (1999) asserted that differences in phonological processing (e.g. problems in associating specific phonemes with specific combinations of letters; cf. Berninger, 2001) could allow poor readers with LD to be distinguished from poor readers without LD. He recommended that a discrepancy between reading ability and listening comprehension should be used in place of the traditional IQ-achievement discrepancy to identify reading disability (Carver & Clark, 1998). This model may prove useful because approximately 90% of students with LD demonstrate academic difficulty primarily in reading ability (Kavale & Forness, 2000). Therefore, although Stanovich's model is intended for a particular form of LD, it may have broader applicability.

While the concept of intrinsic processing deficits may be preferable to discrepancy-based definitions of LD, it has its own drawbacks. Several recent publications (Dean & Burns, 2002; Kavale & Forness, 2000; Scruggs & Mastropieri, 2002) expressed concerns that processing disorders are vague hypothetical constructs requiring more specific definition and research if they are to be useful in explaining the nature of LD.

Zera and Lucian (2001) endorsed another definition of LD involving a pervasive problem in self-organizing systems. Similar to Torgesen (2001a), these authors cited studies supporting the idea that problems in working memory are associated with difficulties in reading, writing, and mathematics. Additionally, they suggested that deficits in self-regulatory executive functions such as planning, decision-making, and self-monitoring, as well as deficits in simultaneous information processing and cognitive flexibility, all might contribute to problems in reading comprehension and mathematical problem-solving. According to Zera and Lucian, a theoretical model of LD that is based on the self-organizational capacities of the brain acknowledges the complexity of the LD construct. While these authors noted that skills specifically related to various academic domains should be assessed, they also emphasized the need for comprehensive evaluation of cognitive processing deficits in such abilities as attention, memory, and sequential reasoning. Zera and Lucian further highlighted the need to assess academic strengths as well as weaknesses, and to consider the dynamic relationship between learning and other factors such as motivation and emotional state, when trying to determine whether a student should be classified as having LD.

Still another conceptualization of LD calls for a "dual discrepancy – the student *both* performs below the *level* evidenced by classroom peers and shows a learning *rate* substantially below that of classroom peers" (Gresham, 2001, p. 6). This model, also known as the treatment validity model (Fuchs et al., 2002) or the response-to-treatment model (Vaughn et al., 2003), considers not only a student's performance relative to peers at a fixed point in time but also his or her rate of academic improvement over time (Fuchs et al., 2002). Fuchs et al. (2002) proposed that LD and the need for remedial intervention might be present if a child fails to progress in an instructional environment in which his or her peers are performing adequately.

Finally, Kavale and Forness (2000) created an operational definition of LD that is comprised of five levels. The first level of this model indicates that academic underachievement and the presence of an ability-achievement discrepancy are necessary for a definition of LD. However, although these characteristics are necessary, they are not sufficient. The second level in this model examines whether deficits are present in specific academic areas such as language, reading, writing, and mathematics. At the third level, learning efficiency is examined in terms of the rate of learning and the kinds of learning strategies that are employed. The fourth level involves an evaluation of deficits in psychological processes such as linguistic processing, attention, memory, perception, social cognition, and metacognition. The fifth level consists of exclusionary criteria, to insure that learning difficulties are not the result of mental retardation, sensory impairment, emotional or behavioral disturbances, cultural differences, or lack of adequate instruction. Kavale and Forness claimed that in current practice, assessment of LD encompasses only the first level in their model. They asserted that their model would provide a more comprehensive definition of LD and would allow greater confidence when assigning an LD diagnosis.

ALTERNATIVE ASSESSMENT PROCEDURES
FOR LD IDENTIFICATION

Alternative conceptualizations of LD will require changes in procedures to assess LD. For example, the use of an intrinsic processing deficit model as the basis for LD identification would require methods by which to evaluate intrinsic processing problems. Instruments that might be suitable for this type of evaluation include the Cognitive Assessment System (Naglieri & Das, 1997, cited in Scruggs & Mastropieri, 2002), the Swanson Cognitive Processing Test (Swanson, 1993, cited in Scruggs & Mastropieri, 2002), the Learning Disabilities Diagnostic Inventory (Hammill & Bryant, 1998, cited in Dean & Burns, 2002), and the Kaufman Assessment Battery for Children (Kaufman & Kaufman, 1983, cited in Dean & Burns, 2002). Dean and Burns (2002), however, expressed skepticism that such instruments truly assess cognitive processing.

Recognizing the difficulty inherent in attempting to directly evaluate processing deficits, Torgesen (2001b) suggested an indirect, two-stage assessment method. He recommended that children from preschool through first grade could be considered at risk for learning disabilities, and eligible for intervention, if they were not mentally retarded yet performed below criteria on predictors of academic achievement. These predictors might include outcome measures associated with processing deficits, such as problems in learning about relationships between letters and sounds. Children identified by this process would receive several years of specialized instruction. If they continued to exhibit significant academic difficulties, they might then be classified as learning disabled.

Several authors have described assessment models pertaining to reading disorder. The phonological process model assumes that reading disorder is caused by deficits in the ability to decode phonemes associated with letters, resulting in word recognition problems (Stanovich, 1999). As a result, LD evaluation would necessitate the use of tests of rapid naming and verbal short-term memory (Scruggs & Mastropieri, 2002).

Badian (1999) investigated whether reading disability could be defined as a discrepancy between listening comprehension and reading comprehension. Stanovich (1993, cited in Badian, 1999) and others have recommended this method as superior to current discrepancy models because they contend that IQ is irrelevant to reading disorder. These authors posit that poor reading comprehension is due to poor decoding skills. Therefore, children who demonstrate good listening comprehension but poor reading comprehension would be considered to have a reading disability (Badian, 1999).

In the Badian (1999) study, over 1,000 children entering kindergarten were administered two subtests of the Wechsler Preschool and Primary Scale of

Intelligence to obtain an estimate of intellectual aptitude. In addition, these participants were annually given the reading comprehension and listening comprehension subtests of the Stanford Achievement Test from Grades 1 through 8. Results indicated that children who were identified with reading disability, as defined by a discrepancy between listening and reading comprehension, possessed at least average intellectual ability and significantly better listening comprehension than non-discrepant poor readers. Badian (1999) interpreted these findings as evidence that using a listening comprehension-reading comprehension discrepancy may be a valid way to define reading disability.

Periera-Laird et al. (1999) proposed a five-stage method to identify students with reading disability. The first step in this method uses teacher recommendations to identify students who might suffer from reading disorder, as suggested by poor reading performance in class. Second, students are suspected of reading disorder if they have a reading achievement test score at or below the 25th percentile. Third, students are selected as possibly having reading disorder if they exhibit variable academic achievement, defined as obtaining some achievement scores below the 25th percentile and other achievement scores at or above the 30th percentile. The fourth step involves the use of exclusionary criteria to insure that students suspected to have reading disorder do not demonstrate neurological or attention deficits, emotional or behavioral problems, and/or visual or auditory impairment. Students for whom English is not their language of origin also are excluded from consideration. The final step in this model employs a short form of the Wechsler Intelligence Scale for Children-Revised to insure that students who may have reading disorder have at least average intelligence, defined as an IQ score of 85 or higher.

Through the use of discriminant analysis, Periera-Laird et al. (1999) found that their model enabled them to correctly classify 95.1% of normally achieving readers and 96.1% of reading disordered readers. These authors reported that attributions about reading success or failure had the greatest predictive power to distinguish normally achieving readers from those with reading disorder, because children with LD may believe that reading success is due to luck or the ease of the reading task, rather than their own efforts (Periera-Laird et al., 1999).

Yet another kind of assessment for reading disorder is based on a so-called rauding diagnostic system (Carver & Clark, 1998). Carver and Clark (1998) derived this system from " 'rauding theory,' which refers to all the theory, constructs, and equations that have been developed to describe, explain, predict, and control the ability to comprehend relatively easy sentences while reading normally" (p. 453). In contrast to discrepancy models that are currently in use, the rauding diagnostic system does not involve the use of IQ tests to identify reading disability. Instead, it examines general reading ability as well as the efficiency and accuracy of text comprehension and the rate of decoding. The rauding system evaluates reading ability at various educational levels, classifying kindergarten through second grade as lower grades, third through seventh grades as middle grades, and adults as eighth grade and older. Regardless of age, individuals who are capable of reading at or above the eighth-grade level are defined as advanced readers and are not considered to have a reading disability. The rauding system categorizes very poor readers as having a reading efficiency level that is two or more grade equivalents below the expected grade level for their age. Once someone is identified as a very poor reader, further examination explores whether reading difficulty results from problems with either reading accuracy or decoding rate. After making this determination, the third step in the evaluation process examines whether disabilities in accuracy or decoding are due to disabilities in verbal knowledge, pronunciation ability, or cognitive speed.

Carver and Clark (1998) wrote that according to the rauding diagnostic system, indicators of potential for improved reading would include strong aptitudes in verbal knowledge, pronunciation, and cognitive speed. They claimed that reading disabilities due to poor knowledge or pronunciation might be remediated through intensive instruction, but that reading problems associated with poor cognitive speed probably would not be alleviated even with remedial instruction.

Assessment based on the dual discrepancy/treatment validity model proposed by Fuchs et al. (2002) demands the use of "curriculum-based measurement" (CBM; Gresham, 2001, p. 6) to identify students with LD. As recommended by Fletcher et al. (2001), "classification should be oriented to results and . . . must ultimately help students master academic skills essential to their capacity to function independently and effectively" (p. 7). CBM can be used to investigate the effectiveness of educational programming and to assist with the planning of such programs. It utilizes measures of educational outcomes that are administered and scored according to standardized procedures, to check whether students are progressing as anticipated in comparison to peers (Fuchs et al., 2002; Helwig et al., 2002).

Fuchs et al. (2002) described their treatment validity model of LD assessment in terms of four phases. In Phase I, a determination is made regarding whether a classroom provides adequate instructional support for its students. Students' performance in the classroom is compared with academic performance in comparable classrooms. If the rate of academic growth lags behind the rate of improvement in similar classrooms, intervention would be directed at strengthening the instructional environment. Phase II entails the identification of students who exhibit a dual discrepancy, meaning that both their level of performance and their rate of academic improvement are significantly less than that of their peers. Evaluation in Phase III focuses on whether modifications in the general educational setting will lead to improved learning for students. If interventions do not lead to improvement, only then would special educational services be considered necessary and only then would a student be classified as having LD (cf. Vaughn et al., 2003). Phase IV examines whether special education results in improved academic performance for a student. According to Fuchs et al. (2002), failure to demonstrate the effectiveness of special education for a student suggests that the student should not be labeled with an LD diagnosis.

Other assessment methods also might be implemented as replacements for current discrepancy models. One such method might employ a neuropsychological test battery to examine visual, auditory, and tactile perceptual skills as well as language abilities (Scruggs & Mastropieri, 2002). Another possibility might rely on a formula to predict LD on the basis of statistical probabilities. This formula would include items from a teacher checklist, with each item on the checklist weighted according to the likelihood of its ability to identify a learning disability. A combination of several different kinds of academic problems might be capable of identifying LD with a high rate of probability (Scruggs & Mastropieri, 2002).

Scruggs and Mastropieri (2002) offered six guidelines for evaluating alternative methods of LD identification. According to these authors, new assessment procedures should meet the following standards: (1) they should examine multiple areas of functioning, to recognize the multifaceted nature of LD; (2) they should be applicable to students of all ages, not only to those in the primary grades; (3) they should possess documented evidence of adequate reliability and validity, as well as standardized administration procedures; (4) in comparison to current practices, they should reduce the likelihood of overidentification of LD; (5) they should lower the variability of LD identification rates across and within states; and (6) they should reduce the likelihood of identifying false positive and false negative cases of LD.

RECOMMENDATIONS FOR THE FUTURE

The possibility exists that at some future date, various technologies to examine brain structure and function (e.g. computerized tomography or functional magnetic resonance imaging) might be capable of consistently identifying brain abnormalities associated with LD. Unfortunately, these technologies presently are unable to pinpoint specific structural or functional differences that can serve as diagnostic markers for LD (Bigler et al., 1998). Therefore, educators and clinicians will continue to rely on theoretical and operational definitions of LD to guide their identification of students who might require specialized instruction to make academic gains. However, the numerous limitations of discrepancy models indicate the need for refinement in the conceptualization of LD.

Several recommendations emerge from the educational literature concerning the kinds of changes that should be made. First, the concept of discrepancy should be considered a component in a more comprehensive definition of LD, rather than the single criterion for determining LD (Hallahan & Kauffman, 1997; Kavale, 2001; Scruggs & Mastropieri, 2002; Zera & Lucian, 2001). The assessment procedures suggested by Kavale and Forness (2000), Periera-Laird et al. (1999), and Torgesen (2001b) all contain elements of current discrepancy-based definitions of LD, but these newer models also incorporate factors such as exclusionary criteria, evidence of inconsistent achievement, and measures of post-intervention performance.

Second, as proposed by Fletcher et al. (2001), revised conceptualizations of LD should emphasize inclusionary criteria. The IDEA definition of LD stipulates that children with mental retardation, sensory impairment, etc., should not be categorized as having LD (Wicks-Nelson & Israel, 2003). Although such exclusions continue to be recommended as part of the LD construct, they do little to elucidate the underlying causes of LD, nor do they offer guidance concerning the kinds of remediation that might prove most beneficial. Fletcher et al. indicated that inclusionary criteria for LD should be specific to the various kinds of learning difficulties (e.g. reading disorder), easily measurable, and relevant to intervention and outcomes assessment.

Third, according to the treatment validity model, an updated definition of LD should acknowledge the role of contextual factors such as the quality of classroom instruction (Fletcher et al., 2001; Fuchs et al., 2002; Vaughn et al., 2003). According to Vaughn et al. (2003), this type of approach to LD identification will demand a "paradigm shift" (p. 392) away from the present focus on intra-individual factors. Instead, students deemed at risk for academic difficulties would receive intervention and only those who demonstrated a poor response to such interventions would be classified with LD (Vaughn et al., 2003).

Perhaps someday, better conceptualizations of LD might facilitate the creation of a multi-axial diagnostic manual for educational disorders, similar to the existing psychiatric manual for the diagnosis of mental disorders (Berninger, 2001). Berninger (2001) proposed that educational researchers could use empirical data to develop this type of classification scheme for use in academic settings. She envisioned a system of axes to describe executive functioning, social-emotional functioning, components of the educational curriculum, language/communication abilities, cognitive factors, motor skills, physical and medical conditions, and pertinent family and community issues that might affect learning.

Whether such a system can be devised for LD, and whether it would constitute an improvement over current conceptualizations, remains to be seen. Thus far, attempts to create a unified classification system for LD have been unsuccessful. Furthermore, it is possible that such an approach might prove harmful for some persons with LD, because it might lead to the use of inadequate assessment procedures as well as a failure to provide appropriate remediation (Zera & Lucian, 2001).

Until the educational community can find and agree upon an improved means of defining and identifying LD, the risk for overidentification and misidentification continues (Scruggs & Mastropieri, 2002; Vaughn et al., 2003). Individuals who exhibit low achievement due to intellectual deficits, inadequate instruction, or other factors may be mistakenly identified as having LD. As suggested by Kavale and Forness (2000), the best solution to this problem might be to make a radical departure from the past and to adopt new approaches to the definition and identification of LD. Further research will be necessary to determine which, if any, of the alternative models discussed in this chapter might provide significant advantages over current definitions. In the meantime, however, strict adherence to existing criteria is important to insure that students with LD will receive the assistance that they need and to which they are legally entitled (Kavale & Forness, 2000).

REFERENCES

American Psychiatric Association (2000). *Diagnostic and statistical manual of mental disorders* (4th ed., text rev.). Washington, DC: Author.

Badian, N. A. (1999). Reading disability defined as a discrepancy between listening and reading comprehension: A longitudinal study of stability, gender differences, and prevalence. *Journal of Learning Disabilities, 32*(2), 138–148. Retrieved January 13, 2003, from the FirstSearch database.

Beitchman, J. H. (1998). Summary of the practice parameters for the assessment and treatment of children and adolescents with language and learning disorders. *Journal of the American Academy of Child and Adolescent Psychiatry, 37*(10), 1117–1119. Retrieved January 8, 2003, from the FirstSearch database.

Berninger, V. W. (2001). Understanding the 'lexia' in dyslexia: A multidisciplinary team approach to learning disabilities. *Annals of Dyslexia, 51*, 23–48. Retrieved January 6, 2003, from the FirstSearch database.

Bigler, E. D., Lajiness-O'Neill, R., & Howes, N. (1998). Technology in the assessment of learning disability. *Journal of Learning Disabilities, 31*(1), 67–82. Retrieved December 19, 2002 from the Expanded Academic ASAP database.

Carver, R. P., & Clark, S. W. (1998). Investigating reading disabilities using the rauding diagnostic system. *Journal of Learning Disabilities, 31*(5), 453–471. Retrieved January 13, 2003, from the FirstSearch database.

Coffey, K. M., & Obringer, S. J. (2000). Culturally diverse rural students: At special risk for LD classification. *Rural Special Education Quarterly, 19*(2), 15–19. Retrieved January 15, 2003, from the EBSCO database.

Colarusso, R. P. (2001). A comparison of eligibility criteria and their impact on minority representation in LD programs. *Learning Disabilities Research and Practice, 16*(1), 1–7. Retrieved January 15, 2003, from the EBSCO database.

Coutinho, M. J., Oswald, D. P., & Best, A. M. (2002). The influence of sociodemographics and gender on the disproportionate identification of minority students as having learning disabilities. *Remedial and Special Education, 23*(1), 49–59. Retrieved December 20, 2002, from the Expanded Academic ASAP database.

Dean, V. J., & Burns, M. K. (2002). Inclusion of intrinsic processing difficulties in LD diagnostic models: A critical review. *Learning Disability Quarterly, 25*(3), 170–176. Retrieved December 20, 2002, from the Expanded Academic ASAP database.

Elksnin, L. K., Bryant, D. P., Gartland, D., King-Sears, M., Rosenberg, M. S., Scanlon, D., Strosnider, R., & Wilson, R. (2001). LD summit: Important issues for the field of learning disabilities. *Learning Disability Quarterly, 24*(4), 297–305. Retrieved January 6, 2003, from the Expanded Academic ASAP database.

Fletcher, J. M., Lyon, G. R., Barnes, M., Stuebing, K. K., Francis, D. J., Olson, R. K., Shaywitz, S. E., & Shaywitz, B. A. (2001). Classification of learning disabilities: An evidence-based evaluation. Paper presented at the 2001 Learning Disabilities Summit: Building a Foundation for the Future. Executive summary retrieved July 8, 2003, from: http://www.air.org/ldsummit.

Fletcher, J. M., Shaywitz, S. E., Shankweiler, D. P., Katz, L., Liberman, I. Y., Stuebing, K. K., Francis, D. J., Fowler, A. E., & Shaywitz, B. A. (1994). Cognitive profiles of reading disability: Comparisons of discrepancy and low achievement definitions. *Journal of Educational Psychology, 86*(1), 6–23.

Fuchs, L. S., Fuchs, D., & Speece, D. L. (2002). Treatment validity as a unifying construct for identifying learning disabilities. *Learning Disability Quarterly, 25*(1), 33–45. Retrieved December 19, 2002, from the Expanded Academic ASAP database.

Gregg, N., Scott, S. S., & McPeek, D. (1999). Definitions and eligibility criteria applied to adolescent and adult population with learning disabilities across agencies. *Learning Disability Quarterly, 22*(3), 213–22. Retrieved January 15, 2003, from the FirstSearch database.

Gresham, F. (2001). Responsiveness to intervention: An alternative approach to the identification of learning disabilities. Paper presented at the 2001 Learning Disabilities Summit: Building a Foundation for the Future. Executive summary retrieved July 6, 2003, from: http://www.air.org/ldsummit.

Gunderson, L., & Siegel, L. S. (2001). The evils of the use of IQ tests to define learning disabilities in first- and second-language learners. *Reading Teacher, 55*(1), 48–55. Retrieved January 15, 2003, from the EBSCO database.

Hallahan, D. P., & Kauffman, J. M. (1997). *Exceptional learners: Introduction to special education* (7th ed.). Boston, MA: Allyn & Bacon.

Helwig, R., Anderson, L., & Tindal, G. (2002). Using a concept-grounded, curriculum-based measure in mathematics to predict statewide test scores for middle school students with LD. *Journal of Special Education, 36*(2), 102–112. Retrieved December 23, 2002, from the Expanded Academic ASAP database.

Jimenez Gonzalez, J. E., & Garcia Espinel, A. I. (1999). Is IQ-achievement discrepancy relevant in the definition of arithmetic learning disabilities? *Learning Disability Quarterly, 22*(4), 291–301. Retrieved January 15, 2003, from the FirstSearch database.

Kavale, K. A. (2001). Discrepancy models in the identification of learning disability. Paper presented at the 2001 Learning Disabilities Summit: Building a Foundation for the Future. Executive summary retrieved July 6, 2003, from: http://www.air.org/ldsummit.

Kavale, K. A., & Forness, S. R. (2000). What definitions of learning disability say and don't say: A critical analysis. *Journal of Learning Disabilities, 33*(3), 239–256. Retrieved January 15, 2003, from the FirstSearch database.

Kidder-Ashley, P., Deni, J. R., & Anderton, J. B. (2000). Learning disabilities eligibility in the 1990s: An analysis of state practices. *Education, 121*(1), 65–72. Retrieved January 15, 2003, from the FirstSearch database.

Little, C. (2001). A closer look at gifted children with disabilities. *Gifted Child Today Magazine, 24*(3), 46–54. Retrieved July 8, 2003, from the EBSCO database.

McEachern, A. G., & Bornot, J. (2001). Gifted students with learning disabilities: Implications and strategies for school counselors. *Professional School Counseling, 5*(1), 34–41. Retrieved December 23, 2002, from the Expanded Academic ASAP database.

Morgan, A. E., Singer-Harris, N., Bernstein, J. H., & Waber, D. P. (2000). Characteristics of children referred for evaluation of school difficulties who have adequate academic achievement scores. *Journal of Learning Disabilities, 33*(5), 489–500. Retrieved December 20, 2002, from the Expanded Academic ASAP database.

O'Malley, K. J., Francis, D. J., Foorman, B. R., Fletcher, J. M., & Swank, P. R. (2002). Growth in precursor and reading-related skills: Do low-achieving and IQ-discrepant readers develop differently? *Learning Disabilities Research and Practice, 17*(1), 19–34.

Periera-Laird, J., Deane, F. P., & Bunnell, J. K. (1999). Defining reading disability using a multifaceted approach. *Learning Disability Quarterly, 22*(1), 59–71. Retrieved January 13, 2003, from the FirstSearch database.

Sarkees-Wircenski, M., & Scott, J. L. (2003). *Special populations in career and technical education.* Homewood, IL: American Technical Publishers.

Sattler, J. M. (1992). *Assessment of children* (rev. and updated 3rd ed.). San Diego: Author.

Scruggs, T. E., & Mastropieri, M. A. (2002). On babies and bathwater: Addressing the problems of identification of learning disabilities. *Learning Disability Quarterly, 25*(3), 155–169.

Silver, A. A., & Hagin, R. A. (2002). *Disorders of learning in childhood* (2nd ed.). New York: Wiley.

Silver, C. H., Pennett, H. D., Black, J. L., Fair, G. W., & Balise, R. R. (1999). Stability of arithmetic disability subtypes. *Journal of Learning Disabilities, 32*(2), 108–119. Retrieved January 13, 2003, from the FirstSearch database.

Sorrell, A. L. (2000). Learning disabilities: From understanding to intervention. In: F. E. Obiakor, S. A. Burkhardt, A. F. Rotatori & T. Wahlberg (Eds), *Intervention Techniques for Individuals with Exceptionalities in Inclusive Settings* (pp. 53–77). Stamford, CT: JAI Press.

Spear-Swerling, L., & Sternberg, R. J. (1998). Curing our 'epidemic' of learning disabilities. *Phi Delta Kappan, 79*(5), 397–401. Retrieved December 19, 2002, from the Expanded Academic ASAP database.

Stanovich, K. E. (1999). The sociopsychometrics of learning disabilities. *Journal of Learning Disabilities, 32*(4), 350–361. Retrieved January 8, 2003, from the Expanded Academic ASAP database.

Sternberg, R. J., & Grigorenko, E. (2001). Learning disabilities, schooling, and society. *Phi Delta Kappan, 83*(4), 335–338. Retrieved January 8, 2003, from the FirstSearch database.

Stuebing, K. K., Fletcher, J. M., & LeDoux, J. M. (2002). Validity of IQ-discrepancy classifications of reading disabilities: A meta-analysis. *American Educational Research Journal, 39*(2), 469–518. Retrieved January 15, 2003, from the FirstSearch database.

Swanson, H. L. (2000). Issues facing the field of learning disabilities. *Learning Disability Quarterly, 23*(1), 37–50. Retrieved January 13, 2003, from the FirstSearch database.

Tanner, D. E. (2001). The learning disabled: A distinct population of students. *Education, 121*(4), 795–798. Retrieved January 15, 2003, from the EBSCO database.

Tomasi, S. F., & Weinberg, S. L. (1999). Classifying children as LD: An analysis of current practice in an urban setting. *Learning Disability Quarterly*, *22*(1), 31–42. Retrieved January 13, 2003, from the FirstSearch database.

Torgesen, J. K. (2001a). Learning disabilities as a working memory deficit: The important next questions. *Issues in Education*, *7*(1), 93–102. Retrieved January 15, 2003, from the EBSCO database.

Torgesen, J. K. (2001b). Empirical and theoretical support for direct diagnosis of learning disabilities by assessment of intrinsic processing weaknesses. Paper presented at the 2001 Learning Disabilities Summit: Building a Foundation for the Future. Executive summary retrieved July 6, 2003 from: http//www.air.org/ldsummit.

Van den Broeck, W. (2002). The misconception of the regression-based discrepancy operationalization in the definition and research of learning disabilities. *Journal of Learning Disabilities*, *35*(3), 194–204. Retrieved December 23, 2002, from the Expanded Academic ASAP database.

Vaughn, S., Linan-Thompson, S., & Hickman, P. (2003). Response to instruction as a means of identifying students with reading/learning disabilities. *Exceptional Children*, *69*(4), 391–409. Retrieved August 3, 2003, from the EBSCO database.

Warner, T. D., Dede, D. E., Garvan, C. W., & Conway, T. W. (2002). One size still does not fit all in specific learning disability assessment across ethnic groups. *Journal of Learning Disabilities*, *35*(6), 501–509. Retrieved December 20, 2002, from the Expanded Academic ASAP database.

Wicks-Nelson, R., & Israel, A. C. (2003). *Behavior disorders of childhood* (5th ed.). Upper Saddle River, NJ: Prentice-Hall.

Willson, V. L., & Reynolds, C. R. (2002). Misconceptions in Van den Broeck's representation of misconceptions about learning disability research. *Journal of Learning Disabilities*, *35*(3), 205–208. Retrieved December 23, 2002, from the Expanded Academic ASAP database.

Zera, D. A., & Lucian, D. G. (2001). Self-organization and learning disabilities: A theoretical perspective for the interpretation and understanding of dysfunction. *Learning Disability Quarterly*, *24*(2), 107–118. Retrieved January 6, 2003, from the Expanded Academic ASAP database.

NON-VERBAL LEARNING DISABILITIES

Sandra Burkhardt

Non-verbal learning disability (NLD) refers to a syndrome whose definition has been emerging over the past 35 years (see Johnson & Myklebust, 1967; Rourke, 1993, 2000; Rourke et al., 1990; Rourke & Fuerst, 1996; Semrud-Clikeman & Hynd, 1990; Tranel et al., 1987). Though well documented in the research literature of learning disabilities and neuropsychology, NLD is seldom directly identified and addressed during multidisciplinary eligibility meetings or through individual education plans (Telzrow & Bonar, 2002). NLD does not currently appear in the Diagnostic and Statistical Manual, 4th Edition, of the American Psychiatric Association (American Psychiatric Association, 2000). Textbooks for teacher preparation seldom mention NLD (Telzrow & Bonar, 2002).

NLD is associated with math disability although the constellation of NLD symptoms extends beyond academic difficulty. Students with NLD are at risk of having the syndrome's defining characteristics, perceptual-motor deficits and awkward social functioning, in addition to math difficulties, mistaken for a multitude of behavior problems and presumed motivational failings. Evaluation methods and educational programming that address the specific learning characteristics and social-emotional behaviors of persons with NLD may differ from those typically associated with verbal learning disabilities (VLD) (Wicks-Nelson & Israel, 2003). Improved assessment and intervention for students with NLD hinge upon increased awareness of the syndrome (Telzrow & Bonar, 2002).

Current Perspectives on Learning Disabilities
Advances in Special Education, Volume 16, 21–33
Copyright © 2004 by Elsevier Ltd.
All rights of reproduction in any form reserved
ISSN: 0270-4013/doi:10.1016/S0270-4013(04)16002-9

PREVALENCE OF NONVERBAL
LEARNING DISABILITY

Research in the area of NLD reports diagnostic criteria, assessment methods and treatment strategies derived from case studies and clinical experiments involving small number of participants and controls. The American Psychiatric Association reported that approximately 1% of school-age children have a mathematics disability (APA, 2003). Wicks-Nelson and Israel (2003) suggested that there is "scant information about prevalence and outcome for mathematics disorder" (p. 277). The prevalence of NLD has not been reported in research literature.

CHARACTERISTICS OF NLD

Brace (1998) identified assets associated with NLD, including excellent auditory memory, precocious reading ability, advanced verbal expression including impressive vocabulary, and superior verbal reasoning. Children with NLD display good rote verbal memory and syntactical strength but weakness in space visualization and visuomotor coordination (Humphries et al., 1996). Rourke et al. (1989) included sustained selective attention for repetitive verbal material associated with excellent rote verbal memory among NLD's assets. Word decoding skills may be evident at an early age and spelling skills for dictated words may develop to a superior level, with misspelling due to phonetic irregularity of the word being spelled.

Deficits displayed by persons with NLD include poor visual memory, tactile-perceptual deficits (often on the left side of the body), coordination difficulties, poor visual-spatial organization, poor arithmetic ability in early grades, difficulty with science theories and concepts, poor written expression, including poor handwriting, confusion regarding directions, distorted perception of time, and inattention, hyperactivity, and social withdrawal and social isolation (Brace, 1998). Cornoldi et al. (1999) linked NLD to deficits in visuospatial working memory and visual imagery, concluding that deficits shown by children with NLD are not due merely to developmental delay but reflect actual disability. Other characteristics summarized by Cornoldi et al. include weak psychomotor and perceptual motor skills, arithmetic deficits, poor adaptation to novel and complex tasks, inflexibility, impulsivity, over-familiarity, mechanical speech pattern, limited awareness of self and others, impoverished sense of humor, and social-emotional adjustment difficulties, including anxiety and depression.

Thompson (1997) described three domains of difficulty for persons with NLD: motoric, visual-spatial organization, and psychosocial. Rourke et al. (1989) identified primary deficits of NLD, including tactile-perceptual difficulties and difficulty with complex psychomotor skills that are more prominent on the left side of the body and of growing significance with age. Rourke et al. also implicated a pattern of attentional deficits that includes poor attention to tactile and visual stimuli and deficient visual attention leading to poor visual memory. Deficits associated with higher functions include poor concept formation, problem solving, and hypothesis testing.

IQ Discrepancy

A "hallmark characteristic" of students with NLD involves "stronger verbal than nonverbal cognitive abilities" (Telzrow & Bonar, 2002, p. 9). Rourke et al. (1989) identified as a marker of NLD a statistically significant discrepancy between Verbal Scale IQ and Performance Scale IQ on the Wechsler measures of intellectual functioning, such that verbal abilities are superior to nonverbal abilities. The left to right hemisphere functioning discrepancy has been defined as a Verbal Scale IQ that is 15 points greater than the Performance Scale IQ. Verbal abstract reasoning is usually at or above average, while measures of nonverbal abstract reasoning, such as Block Design and Object Assembly, are below average. Other nonverbal deficits evident on Wechsler Performance subtests include below average social perception, as measured by Picture Arrangement, and visual-motor coordination, as measured by Coding (Foss, 2001).

Achievement Characteristics

Achievement scores in oral reading, decoding, and spelling typically exceed reading comprehension scores for students with NLD. Mathematical computation usually exceeds mathematical applications (Foss, 2001).

For persons with NLD expressive vocabulary, while quite good, may manifest in verbosity (excessively verbal and dramatically expressive) or social communication typified by monologues and rambling without making a point (Foss, 2001). Hyperlexia and superior ability to decode and recognize words may initially mask the deficits of NLD associated with limited reading comprehension, poor inferences about the motivation of characters, and inability to identify literary devices such as theme and plot (Brace, 1998; Thompson, 1997).

Behavioral and Language Characteristics

The behavioral and language patterns of children with NLD include gaze avoidance (poor eye contact), communication and learning disabilities, and emotional dysfunction resulting in interpersonal problem (Gross-Tsur et al., 1995). Students with NLD demonstrated fewer behaviors associated with school success than children with verbal learning disabilities (VLD) and children with low verbal abilities in terms of day-to-day organization and coping ability (Badian, 1992). Routine childhood milestones may be delayed for children with NLD, such as learning to ride a bicycle or copying accurately from the blackboard in the classroom (Thompson, 1997). Linguistic dysfunction has been associated with NLD, including difficulties with linguistic inferences, particularly related to spatial and emotional aspects (Rourke & Tsatsanis, 1996; Worling et al., 1999). Rourke et al. (1989) identified speech and language patterns associated with NLD that include mild oral-motor praxis, strange prosody, verbosity, and poor pragmatic language. The authors indicated that most of the language related difficulties become more evident with age. Lastly, Thompson (1997) reported other factors related to impaired social communication for persons with NLD that included missing nonverbal social cues, lack of reciprocity and turn-taking in conversation, limited shared interests, literal interpretations of verbal communication and social rules, over reliance on asking many questions and subvocalization (self-talk) during motor tasks.

Social Deficits

Persons with NLD exhibit social difficulties including a paucity of friendships, failure to monitor audience reactions to social interactions, interrupting others, and invading others personal space (Foss, 2001; Morris, 2002). Persons with NLD may have difficulty processing nonverbal, nonlinguistic information, in the presence of good ability to process verbal information. Brumback et al. (1996) determined that facial expressions and gestures, as aspects of nonverbal social communication, are associated with the right cerebral hemisphere functioning, and that right hemisphere dysfunctions associated with NLD are correlated with social difficulties.

Children with NLD were found to be particularly vulnerable to social imperception (Dimitrovsky et al., 1998) and experience a poor sense of self due to little ability to perceive self as seen by others (Foss, 2001).

Rourke and Fuerst (1992) assert that the assets and deficits of NLD negatively impact psychosocial functioning, speculating that social deficits do not have a direct basis in central nervous system (CNS) dysfunction but rather develop as a function of neuropsychological deficits. Morris (2002) identified social skills deficits associated with NLD, including difficulty with initiating play and conversation with peers, working in groups, displaying empathy, resolving conflict, and managing frustration.

The social behavior of persons with NLD during the early years is likely to be experienced as annoying rather than bad or disruptive (Thompson, 1997). Students with NLD may be at higher risk for bullying and teasing than other students, including other students with disabilities (Telzrow & Bonar, 2002). Peer and sibling shunning and victimization were common among children with NLD (Little, 2001).

NEUROPSYCHOLOGICAL FEATURES OF NLD

The neurological underpinnings of NLD may be dysfunction of white matter (long myelinated fibers) affecting right hemisphere functions and interhemispheric communication (Gunter et al., 2002; Regan & Reeb, 1998; Rourke et al., 2002). Sandson et al. (2000) provide evidence to support right hemisphere dysfunction in a subgroup of persons with attentional difficulties. NLD as a function of right hemisphere dysfunction (RHD) has been described as a learning disability of the right hemisphere with suspected visuoperceptive/simultaneous information processing deficits (Denckla, 1991).

Factors associated with nonverbal abilities include visuospatial-motor skills, psychomotor speed, visual-attentional abilities and a factor, *visual learning*, which is comprised of visual sequencing and complex-processing speed (Williams & Dykman, 1994). NLD is associated with sensory integrative dysfunction (Humphries et al., 1996). NLD may be identified by impaired performance on neuropsychological tests that are associated with visual perceptual organization, psychomotor coordination, and complex tactile-perceptual skills, such as the Target Test, Trail Making Tests, Tactual Performance Test, and Grooved Pegboard (Harnadek & Rourke, 1994).

DISORDERS ASSOCIATED WITH NLD

The pattern of assets and deficits that define the NLD syndrome has been associated with various neurological and neuropsychological disorders. Gross-Tsur et al. (1995) found that many children with NLD had been previously diagnosed with Attention Deficit Hyperactivity Disorder (ADHD). Like ADHD, frequently the identification of NLD depends upon observation and non-standard interpretation of standardized test findings. NLD and ADHD as co-occurring disorders or ones that require differential diagnosis remains an issue for future research (Thompson, 1997).

NLD is one of seven disorders beginning in childhood that are associated with impaired reciprocal social interaction (Scheeringa, 2001). In addition to NLD the other categories of disorders include *developmental disorders, semantic-pragmatic language disorders, attachment disorders, schizoid personality disorder* and *other Pervasive Developmental Disorder-Not Otherwise Specified (PDD-NOS)*.

NLD is associated with Autistic Spectrum Disorders, including Asperger's Syndrome (Gunter et al., 2002; Klin et al., 1995; Semrud-Clikeman & Hynd, 1990). Like individuals with high functioning autism (HFA), students with NLD have difficulty with reading comprehension even in the presence of good rote reading and spelling skills (Minshew et al., 1994).

NLD has been linked to William's Syndrome (Rourke et al., 2002), Triple X Syndrome in females (Ryan et al., 1998); cranial irradiation for the treatment of childhood leukemia (Regan & Reeb, 1998); prematurely (< 30 weeks gestation) (Wocadlo & Rieger, 2000); and, velo-cardo-facial syndrome (VCFS) (Swillen et al., 1999). NLD syndrome was in evidence in patients with lesions associated with Periventricular Leukomalacia (PVL) and white matter dysfunction (Woods et al., 2000).

Children of parents with bipolar disorder have been found to have characteristics similar to children with NLD, including Verbal Subscale IQ greater than Performance Subscale IQ, however, math and spelling deficits were not necessarily present in the children of bipolar parents. Findings were inconclusive regarding persons with NLD demonstrating greater risk of bipolar disorder (McDonough-Ryan et al., 2002).

NLD AND PSYCHIATRIC SYMPTOMS INCLUDING SUICIDALITY

NLD has been linked to depressive symptoms and increased incidence of suicidality (see Bigler, 1989; Cleaver, 1998; Groffman, 1994; Rourke et al., 1989). Fletcher (1989) suggested that assessment of cognition, adaptive behavior and academic achievement is needed for suicide prevention efforts. Cleaver (1998) found that young adults with NLD were more likely to be depressed than cohorts who were either reading disabled or non-disabled. The author also determined that young adults in a psychiatric population who displayed NLD were at greater risk for depression than other psychiatric patients who did not show the classic NLD pattern of characteristics.

Pettit et al. (2003) determined that children with NLD were less accurate in interpreting adult facial expressions and much more likely to be diagnosed with internalizing disorders. Children with NLD were found to be at greater risk for personality disturbance and behavior problems than children without NLD (Greenham, 1999). Palombo (1993) examined NLD from a psychoanalytic perspective, suggesting that individuals with NLD do not develop intrapsychic cohesiveness.

NLD: TO BE OR NOT TO BE A REAL LD?

NLD shares the characteristics of other learning disabilities (LD) in several key areas. NLD is associated with a failure to acquire new learning, such as reading comprehension and arithmetic skills, in a person with average intellectual aptitude after exposure to formal teaching efforts. Lerner (2000) estimates that more than one-third of students with LD display problems with social skills. Like students with dyslexia, students with NLD may continue to struggle with generalization even after learning has occurred. Like students with other LD, students with NLD may require continuing assistance to compensate for areas of deficit. Like students with ADHD, students with NLD display difficulties in social and behavioral self-regulation in the presence of average to above average intelligence and good home and school environments.

Finally, LD in general are associated with baffling mixtures of capability and deficit – the student who can read, but can not spell, can verbally respond, but can not write the answer, can complete the first half of the paper accurately, but makes careless mistakes working on the second half. Similarly, students with NLD may automatically acquire precocious verbal abilities while displaying naïve and inappropriate verbal social communication.

NLD is distinct from Verbal Learning Disabilities (VLD) in the obvious feature that NLD involves intact, average to above average verbal ability. Among students with LD, NLD has been distinguished from VLD in the preference of students with NLD for serial verbal learning strategies rather than semantic learning strategies as measured by the California Verbal Learning Test (Fisher & DeLuca, 1997). Chow (1999) reported that in a sample of 19 children with NLD who were compared to 16 children with language disorder, the children with NLD were found to have greater difficulty with sequential processing than simultaneous processing. Because NLD has been linked to right hemisphere dysfunction that impairs spatial skills but leaves language intact, the social and behavioral deficits found in NLD may have a different origin than similar problems "linked to language-based disabilities" (Wicks-Nelson & Israel, 2003, p. 278).

It is likely that the association between NLD characteristics and neurological, medical and developmental disorders contributes to uncertainty as to the true nature of NLD as solely, or primarily, a distinctive learning disability. The principle of equifinality refers to the fact that various developmental paths can result in the same outcome (Cicchetti & Cohen, 1995). For example, various disorders or conditions may affect the white matter of the brain, potentially resulting in the NLD syndrome. Thus, the presumed etiology of the NLD characteristics – physical illness, genetic abnormality, prematurely, or medical treatment – influences if an LD label is considered.

For example, a student with a math disability who has Williams Syndrome is most likely to have the deficit attributed to developmental disability. Another student with a math deficit may be considered LD secondarily to processing difficulties associated with ADHD. In a third scenario a child with leukemia whose successful treatment actually caused NLD symptoms may be categorized as health impaired and have the math deficit misattributed to excessive absenteeism.

Similarly, behavioral manifestations of NLD may be interpreted in light of the perceived disabling condition. The blunt and naïve student with Williams Syndrome may be viewed as socially inept due to cognitive limitations. The child with NLD who also displays attentional deficits may be labeled impulsive. The child with NLD as a result of treatment for leukemia may be viewed as outspoken and immature due to being spoiled and overprotected by concerned adults. In sum, it may be that NLD is not readily identified as a specific type of learning disability because the characteristics may be associated with and attributed to a host of real and imagined causes.

If NLD is true LD then educators should promote assessment and intervention. Steps to advancing the understanding of NLD include helping parents and teachers understand the distinctive characteristics of NLD, including an awareness of the assets associated with the syndrome, and promotion of interventions for deficits that negatively affect development.

INTERVENTION FOR NLD

Telzrow and Bonar (2002) suggest responsive educational efforts that include specific *remedial, compensatory* and *therapeutic* interventions for NLD. *Remedial* interventions for NLD include intensive training and practice in arithmetic, handwriting, and reading facial expressions. *Compensatory* strategies for NLD address deficits by promoting the use of calculators, word processing, organizers, and explicit rules to guide social behavior. Finally, *therapeutic* interventions for NLD involve specialized methods to address deficits, such as adapted gym class, occupational therapy, social skills training, pragmatic language therapy, and cognitive-behavioral therapy for depressive symptoms.

Foss (2001) promotes remediation for areas of deficit found in NLD that includes explicit, direct instruction using verbal strengths to address nonverbal weaknesses as well as using verbal skills to mediate situations and enhance self-direction.

Principles for intervention include the following: (a) clarity in addressing difficulties; (b) identify weaknesses and getting the person with NLD to commit to improvement; (c) starting with familiar material and moving to more complex material; (d) using the student's verbal and analytic strengths; (e) modeling verbal mediation of nonverbal information; (f) describing concrete object actions and experiences; (g) designing lessons to be sequential and step-by-step; (h) promoting generalization; and (i) providing multisensory integration in instruction (read it, see it, hear it, touch it, say it, write it, do it).

Additional interventions made by Foss (2001) include educating general education teachers about NLD, structuring priorities for multiple tasks, and setting a work schedule such that not all assignments or tests are due at the same time. Social interventions include antecedent behavior management that avoids behavior that lead to criticism, teasing and shunning and signaling social errors (Vacca, 2001).

Numerous remedial instructional programs have been proposed. Tanquay (2002) delineated curricular modification and teaching strategies for work with children with NLD, including methods for instruction in writing, mathematics and reading comprehension. Aloyzy-Zera (2001) promoted the use of a *self-organizing system* (SOS) for students with NLD. Williams et al. (1992) endorsed problem-solving strategy training using cognitive behavioral modification to verbally mediate spatial tasks.

Minskoff (1980) was among the first to promote training social perception skills, including the discrimination of social cues with body language or kinesthetic cues including proxemics and vocalics. A Social Competence Intervention Program (SCIP), which uses drama methods for children with perceptual deficits, may increase social perception and self-awareness (Glass et al., 2000). Gutstein and Sheely (2002) developed activities for social-emotional development for individuals with Autism Spectrum Disorders, including NLD.

SUMMARY

NLD is a syndrome that has been receiving more attention the past ten years even though it has been reported in the literature since the late 1960s. Educators and clinicians are now realizing the need to identify students with NLD and provide intervention due to the disabling academic, social and affective aspects of this syndrome. This chapter has delineated NLD characteristics in cognitive, academic, social, behavioral and language domain areas so as to differentiate it from VLD. Professionals, who work with students with NLD, must educate other professionals that this syndrome is a distinctive learning disability. This is necessary due to its association with neurological, medical, and developmental disorders which have contributed to uncertainty as to the nature of NLD.

Positively, progress has been made in the development of academic and social-emotional interventions to treat students with NLD.

REFERENCES

Aloyzy-Zera, D. (2001). A reconceptualization of learning disabilities via a self-organizing systems paradigm. *Journal of Learning Disabilities, 34*(1), 79–94.

American Psychiatric Association (2000). *Diagnostic and statistical manual of mental disorders* (4th ed., text rev.). Washington, DC: American Psychiatric Association.

Badian, N. A. (1992). Nonverbal learning disability, school behavior, and dyslexia. *Annals of Dyslexia, 42*, 159–178.

Bigler, E. D. (1989). On the neuropsychology of suicide. *Journal of Learning Disabilities, 22*(3), 180–185.

Brace, P. (1998). What are nonverbal learning disabilities? Retrieved December 20, 2003, from http://www.ldao.on.ca/about_ld/articles/general/nld.html.

Brumback, R. A., Harper, C. R., & Weinberg, W. A. (1996). Nonverbal learning disabilities, Asperger's syndrome, pervasive developmental disorder-should we care? *Journal of Child Neurology, 11*(6), 427–429.

Chow, D. (1999). Simultaneous and successive cognitive processing in children with nonverbal learning disabilities. *School Psychology International, 20*(2), 219–231.

Cicchetti, D., & Cohen, D. J. (1995). Perspectives on developmental psychopathology. In: D. Cichetti & D. J. Cohen (Eds), *Developmental Psychopathology* (pp. 1–10). New York: Wiley.

Cleaver, R. L. (1998). Right hemisphere, white-matter learning disabilities associated with depression in an adolescent and young adult psychiatric population. *Journal of Nervous & Mental Disease, 186*(9), 561–565.

Cornoldi, C., Rigoni, F., Tressoldi, P. E., & Vio, C. (1999). Imagery deficits in nonverbal learning disabilities. *Journal of Learning Disabilities, 32*(1), 48–57.

Denckla, M. B. (1991). Academic and extracurricular aspects of nonverbal learning disabilities. *Psychiatric Annals, 21*(12), 717–724.

Dimitrovsky, L., Spector, H., Levy-Shiff, R., & Vakil, E. (1998). Interpretation of facial expressions of affect in children with learning disabilities with verbal or nonverbal deficits. *Journal of Learning Disabilities, 31*(3), 286–292.

Fisher, N. J., & DeLuca, J. W. (1997). Verbal learning strategies of adolescents and adults with the syndrome of nonverbal learning disabilities. *Child Neuropsychology, 3*(3), 192–198.

Fletcher, J. M. (1989). Nonverbal learning disabilities and suicide: Classification leads to prevention. *Journal of Learning Disabilities, 22*(3), 176, 179.

Foss, J. M. (2001). Nonverbal learning disability: How to recognize it and minimize its effects. *ERIC Clearinghouse on Disabilities and Gifted Education, ERIC EC Digest #E619* (2001, December). Retrieved December 31, 2003, from http://ericec.org/digests/e619.html.

Glass, K. L., Guli, L. A., & Semrud-Clikeman, M. (2000). Social competence intervention program: A pilot program for the development of social competence. *Journal of Psychotherapy for Independent Practice, 1*(4), 21–33.

Greenham, S. L. (1999). Learning disabilities and psychosocial adjustment: A critical review. *Child Neuropsychology, 5*(30), 171–196.

Groffman, S. (1994). Can optometrists prevent suicide? *Journal of Optometric Vision Development, 25*(1), 1–3.

Gross-Tsur, V., Shalev, R. S., Manor, O., & Amir, N. (1995). Developmental right-hemisphere syndrome: Clinical spectrum of the nonverbal learning disability. *Journal of Learning Disabilities, 28*(2), 80–86.

Gunter, H. L., Ghaziuddin, M., & Ellis, H. D. (2002). Asperger syndrome: Tests of right hemisphere functioning and interhemispheric communication. *Journal of Autism & Development Disorders, 32*(4), 263–281.

Gutstein, S. E., & Sheely, R. K. (2002). *Relationship development intervention with children, adolescents and adults: Social and emotional development activities for Asperger syndrome, autism, PDD and NLD.* London: Jessica Kingsley Publishers.

Harnadek, M. C., & Rourke, B. P. (1994). Principal identifying features of the syndrome of nonverbal learning disabilities in children. *Journal of Learning Disabilities, 27*(3), 144–154.

Humphries, T., Krekewich, K., & Snider, L. (1996). Evidence of nonverbal learning disability among learning disabled boys with sensory integrative dysfunction. *Perceptual & Motor Skills, 82*(3), 979–987.

Johnson, D., & Myklebust, H. R. (1967). *Nonverbal disorders of learning. Learning disabilities: Educational principles and practices.* New York: Grune and Stratton.

Klin, A., Volkmar, F. R., Sparrow, S. S., & Cicchetti, D. V. (1995). Validity and neuropsychological characterization of Asperger syndrome: Convergence with nonverbal learning disabilities syndrome. *Journal of Child Psychology & Psychiatry & Allied Disciplines, 36*(7), 1127–1140.

Lerner, J. (2000). *Learning disabilities: Theories, diagnosis and teaching strategies.* Boston: Houghton Mifflin.

Little, L. (2001). Peer victimization of children with Asperger spectrum disorders. *Journal of the American Academy of Child & Adolescent Psychiatry, 40*(9), 995–996.

McDonough-Ryan, P., DelBello, M., Shear, P. K., Ris, M. D., Soutullo, C., & Strakowski, S. M. (2002). Academic and cognitive abilities in children of parents with bipolar disorder: A test of the nonverbal learning disability model. *Journal of Clinical and Experimental Neuropsychology, 24*(3), 280–285.

Minshew, N. J., Goldstein, G., Taylor, H. G., & Siegel, D. J. (1994). Academic achievement in high functioning autistic individuals. *Journal of Clinical & Experimental Neuropsychology, 16*(2), 261–270.

Minskoff, E. H. (1980). Teaching approach for developing nonverbal communication skills in students with social perception deficit: Proxemics, vocalic, and artifactual cues. *Journal of Learning Disabilities, 13*(4), 203–208.

Morris, S. (2002). Promoting social skills among students with nonverbal learning disabilities. *TEACHING Exceptional Children, 34*(3), 66–70.

Palombo, J. (1993). Neurocognitive deficits, developmental distortions, and incoherent narratives. *Psychoanalytic Inquiry, 13*(1), 85–102.

Pettit, V. L., Voelker, S. L., Shore, D. L., & Hayman-Abello, S. E. (2003). Perception of nonverbal emotion cues by children with nonverbal learning disabilities. *Journal of Developmental & Physical Disabilities, 15*(1), 23–36.

Regan, J. M., & Reeb, R. N. (1998). Neuropsychological functioning in survivors of childhood leukemia. *Child Study Journal, 28*(3), 179–200.

Rourke, B. P. (1993). Arithmetic disabilities, specific and otherwise: A neuropsychological perspective. *Journal of Learning Disabilities, 26*(4), 214–226.

Rourke, B. P. (2000). Neuropsychological and psychosocial subtyping: A review of investigations within the University of Windsor laboratory. *Canadian Psychology, 41*(1), 34–51.

Rourke, B. P., Ahmad, S. A., Collins, D. W., Hayman-Abello, B. A., Hayman-Abello, S. E., & Warriner, E. M. (2002). Child clinical/pediatric neuropsychology: Some recent advances. *Annual Review of Psychology, 53*(1), 309–339.

Rourke, B. P., del Dotto, J. E., Rourke, S. B., & Casey, J. E. (1990). Nonverbal learning disabilities: The syndrome and a case study. *Journal of School Psychology, 28*(4), 361–385.

Rourke, B. P., & Fuerst, D. R. (1992). Psychosocial dimensions of learning disability subtypes: Neuropsychological studies in the Windsor laboratory. *School Psychology Review, 21*(3), 361–374.

Rourke, B. P., & Fuerst, D. R. (1996). Psychological dimensions of learning disability subtypes. *Assessment, 3*(3), 277–290.

Rourke, B. P., & Tsatsanis, K. D. (1996). Syndrome of nonverbal learning disabilities: Psycholinguistic assets and deficits. *Topics in Language Disorders, 16*(2), 30–44.

Rourke, B. P., Young, G. C., & Leenaars, A. A. (1989). A childhood learning disability that predisposes those afflicted to adolescent and adult depression and suicide risk. *Journal of Learning Disabilities, 22*(3), 169–175.

Ryan, T. V., Crews, W. D., Cowen, L., Goering, A. M., & Barth, J. T. (1998). A case of triple X syndrome manifesting with the syndrome of nonverbal learning disabilities. *Child Neuropsychology, 4*(3), 225–232.

Sandson, T. A., Bachna, K. J., & Morin, M. D. (2000). Right hemisphere dysfunction in ADHD: Visual hemispatial inattention and clinical subtype. *Journal of Learning Disabilities, 33*(1), 83–90.

Scheeringa, M. S. (2001). The differential diagnosis of impaired reciprocal social interaction in children: A review of disorders. *Child Psychiatry & Human Development, 32*(1), 71–89.

Semrud-Clikeman, M., & Hynd, G. W. (1990). Right hemisphere dysfunction in nonverbal learning disabilities: Social, academic, and adaptive functioning in adults and children. *Psychological Bulletin, 107*(2), 196–209.

Swillen, A., Vandeputte, L., Cracco, J., Maes, B., Ghesquiere, P., Devriendt, K., & Fryns, J. (1999). Neuropsychological, learning and psychosocial profile of primary school aged children with the velo-cardio-facial syndrome (22q 11 deletion): Evidence for a nonverbal learning disability? *Child Neuropsychology, 5*(4), 230–241.

Tanquay, P. B. (2002). *Nonverbal learning disabilities at school: Educating students with NLD, Asperger syndrome and related conditions.* London: Jessica Kingsley Publishers.

Telzrow, C. F., & Bonar, A. M. (2002). Responding to students with nonverbal learning disabilities. *TEACHING Exceptional Children, 34*(6), 8–13.

Thompson, S. (1997). *The source for nonverbal learning disorders.* East Moline, IL: LinguiSystems.

Tranel, D., Hall, L. E., Olson, S., & Tranel, N. N. (1987). Evidence for a right-hemisphere developmental learning disability. *Developmental Neuropsychology, 3*(2), 113–127.

Vacca, D. M. (2001). Confronting the puzzle of nonverbal learning disabilities. *Educational Leadership, 59*(3), 26–31.

Wicks-Nelson, R., & Israel, A. C. (2003). *Behavior disorders of childhood* (5th ed.). Upper Saddle River, NJ: Prentice-Hall.

Williams, J., & Dykman, R. A. (1994). Nonverbal factors derived from children's performances on neuropsychological test instruments. *Developmental Neuropsychology, 10*(1), 19–26.

Williams, J. K., Richman, L. C., & Yarbrough, D. B. (1992). Comparison of visual-spatial performance strategy training in children with turner syndrome and learning disabilities. *Journal of Learning Disabilities, 25*(10), 658–664.

Wocadlo, C., & Rieger, I. (2000). Very preterm children who do not cooperate with assessment at three years of age: Skill differences at five years. *Journal of Development & Behavioral Pediatrics, 21*(2), 107–113.

Woods, S. P., Weinborn, M., Ball, J. D., Tiller-Niven, S., & Pickett, T. C. (2000). Periventricular Leukomalacia (PVL): An identical twin case study illustration of white matter dysfunction and nonverbal learning disability (NLD). *Child Neuropsychology, 6*(4), 274–285.

Worling, D. E., Humphries, T., & Tannock, R. (1999). Spatial and emotional aspects of language inferencing in nonverbal learning disabilities. *Brain & Language, 70*(2), 220–239.

MULTICULTURAL LEARNERS WITH LEARNING DISABILITIES: BEYOND EUROCENTRIC PERSPECTIVES

Festus E. Obiakor and Cheryl A. Utley

A myriad of legislative mandates to reform and restructure special education practices has been promulgated to benefit all students despite their racial, cultural, and socioeconomic backgrounds (Obiakor & Ford, 2002). For example, the *1964 Civil Rights Act*, and the *Goals 2000 Educate America Act* (U.S. Department of Education, 1994) have been well-meaning societal efforts to assist all students in maximizing their full potential. More recently, the *No Child Left Behind Act of 2001: Reauthorization of the Elementary and Secondary Education Act* (Council for Exceptional Children, 2002) has been designed to ensure that the goals of high expectations and achievement in U.S. schools are reached. Ironically, these legislative efforts appear to have had little or no effect on the traditional Eurocentric educational system. MacMillan and Siperstein (2001) reported that the population of students with learning disabilities (LD) has dramatically changed as public schools have responded to policy changes affecting general and special education. They also noted that "between 1976–1977 and 1992–1993, the number of children served as LD nationwide increased by 198%" (U.S. Department of Education, 1995, p. 1). During the 1999–2000 school year students served under the LD category represented 50.5% of all students served ages 6–21 under IDEA (see U.S. Department of Education, 2001).

Osher et al. (2002) observed that "the success or failure of schools in supporting positive outcomes for all students depends on their structure, organizational

Current Perspectives on Learning Disabilities
Advances in Special Education, Volume 16, 35–64
Copyright © 2004 by Elsevier Ltd.
All rights of reproduction in any form reserved
ISSN: 0270-4013/doi:10.1016/S0270-4013(04)16003-0

culture, cultural competence, and capacity to provide every student, regardless of background with the academic, behavioral, and emotional supports to build on their strengths and fully address their needs" (p. 109). Unfortunately, the traditional Eurocentric public educational system has exacerbated the odds that multicultural learners with disabilities will experience school failure. In addition, it has resisted meaningful modifications to accommodate multicultural learners with disabilities, particularly students with LD (Losen & Orfield, 2002; National Research Council, 2002). The failure of schools to provide a quality education is substantiated through the race/ethnic distribution of students served under IDEA. During the 1999–2000 school year the percentage of students, ages 6–21, in each of the "high incidence categories" (i.e. specific learning disabilities, severe language impairment, and mental retardation) differed from that of the resident population of 6–21 year olds (U.S. Department of Education, 2001) (see Table 1).

The institution of the *1997 Individuals with Disabilities Education Act* (IDEA, 1997, P.L. 105–117) elucidated many fundamental concepts of special education. The public was reassured that multicultural students with and without disabilities would receive: (a) unbiased identification and nondiscriminatory assessment procedures; (b) placement in the least restrictive environment; (c) confidentiality of information; (d) parental consent; (e) procedural safeguards; and (f) individualized educational programming (Utley & Obiakor, 2001). The general consensus was that old mistakes would be remedied. Today, the old troublesome debates

Table 1. Race/Ethnicity of Students with Disabilities Served.

Disability	American Indian/ Alaska Native	Asian/ Pacific Islander	Black (Non-Hispanic)	Hispanic	White (Non-Hispanic)
Specific learning disabilities	1.4	1.6	18.4	16.6	62.1
Speech and language impairment	1.2	2.4	16.1	12.7	67.6
Mental retardation	1.1	1.8	34.2	9.1	53.8
Emotionally disturbed	1.1	1.2	27.3	8.9	61.5
Developmental disabilities	0.9	0.8	30.5	4.1	63.7
All disabilities	1.3	1.8	20.3	13.7	62.9
Resident population	1.0	3.8	14.5	16.2	64.5

Source: Office of Special Education Programs (2001). *Twenty-third report to Congress on the implementation of the Individuals with Disabilities Education Act.* Washington, DC: U.S. Department of Education.

continue to rage and two critical questions seem to surface: What general and special education reform and restructuring programs will best meet the needs of multicultural learners who are at-risk of misidentification, misassessment, mislabeling, and misinstruction? Can real progress be made in special education without at least modifying the entrenched culture of traditional Eurocentric educational pedagogy?

The field of LD is one aspect of special education where issues of definition, identification, appropriate assessment, and evidence-based instructional practices continue to be heavily debated. Over the past ten years, the category of LD has changed its definition and identification parameters to incorporate a significant number of multicultural learners, with low intelligence, underachievers, and students who are low achievers. Distinguishing the child with true learning disabilities from the underachiever and low achiever has become very challenging (Fuchs et al., 2001). Kavale (2001) acknowledged that "even though discrepancy remains the primary criterion for LD identification, it seems to be ignored in actual practice. Studies have identified large percentages of students with LD with intelligence quotient (IQ) scores in the low to low-average range (p. 3)." Consequently, leaders in the field have proposed that there are generalized characteristics which are representative of many individuals identified as having a mild intellectual, learning, or behavioral disability (Henley et al., 1993; Kavale & Forness, 1998; MacMillan & Reschly, 1997). For instance, Kavale and Forness agreed that:

> The LD category has thus become a catch-all classification with little substantive foundation. Research demonstrating a decline in IQ scores and the increasing recognition of social/emotional deficits among students with LD reveals a fundamental change in the nature of LD caused by incorporating students who would previously have been designated mentally retarded (MR) or emotionally/behaviorally disordered (E/BD). Thus, LD covers not only students experiencing specific academic difficulties but also those who possess learning problems with an overlay of lowered intellectual ability or mild behavior problems. When combined with this perception that LD is a "better," less stigmatizing, and more acceptable classification, the desire for LD, rather than MR or E/BD, designation becomes irresistible and the political climate appears quite willing to accommodate this desire (p. 250).

The current state of affairs reveals that multicultural learners are still confronted with multidimensional problems because urban schools are not structured to serve their interests and the interests of students from low-income backgrounds, or students whose first language is not English (Artiles & Trent, 1994; Hallahan & Mercer, 2001; Sleeter & Hartney, 1992; Tomasi & Weinberg, 1999). In other words, multicultural learners are at-risk for being put in the disability status because schools are not well-prepared to deal with differences in learning behavior, culture, and language either separately or in combination. As it appears, general and special educators have recognized properly the important role of cultural, linguistic, and environmental influences on children's learning problems (Obiakor, 2001; Obiakor & Ford, 2002; Obiakor et al., 2002). Therefore, they must acknowledge different approaches to understanding LD and incorporate this knowledge base in assessment and evidence-based instructional practices in teaching multicultural learners. This fundamental premise is the major focus of this chapter.

DISPROPORTIONATE REPRESENTATION OF MULTICULTURAL LEARNERS WITH LEARNING DISABILITIES

For more than 30 years, the overrepresentation of minority learners in special education programs has sparked controversy (Artiles & Trent, 1994; Cunningham, 1998; Gottlieb et al., 1994; Harry, 1994; McIntosh, 2002; Obiakor et al., 2003). The National Institute for Urban School Improvement (2001) recently published a document titled, *On the Nexus of Race, Disability, and Overrepresentation: What Do We Know? Where Do We Go?* Based on the ideas encapsulated in this document:

(1) African American students tend to be overrepresented in classrooms for students with mild disabilities and emotional and behavioral disabilities (Midgette, 1995).
(2) Almost 75% of diagnoses of mild mental retardation (MMR) are linked to various socioeconomic-related environmental contingencies. Poor children are more likely than wealthier children to receive special education (U.S. Department of Education, 1998).
(3) Although African Americans represent 16% of elementary and secondary enrollments, they constitute 21% of total enrollments in special education (U.S. Department of Education, 1998).
(4) Poor African American children are 2.3 times more likely to be identified by their teacher as having mental retardation than their White counterparts (McIntosh, 2002).
(5) The population of Native American children who receive special education services is one-and-one-half times greater at 16.8% vs. 11% for the general population (National Research Council, 2002).
(6) African Americans, especially males, who engage in certain behaviors that represent artifacts of their culture-such as language (Ebonics), movement patterns (verve), and a certain "ethnic" appearance-have been found to be over-referred for special education placement (Obiakor, 1994, 1999).

(7) Although Latino students are often not overrepresented in state and national data, they are likely to be overrepresented in special education when their proportion of a district's diverse student body increases (Ortiz, 1997).

More recently, the National Research Council (NRC) (2002) examined the 1998 Office for Civil Rights placement data and Office of Special Education Programs (OSEP) Child Count data on the enrollment of students in special education programs broken down by racial/ethnic group. In the federal reporting of data by race/ethnicity, the following five groups were identified: (1) American Indian/Alaskan Natives; (2) Asian/Pacific Islander; (3) Hispanics; (4) Blacks; and (5) non-Hispanic Whites. As a means of understanding the overrepresentation of multicultural learners with LD, three different types of indices have been used to compare placement rates for different racial/ethnic groups: (1) the risk index (RI); (2) odds ratio; and (3) composition index (CI) (see Table 2).

Based on the aforementioned data, the risk index (RI) identifies the percentage of all students of a given racial/ethnic group in a given disability category. The RI is calculated by dividing the number of students in a given racial/ethnic group served in a given disability category (e.g. LD) by the total enrollment for that racial/ethnic group in the school population. The 1998 OCR data revealed risk indices for all racial/ethnic groups that were higher for LD than those found for MR. The NRC (2002) report stated that, "Asian/Pacific Islander have placement rates of 2.23%. Rates for all other racial/ethnic groups exceed 6%, and for American

Table 2. Indices of Placement for Learning Disabilities by Race/Ethnicity: 1998 OCR and OSEP Data.

Characteristics	Risk Index		Odds Ratio		Composition Index	
	OCR	OSEP	OCR	OSEP	OCR	OSEP
American Indian/Alaskan native	7.45	7.30	1.24	1.20	1.38	1.37
Asian/Pacific Islander	2.23	2.25	0.37	0.37	1.51	1.43
Black	6.49	6.58	1.08	1.08	18.48	18.19
Hispanic	6.44	6.81	1.07	1.12	16.04	16.50
White	6.02	6.08			62.60	62.51
Total	6.02	6.07			100.00	100.00

Notes: OCR placement and membership dates are taken from the *Fall 1998 Elementary and Secondary School Civil Rights Compliance Report, National Projections.* OSEP data are taken from the 1998–1999 Child Count, and the indices were calculated using estimated K-12 total enrollment data from the U.S. Department of Education, *National Center for Education Statistics, Common Core of Data, School Universe Study,* 1998–1999, compiled by Mark Glander, National Education Data Resource Center.

Source: National Research Council (2002).

Indian/Alaskan Natives, the rate reached 7.45%" (p. 47). The second index, odds ratio, provides a comparative index of risk and is calculated by dividing the risk index on one racial/ethnic group by the risk index of another racial/ethnic group. In the OCR and OSEP databases, the odds ratios are reported relative to White students. If the risk index is identical for a particular minority group and White students, the odds ratio will equal 1.0. Odds ratios greater than 1.0 indicate that minority group students are at a greater risk of identification, while odds ratios of less than 1.0 indicate that they are less at risk. Using the 1998 OCR placement rates, the LD odds ratio for American Indian/Alaskan Natives is 1.24, showing that they have a 24% greater likelihood of being assigned to the LD category than White students. Odds ratios for Asian/Pacific Islander are low (0.37). For both Black and Hispanic students, the odds ratios are close to 1.0. The third index, composition index (CI), shows the proportion of all children served under a given disability category who are members of a given racial/ethnic group and is calculated by dividing the number of students of a given racial or ethnic group enrolled in a particular disability category. Two underlying assumptions of the CI are that the sum of composition indices for the five racial/ethnic groups will total 100%, and baseline enrollment of a given racial/ethnic group is not controlled. More specifically, the CI may be calculated using the percent of 6- through 21-year old population with the racial/ethnic composition of IDEA and U.S. census population statistics. For example, if 64% of the U.S. population is White, 15% is Black, 16% is Hispanic, 4% is Asian, and 1% is American Indian these data not interpretable without knowing the percentage of the racial/ethnic composition with IDEA. Hypothetically, IDEA data may show that of the 6–21 year olds served under IDEA, 63% are White, 20% are Black, 14% are Hispanic, 2% are Asian, and 1% is American Indian. To calculate disproportionality, a benchmark (e.g. 10%) against which to measure the difference between these percentages must be used. If the difference between the two percentages and the difference represented as a proportion of the group's percent of population exceeds +10, then the racial/ethnic group is overrepresented. Conversely, if the difference between the two percentages and the difference represented as a proportion of the group's percent of the population is larger than −10, then, the racial/ethnic group is underrepresented.

A thorough understanding of the phenomenon of disproportionate representation involves a very complex combination of theories (Gottlieb et al., 1994; National Research Council, 2002; Utley & Obiakor, 2001). The National Academy of Sciences Panel (NASP) (Heller et al., 1982), national data from OCR (1997), the National Longitudinal Transition Study (NLTS) (2002), the National Early Intervention Longitudinal Study (NEILS) (2000), and the Committee on Minority Representation in Special Education (National Research Council, 2002) have presented unique perspectives on the issue of overrepresentation (Hebbeler

& Wagner, 2001; Office for Civil Rights, 1997). According to the NASP, the overrepresentation issue implicates the entire special education process as being unfair to students: the quality of instruction prior to referral, the decision to refer, the assessment, placement in special education programs, and the quality of instruction that occurs in that program. Problematic circumstances include the invalid assessment and placement in programs for students with cognitive disabilities where educational progress may be hindered because of teachers' lowered expectations and goals, opportunities for success are restricted, and low-quality instruction exists. OCR investigations have disclosed school discriminatory practices, such as: (1) extensive pre-referral interventions in school districts with predominantly White students than in schools with predominantly African American students; (2) a greater emphasis on students' behavioral problems as opposed to academic reasons; (3) a greater reliance on IQ tests in the evaluation of minority students; and (4) a disproportionate number of minority students labeled as cognitively disabled and placed in restrictive classroom settings. According to the National Institute for Urban School Improvement (2001):

> Two elements have emerged as keys to understanding the nexus of race, disability, and overrepresentation. There is a disconnect between the race, culture, and class of teachers in most schools on one hand, and the culture, race, and SES [socioeconomic status] of learners they serve on the other. This disconnect is associated with underachievement which contributes significantly to the disproportionate representation of these learners in special education.... Increasingly numbers of traditionally trained teachers from the dominant American culture are teaching students who are often nontraditional learners, resulting in cultural, race, and class chasms in our classrooms and schools. Further, too few teachers have been educated to recognize and deal with the cultural, class, and gender "knapsacks" of these learners, or of their own, and may have low expectations shaped by inaccurate assumptions about the innate ability of racial minorities and poor children (p. 6).

CONCEPTUAL UNDERSTANDING OF LEARNING DISABILITIES

Within the field of special education, the category of LD is a relatively new field of exceptionality. Hardman et al. (1999) described the field of LD as controversial, confused, and polarized because it represents the largest single service delivery program for exceptional children in the United States. They agreed that "in the past, many children now identified as having specific LD would have been labeled as remedial readers, remedial learners, or emotionally disturbed or even mentally retarded, if they received any special attention or additional instructional support at all" (p. 173). The percentage of students with LD, ages 6–21, comprised 51% of all students identified in 1995–1996, and tend to be served primarily in general education and resource room classrooms (U.S. Department of Education, 1998). Many professionals agree that the controversial issues about this specific disability category are rooted in variations of the definition and identification procedures.

Traditional Definitions of LD

There are many definitions by professional organizations and state education agencies. However, P.L. 94–142, included in its legislation, the definition recommended by the National Advisory Committee on Handicapped Children (NACHC). The National Joint Committee on Learning Disabilities (NJCLD) (1994) reiterated the 1967 NACHC's definition, which reads:

> *Specific learning disability* means a disorder in one or more of the basic psychological processes involved in understanding or in using language, spoken or written, which manifest itself in an imperfect ability to listen, think, speak, read, write, spell, or to do mathematical calculations. The term includes such conditions as perceptual handicaps, brain injury, minimal brain dysfunction, dyslexia, and developmental aphasia. The term does not include children who have learning problems which are primarily the result of visual, hearing or motor handicaps, of mental retardation, of emotional disturbance, or of environmental, cultural, or economic disadvantage (p. 4).

Over the years, this definition has been misinterpreted and has resulted in a number of issues and problems affecting the delivery of services to students. Following are three apparent definitional problems:

(1) This definition does not recognize the developmental nature of LD and that this disability may occur in early childhood and continue into adult life. The definition limits the applicability of this term to individuals 0–21 years of age.
(2) The etiology of LD is not stated clearly in the definition. Disorders represented by the term LD should be viewed as intrinsic to the individual and that the basis of the disorder is presumed to be due to central nervous system dysfunction.
(3) The wording of the "exclusion clause" in the definition lends itself to the misinterpretation that individuals with LD cannot have multiple disabilities, gifted, or be from cultural and linguistic backgrounds.

In 1981, a revised definition of LD was developed by the National Joint Committee on Learning Disabilities (NJCLD) and adopted by the following NJCLD member organizations: American Speech-Language-Hearing Association, Council for Learning Disabilities, Division for Children with Communication Disorders, International Reading Association, Learning Disabilities Association, National Association of School Psychologists, and Orton Dyslexia Society. The revised definition reads as follows (see NJCLD, 1994):

Learning disabilities is a general term that refers to a heterogeneous group of disorders manifested by significant difficulties in the acquisition and use of listening, speaking, reading, writing, reasoning, or mathematical abilities. These disorders are intrinsic to the individual, presumed to be due to central nervous dysfunction, and may occur across the life span. Problems in self-regulatory behaviors, social perception, and social interaction may exist with learning disabilities but do not by themselves constitute a learning disability. Although learning disabilities may occur concomitantly with other "handicapping" conditions (for example, sensory impairments, mental retardation, serious emotional disturbance), or with extrinsic influences (such as cultural differences, insufficient or inappropriate instruction),they are not the result of those conditions or influences (p. 65).

This revised definition of LD addressed a number of issues resulting from the earlier definition. These issues included: (a) recognizing "LD"as a general term consisting of a heterogeneous group of disorders with difficulties in listening, speaking, reading, writing, reasoning, and mathematical abilities; (b) identifying different subgroups of individuals with LD; (c) using a multifaceted approach in the identification, assessment, instruction, remediation, and management in programs for persons with LD; (d) identifying problems in the ability of individuals with LD to self-regulate their behaviors and to engage in appropriate social interactions; (e) recognizing the developmental nature of LD continuing from early childhood throughout adult life; (f) understanding that the etiology of LD may be due to several reasons such as a central nervous system dysfunction, failure to learn because of inherently altered processes of acquiring and using information, poor instruction, and the interaction between the learner and his/her social and cultural environment; and (g) recognizing that LD may occur within the different disability categories as well as different cultural and linguistic groups.

There are popular scientific terminologies that explicate learning disabilities (e.g. agraphia and dysgraphia, alexia and dyslexia, acaculia and dyscalculia, and aphasia and dysphasia) (Hallahan et al., 1999; Raymond, 2000). To a large measure, these terminologies represent the 3R's (reading, writing, and arithmetic). More than two decades ago, Faas (1980) defined agraphia as the "inability to recall the kinesthetic patterns requested to write words or express oneself in writing" (p. 399), and dysgraphia is the "partial inability to express ideas by means of writing or written symbols; usually associated with being dysfunctional" (p. 403). He defined alexia as the "loss of the ability to read written or printed language" (p. 399), and dyslexia as the "partial inability to read, or understand what one reads, silently or aloud; usually, but not always, associated with brain impairment" (p. 403). He explained acaculia as the "loss of the ability to manipulate arithmetic symbols and perform simple mathematical calculations" (p. 399), and dyscalculia as the "partial loss of the ability to calculate and to manipulate number symbols" (p. 403). Additionally, he defined aphasia as the "loss of the ability to comprehend spoken words in speech, words, or signs" and dysphasia as the "partial inability to comprehend the spoken word (receptive aphasia) and to speak (expressive aphasia), believed to be the result of injury, disease, and maldevelopment of the brain" (p. 403). These explanations make learning disability a perplexing disability, even though it is tied to academic instruction. While the category of LD creates classification problems, general and special educators must be cognizant of certain "red flags." For example, students must be identified when they demonstrate: (a) linguistic deficits; (b) academic deficits; (c) neuro-psychological deficits; and (d) social behavior deficits (Blackhurst & Berndine, 1993). But then, general and special educators must be careful that they do not classify students without discovering their specific problems. This is especially important for multicultural learners with school problems.

Fundamental Frameworks and Causes of LD

Many conceptual frameworks or models have been used to identify the causes of learning disabilities: medical (i.e. neurological, genetic, and biochemical), intrinsic processing (Torgenson, 2001), cognitive-information processing, and achievement-behavioral (Cunningham, 1998; Smith et al., 1986). From a medical perspective, neuropsychological models attempt to explain certain types of academic failure in terms of damage to specific brain functions. The category of major organic problems includes organic brain damage, brain injury, neurological disabilities, and central processing disorders. Research on the genetic transmission of reading disabilities has demonstrated that approximately 50% of all variability in the phonological processes that cause specific reading disabilities can be attributed to genetic factors (Olson, 1997; Torgensen, 1998). In addition, brain mapping research has demonstrated that a relationship exists between learning disabilities and subtle abnormalities in parts of the brain that process language (e.g. word-finding problems and identifying 40 segments or phonemes in spoken words) (Manis, 1996).

Biochemical imbalances have been identified as one of the causes of learning disabilities. This category, also referred to as "minor organic problems that are compounded by poor environments" includes maturational lags, vitamin deficiencies, allergic reactions, and sugar or food additives (Smith, 1998). Biochemical research related to learning disabilities has revealed that there is no scientific evidence linking the nature or extent of this factor on learning and behavior problems in children identified as LD. A cognitive-information processing model taps psychological processes that attempts to understand how individuals with LD acquire, retain, and interpret information received through the senses. General and special educators attempt to understand how thinking processes operate in order to complete such complex cognitive tasks as summarizing a chapter in a book, solving complex math problems, writing a mystery novel, and comparing and contrasting theories of learning. An achievement-behavioral model is based upon the assumption that academic failure in one or more of academic skill areas is due to inadequate learning environments. This category (without organic problems) includes poor teaching, poor curricula and focused on observable academic behaviors for the purposes of remediation of skill deficits (Berninger & Abbott, 1994; Greenwood, 1996).

Assessing Learners with LD

Given the controversy surrounding the definition of LD, the question remains as to how to assess individuals with LD accurately. Embedded within the definition are four major components related to the types of assessment used to document eligibility for services: an ability-achievement discrepancy clause, an emphasis on psychological processes, a central nervous system dysfunction etiology, and an exclusion clause differentiating the category of learning disability from other disability categories. Bender (1995) outlined the components of the LD definition in relation to the types of assessments suggested to document eligibility for services. The psychological processes component examines the types of ability deficits (i.e. intelligence, visual perception/motor, auditory perception, and language) that hinder learning. Earlier research studies conducted by McKinney and Feagans (1981), Kaufman (1981), and Galagan (1985) showed that the assessment of basic psychological processes is not possible psychometrically due to the low reliability and validity of the majority of instruments. In addition, eligibility for special education services was not based on the assessment of psychological or intrinsic processes in children with LD. Rather, children were diagnosed primarily in terms of a discrepancy between measures of intelligence and measures of achievement in specific areas of learning. The discrepancy component is based on the observation that children with LD score below their age-mates in overall achievement and perform below expectations on their measured potential. A major discrepancy between the verbal IQ and performance IQ on an intelligence test has been used as an indicator of a potential learning disability. Two types of discrepancies (i.e. intraindividual and ability-achievement) and four major types of ability-achievement discrepancy formulas (e.g. standard score calculations, regression-score tables, discrepancies between grade placement and achievement, and discrepancies based upon achievement, intelligence, and grade placement) have been derived using ability-achievement discrepancy calculations to document deficits in the psychological processes and academic achievement. More recently, Gresham (2001) noted that:

These discrepancy approaches to quantifying LD have been used to qualify students for special education and related services. However, each method has a number of conceptual and statistical drawbacks. Further, a major controversy in discrepancy-based notions of defining LD is the central importance assigned to IQ tests in the process, because they contribute little reliable information for planning, implementing, and evaluating instructional interventions. Although the system now in place does identify students in need of services, expensive and time-consuming assessments at three different steps could be streamlined and articulated to be more respectful of the judgment of both teachers and school professionals about a student's need for immediate intervention services (9, p. 4).

Lyon (1996) remarked that "there is no universally accepted test, test battery or standard for identifying children with LD. While a discrepancy between intelligence quotient (IQ) and achievement has been widely accepted criteria for the identification of LD and still serves as the driving clinical force in the diagnosis of LD, there is considerable variation in how the discrepancy is derived and quantified" (pp. 58–59). The operationalization of the exclusionary clause has been very difficult because assessment methods distinguishing characteristics describing the categories of MR, EB/D, and medically based conditions have been vague with very little information available. In addition, the use of assessment methods for differentiating children from different cultural backgrounds, who have been raised in poor and low-socioeconomic (SES) environments, and students who are low achieving continues to be problematic. Criteria for assessing individuals with LD must be clear, observable, measurable, and agreed upon by professionals in the field. However, the federal definition of LD does not specify criteria or guidelines for distinguishing the disability category of learning disability from other disability categories nor does it stipulate that students with LD cannot demonstrate deficits related to other categories of disability (Utley, 2002).

CONTEMPORARY PERSPECTIVES ON LD: BEYOND EUROCENTRISM

To move beyond Eurocentric views on LD, some contemporary perspectives (i.e. sociocultural, transactional, and ecobehavioral analysis) must be strongly considered. The sociocultural perspective addresses issues of definition, classification, and student characteristics, and the interplay of these variables in relation to cultural and linguistic contextual factors. The transactional model is based upon the interaction of person and environmental factors and their effects on the learning outcomes of children. The ecobehavioral analysis approach examines classroom and instructional factors that are "temporarily and spatially removed from the behavior of individuals, including those in 'the broader social, professional, institutional, and cultural contexts' " (Morris & Midgley, 1990, p. 11).

Sociocultural Perspective

The social construction of LD has been a topic of great debate by scholars (e.g. Kavale & Forness, 1998). As mentioned earlier, scholars espoused the philosophy that the field of LD originated from a medical model focused on the neurobiological and organic bases of learning problems, while other researchers asserted that LD is a construct of society and that its etiology and history directly correlate with the changing standards in education as a result of societal beliefs (Sleeter, 1986). Kavale and Forness noted that the process of identifying children as LD is primarily a function of ideology that is "shaped by the social forces in the environment" (p. 254). In order to promote change in the system of classifying individuals with LD, researchers and educators need to understand how society, culture, and language influence education and the learning process. Recently, Keogh et al. (1997) suggested that researchers and educators examine a sociocultural perspective on LD in order to understand learning problems within multicultural groups. They further remarked that without a "sociocultural perspective it is impossible to separate the learning competencies and problems of individual children from the contexts in which they live and function" (p. 107). Garcia et al. (1997) explained that "difficulties experienced by educators in distinguishing cultural or linguistic differences from disabilities can be partially explained by their unfamiliarity with cultural, linguistic, and other influences on student learning, attitudes, and behavior" (p. 441). Other researchers (e.g. Cole & Means, 1981; Garcia & Dominguez, 1997; Garcia & Malkin, 1993; Garcia & Ortiz, 1988; Gindis, 1995; Moll, 1992; Rogoff & Chavajay, 1995; Wertsch, 1991) have observed that sociocultural activities and how people think, remember, reason, and express their ideas influence the intellectual and social development of children. Also, in non-Western cultures, learning is affected by neurological and biological factors in addition to sociocultural contexts in which children live. As a result, the development of LD in children is inherently related to children's sociocultural experiences and biological and organic factors. Therefore, an examination of a sociocultural perspective has implications for defining the construct of LD and the assessment and intervention of multicultural learners.

In today's society and school-based settings, literacy, technology, education, and performance on standardized assessments are highly valued. If educational performance is used as an index of learning, then *one* critical component of defining LD is the normative performance of individuals in reading, mathematics, science, and other academic areas. However, in non-Western countries where intelligence test scores or performance on cognitive ability tests have little relevance to survival in society, educational competencies related to literacy are not emphasized and relevant to being productive members in society. In examining a sociocultural perspective, Keogh et al. (1997) questioned many assumptions about the concepts of ethnicity and culture in defining and classifying individuals with LD. These issues are focused on: (a) using ethnicity as a marker variable for culture in the classification of persons as learning disabled; (b) defining cultural characteristics of multicultural groups with precision and accuracy; (c) identifying characteristics of subgroups and of individuals within specific ethnic and cultural groups; and (d) distinguishing ethnicity and culture by acknowledging variations in three different ways: among ethnically defined groups, within ethnically defined groups, and among individuals within ethnic and cultural groups. In differentiating aspects of culture and ethnicity, Longstreet (1978) and Byrd (1995) outlined five areas that must be taken into consideration: (a) intellectual modes (e.g. ethnic influence and emphasis on the development of intellectual abilities and approaches to learning); (b) verbal communication (e.g. categories describing oral language, verbal communications, and sociability); (c) nonverbal communication (e.g. gestures and body language, personal space, and touching); (d) orientation modes (e.g. body and spatial orientations, and attention modes); and (e) social value patterns.

As researchers and educators become aware of the influence of the role of sociocultural factors on children's learning, they must conceptually and empirically validate the concepts of ethnicity and culture. Bos and Fletcher (1997) concurred with Keogh et al. (1997) and proposed adopting a sociocultural framework that includes student and contextual variables to reflect the dynamic interactions between learner and context. Student variables include: (a) sex; (b) age; (c) race and ethnicity; (d) socioeconomic status; (e) geographic region and locale; (f) grade level; (g) intelligence; (h) academic achievement; (i) time in special education placement; (j) level of special education placement; (k) primary and secondary language (proficiency); (l) cultural background; and (j) linguistic background. Contextual variables involve multiple layers of contexts within students' formal education programs. Three broad categories of contextual variables include community and family contexts (e.g. family and community cultures), district and school contexts (e.g. educational philosophy, size, location, curriculum, student achievement levels), and classroom context (e.g. size of class, students' and teachers' characteristics, curriculum, and culturally relevant pedagogy). In order to further understand multicultural learners, general and special educators must recognize, examine, incorporate, and document student variables within the broader sociocultural context.

Because of the aforementioned contexts, it is important to differentiate cultural and linguistic differences from LD. No doubt, the United States' multicultural and pluralistic society that is enriched, enhanced, and augmented by the traditions and values of people from different national origins, language backgrounds, and countries. Linguistic diversity in the U.S. varies regionally and socially – languages are distributed geographically and along income and socioeconomic levels, education, occupation, and racial/ethnic group membership. Adler (1993) remarked that:

> Each year children from ghettos, barrios, and reservations enter our public schools with substantial handicaps in education readiness related to their culturally different heritages. These children bring with them unique experiences and differences in standards and values. They possess a culture of their own with different learning and living styles and different speech and language patterns. The manifestations both of speech and language patterns and of other cultural styles that differ significantly from those used by members of the dominant culture, however, are frequently rejected not only by their peers, but also, too frequently, by their instructors (p. 15).

Massey (1996) further stated that the "study of language development cannot be separated from the study of the cultural dictates of the community that the language user is a part of. As important, the relation between primary language, the cultural experiences that shape the use of that language, and success with later societal demands (e.g. school) cannot be ignored" (p. 290).

Educational and research priorities have identified differentiating students with LD, communication and language disorders, and developmental delay from multicultural learners who have normal language skills (Craig, 1996; Hallahan et al., 1999; Hamayan & Damico, 1991; Ortiz, 1997; Perkins-Gordon, 1996; Schmidt et al., 1996; Seymour & Bland, 1991; Taylor, 1986). Smith (1998) noted that "many children who are multiculturally and linguistically diverse enter school with sociolinguistic conventions that are mismatched with the content and structure of the school curriculum, thereby causing confusion and misunderstanding" (p. 106). Unfortunately, the cultural mismatch between the school's expectations and students' cultural, linguistic, and socioeconomic backgrounds has resulted in serious problems in teacher attitudes, classification, assessment, and educational services provided to multicultural learners who speak African American English (AAE) (also referred to Black English and Ebonics) and Limited English Proficient (LEP) learners. For example, Seymour et al. (1995, p. 98) reported that teacher attitudes about child AAE speakers were that: (a) they equated a lack of school vocabulary with an overall lack of vocabulary; (b) they characterized children as not speaking in sentences or in complete thoughts and as strange grammatical constructions; (c) they complained that children's mispronunciations resulted from failure to use their tongue, teeth, and lips; and (d) they thought children did not know the correct English sounds. Kretschmer (1991) noted that there has been an overlap between the classification of LEP students as "language-learning disabled," "language disordered," or "learning disabled." When language profiles show difficulties in conversational interaction and oral communication, LEP students are typically labelled "language disordered," while profiles of LEP students that show evidence of academic problems result in the classification of students as "learning disabled." Some of the problems manifested by language-learning disabled students, as identified by Roseberry-McKibbin (1995), include: (a) problems in earning language at a normal rate; (b) a family history of learning difficulties; (c) maturational lag in development than siblings; (d) communication difficulties (e.g. poor sequencing skills, lack of organization, structure, and sequence in spoken and written language, poor conversational and social interaction skills); (e) difficulties in using precise vocabulary words (e.g. noting and producing homophones and synonyms); (f) using concrete word meanings, deictic spatial terms, and syntax; and (g) using appropriate grammar, generating simple sentences. Collier (1998b) described several characteristics of multicultural learners who are suspected of having LD. Four areas characteristic of specific LD are under the categories of: (a) achievement below ability; (b) receptive expressive language deficits; (c) behavior problems; and (d) problems associated with cognitive learning strategies. A detailed analysis of the sociocultural characteristics of African American, Asian/Pacific Islander, Hispanic, and American Indian students with LD and their instructional implications are described in Table 3.

Transactional Perspective

The transactional model is based upon the reciprocal interplay of person and his/her environment and this encompasses a comprehensive perspective to understanding learning problems in children (Adelman & Taylor, 1993). Theoretically, a transactional model describes person and environmental factors as the "locus of cause" of learning problems on a continuum of types of learning problems: Type I, Type II, and Type III. Type I learning problems are caused by factors in the environment. These factors include: (a) insufficient stimuli; (b) excessive stimuli; and (c) intrusive and hostile stimuli. Type II learning problems are caused by factors in the environment and person. These factors include: (a) physiological insult; (b) genetic anomaly; (c) cognitive activity and affective states experienced by self as deviant; (d) physical characteristics shaping contact with the environment and/or experienced by self as deviant; and (e) deviant actions of the individual. Type III learning problems are caused by factors in the person (e.g. LD). These factors include: (a) severe to moderate personal vulnerabilities and environmental defects and differences; (b) minor personal vulnerabilities not accommodated by the situation; and (c) minor environmental defects and differences not accommodated by the individual. In studying the learning problems of children, Adelman and Taylor (1993) suggested that learning is a function of the transactions between the learner

Table 3. Characteristics of Multicultural Learners with Learning Disabilities.

Characteristics of Exceptionality	Sociocultural Characteristics	Instructional Implications
African American		
Achievement below ability Difficulty perceiving and interpreting patterns in language environment (e.g. words, sounds, numbers hyperactive, attention deficit disorders)	Ability often misjudged because of test bias Words not spoken with familiar intonation not paid attention to interactive style Boredom can lead to distractibility	Students with learning disabilities may be misdiagnosed as mentally retarded Students may appear to have auditory perceptual problems when there is simply a failure to recognize meaning without the cues of dialect Teacher may view student as hyperactive when he/she interacting normally with peers
Asian American		
Achievement below ability Difficulty perceiving and interpreting patterns in language environment (e.g. words, sounds, numbers) Attention deficit disorders Limited level of educational achievement	Value placed on high academic achievement, industriousness Failure to perceive unfamiliar sounds; or remember words out of context for non-English speaking children Culture values appearances of self-control, but expects emotion Social class and self-esteem determined by level of education	Student may try to compensate for disability by working extra hard, memorizing materials, etc., so as not to bring shame on family Teacher should use alternative assessment strategies Behavior may be a source of shame to parents and self Teacher needs to assist student with culturally appropriate strategies Teacher will need to assist student with self esteem and guide out of learned helplessness
Hispanic American		
Achievement below ability Difficulty perceiving and interpreting patterns in language environment (e.g. words, sounds, numbers) Hyperactive, attention deficit disorders	Impact of inadequate disrupted education Differences in learning deficiencies Disrupted early experiences result in both native language and English differences Many English words sound alike to Spanish speakers	Teacher needs to use appropriate alternative assessment Teacher needs to assist student with a variety of appropriate cognitive learning strategies Teacher should assist student in using active-processing, analogy and other cognitive learning strategies related to language development

Table 3.   (*Continued*)

Characteristics of Exceptionality	Sociocultural Characteristics	Instructional Implications
American Indian		
Achievement below ability Difficulty perceiving and interpreting patterns in language environment (e.g. words, sounds, number) Attention deficit disorders	Impact of inadequate instruction Children are taught to observe first and not to act until they are sure of doing it correctly Disrupted by experiences may lead to both native language and English deficiencies	Teacher should facilitate cognitive learning strategies Teacher needs to learn to separate learning and behavior problems due to difference from disability Teacher should assist student in using active-processing, analogy, and other cognitive learning strategies related to self monitoring and learning to learn

Source: Adapted from Collier (1998c), Nazzaaro (1981), Utley (1993).

and classroom environment. They described the learning situation in classrooms as follows:

> . . . a learner brings to a learning situation both capacities and attitudes that have been accumulated over time, and current states of being and behavior. These transact with each other and also with the learning environment. The learning environment consists of not only of instructional processes and content, but also the physical and social context in which instruction takes place. Each part of the environment transact with the others. The outcome of all of these transactions may be positive learning or learning problems. Because the nature of the transactions can vary considerably, so can the outcomes. In general, the types of outcomes can be described as: (a) deviant learning (i.e. capacities and attitudes change and expand, but not in desirable ways); (b) disrupted learning (i.e. interference with learning and possibly a decrease in capacities); (c) delayed and arrested learning (i.e. little change in capacities); and (d) enhanced learning (i.e. capacities and attitudes change and expand in desirable ways) (pp. 21–23).

In any school situation, multicultural learners bring characteristics (e.g. race/ethnicity, language, and culture, family, and economic status) to classrooms that differ significantly from monolingual, English-speaking Caucasian learners who have no apparent physical or cognitive disabilities (Collier, 1998a). Gonzalez et al. (1997) pointed out:

> Strong relationships exist between certain characteristics of these students and indicators of school failure, including those between poverty and low reading and math scores, racial and ethnic minority status and high drop-out rates, and disability and under-or unemployment after graduation. Less attention, unfortunately, has been paid to analyzing relationships between characteristics of the learning environment itself and aspects of school failure. While culturally and linguistically diverse students may have personal characteristics that contribute to a lack of

academic progress (e.g. a genuine disability or an unstable home life), they may also be at-risk because characteristics of the school setting are detrimental to the learning process (pp. 5–6).

By examining transactions between person and environmental factors, researchers and educators become knowledgeable about the influence of sociocultural characteristics of multicultural learners (e.g. cultural values, beliefs, and customs) and how these factors interact within the classroom environment. The transactional model is focused on interactions of the student with the environment as an explanation of academic learning and social development. Environmental variables that influence the learning environment may be broadly categorized as: (a) setting and context characteristics (e.g. organizational format, locale and geographic location, and climate); (b) characteristics of the participants (e.g. parent, student, demographics, individual differences in current motivation and development, and criteria for judging person characteristics); and (c) task-process-outcome characteristics (e.g. quantitative and qualitative features of instruction, types of tasks, and procedural methods, materials, and techniques).

For multicultural learners, the environment consists of the society, community, school, and family and the interactions across these contexts dramatically affects children's abilities, strengths, and weaknesses. Thus, a classroom learning environment can work to habilitate or further debilitate a student's potential to learn (Kea & Utley, 1998; Ruiz, 1995). Garcia et al. (1997) remarked that:

> Although instruction occurs primarily in a classroom context, other factors beyond that context are important influences on decisions that teachers make during the instructional process. For example, at the societal level, the low performance of language minority students is embedded in the interactions between majority and "minority" groups, which influence educator role definition and the school climate . . . The societal interaction also influences orientations of language minority students and their families toward education and schooling, thereby affecting the quality of home-school, parent-teacher, and student-teacher interactions (pp. 444–445).

Evaluating Instructional Contexts: The Ecobehavioral Analysis Model

General and special educators face unique challenges in teaching multicultural learners, some of which include: (a) their lack of understanding of how to incorporate language effectively in the classroom; (b) difficulty in designing a classroom where teachers make instructional time challenging for students; (c) teachers' use of native language while teaching a second language; and (d) developing a classroom atmosphere of mutual understanding and accommodation. Over the past years, an emerging knowledge base has developed to address these classroom-based instructional challenges (Mitchem & Richards, 2003). Two instructional questions appear critical for a general or special educator. Can a classroom environment be designed to optimize learning and student performance in multicultural learners? What are the most crucial instructional variables that are likely to affect student outcomes? Researchers at the Juniper Gardens Children's Project of the University of Kansas, have adopted an ecobehavioral analysis approach to: (a) analyzing a broad range of environmental variables that are temporarily and spatially removed from the behavior of individuals, including those variables that are within environmental, social, and cultural contexts; and (b) evaluating the effectiveness of instruction and interventions in special education and bilingual education settings as a means of addressing classroom contextual factors that affect student outcomes of multicultural children with and without disabilities. By examining classroom process variables (i.e. the assessment of teacher behavior, student behavior, and contextual variables), students' interactions with the environment (or ecological factors) can be studied to determine if instruction is optimizing or limiting the performance of multicultural learners. Thus, ecobehavioral analysis is a technology for evaluating instructional interventions in relation to program aspects (e.g. instructional environment components, teacher behaviors, and student behaviors) and identifying instructional variables that reliably influence academic and linguistic performance and the design of instructional technology based on this knowledge (Arreaga-Mayer et al., 1994).

In research studies with teachers, the concepts of "opportunity to respond" and "student engagement" were identified as important variables that facilitate academic achievement. Opportunity to respond refers to "the need to promote higher rates of academic behavior for all students for longer periods by ensuring that instruction occasioned active academic responding in the classroom" (Greenwood et al., 1994, p. 214). More specifically, "opportunity to respond (also referred to as student engagement) can be defined as the interaction between: (a) teacher formulated instruction . . . (the materials presented, prompts, questions asked, signals to respond); and (b) its success in establishing the academic responding desired or implied by materials, the subject matter goals of instruction" (Greenwood et al., 1984, p. 64). Observational instruments have been developed and validated through empirical research studies (Arreaga-Mayer et al., 1994; Carta et al., 1985, 1987; Greenwood et al., 1997; Greenwood & Delquadri, 1988; Stanley & Greenwood, 1981). Emerging from this database are descriptive studies conducted with: (a) students with LD (e.g. Bulgren & Carta, 1993); (b) at-risk students in urban poverty environments (Greenwood, 1991), and bilingual students with developmental disabilities (Arreaga-Mayer, 1992; Arreaga-Mayer et al., 1994) documenting causal relations between achievement, academic responding, and instruction.

Over the years, a knowledge base has developed documenting why children living in urban poverty communities are academically delayed as early as kindergarten and first grade (Snow et al., 1998). To address questions regarding the causes and solutions to academic delay, learning disability, and school failure in urban poverty classrooms, Greenwood et al. (1991) remarked that "ecobehavioral analysis offers education a powerful, expanded process measure for the study of the delivery of teaching and its effects on students, including the causes of academic success and failure" (p. 63). Earlier studies of ecobehavioral assessments describing the ecological features of classroom practices in second, third, and fourth grade samples revealed important differences in practices and school achievement levels between at-risk students in low-SES schools compared to students schools in middle-high SES schools (Greenwood et al., 1989). Greenwood et al. (1991) summarized these results as follows:

> First, high-SES students received significantly more time per day in subject matter instruction. Second, the ecological structure of instructional programs serving these students differed in terms of multiple qualitative and quantitative factors (e.g. materials used, grouping arrangements, and teachers' behaviors) compared to those received by low-SES students. Third, low-SES students who were significantly less skilled on academic tests and measured IQ, were also significantly less engaged in academic behaviors ($M_{difference} = 11$ minutes per day, range $= 9$–110 minutes of engagement per day) during their daily lessons than were high-SES, higher-skilled students. Fourth, the instructional arrangements employed by teachers of high-SES students covaried with higher levels of students' academic engagement (p. 66).

These descriptive data provide important evidence that the ecological arrangements of classrooms and the delivery of instructional practices in classrooms can accelerate or decelerate academic responding and engagement and affect the overall rate of academic development, especially in children divergent in SES, achievement levels, and measured intelligence. When teachers implement instructional practices (i.e. ecological features of instruction) that promote low levels of academic responding and engagement, then, slower rates of academic growth on weekly test scores are observed. Conversely, when teachers implement instructional practices that promote high levels of academic responding and engagement, then, higher rates of academic growth on weekly test scores are observed. Recently, Arreaga-Mayer et al. (2003) reported the results of a study using *The Ecobehavioral System for the Contextual Recording of Interactional Bilingual Environments* (ESCRIBE) to describe in quantifiable terms assessment, methodological, and instructional variables related to the delivery of services for bilingual students at risk for developmental disabilities. Collectively, the results revealed that: (a) the most frequently occurring activities were math (20%), reading (18%), and language arts (16%); (b) English was the most frequently used language of instruction (58%); and (c) the total "active engagement" of students in academic behaviors (44%) was slightly less than one-half of a typical school day.

NEW VISION FOR EDUCATING MULTICULTURAL LEARNERS WITH LD

Multicultural education is the ultimate antidote for misidentification, misassessment, miscategorization, misplacement, and misinstruction of culturally and linguistically diverse learners of LD. The definition of multicultural education is based on different frameworks, typologies, or approaches. Collectively, these approaches emphasize one of many aspects of multicultural education such as: (a) educational equity; (b) cultural pluralism; (c) human relations; (d) social reconstruction; (e) school reform and restructuring; (f) teachers' educational practices; (g) cross-cultural competence. Consequently, definitions have been misinterpreted and have led to misconceptions and myths about basic assumptions, beliefs, and structures within schools that attempt to educate learners with LD. To advance the field and reduce the multiple meanings of multicultural education, scholars need to develop a higher level of consensus about what the term means. Such agreement is beginning to form among academics. The consensus centers around a primary goal of increasing educational equality for both gender groups, for students from diverse ethnic and cultural groups, and for exceptionalities (e.g. LD). In the same vein, Grant and Ladson-Billings (1997) stated that "as scholars continue to study multicultural education and try to define it to meet the context of the ever-changing society, the meanings that characterize the different approaches will change, and/or some of the approaches will give way to make room for new ideas and meanings" (p. 176). Recently, Nieto (2001) defined multicultural education as:

> ... a process of comprehensive school reform and basic education for all students. It challenges and rejects racism and other forms of discrimination in schools and society and accepts and affirms the pluralism (ethnic, racial, linguistic, religious, economic, and gender, among others) that students, their communities, and teachers reflect. Multicultural education permeates the schools' curriculum and instructional strategies, as well as the interactions among teachers, students, and families, and the very way that schools conceptualize the nature of teaching and learning. Because it uses critical pedagogy as its underlying philosophy and focuses on knowledge, reflection, and action (praxis) as the basis for social change, multicultural education promotes democratic principles of social justice (p. 305).

Banks (1992, cited in Lockwood) summarized the underlying assumptions of multicultural education, as follows:

(1) Multicultural education is a reform movement designed to bring about educational equity for all students, including those from different races, ethnic groups, social classes, exceptionality, and sexual orientation.

(2) Multicultural education should help students to develop the knowledge, attitudes, and skills to participate in a democratic and free society . . . Multicultural education promotes the freedom, abilities and skills to cross ethnic and cultural boundaries to participation in other cultures and groups.

(3) Multicultural education is for all children, not just for African Americans or Hispanics or Native Americans, but for all students.

(4) The multicultural classroom, students hear multiple voices and multiple perspectives. They hear the voice of different ethnic and cultural groups.

(5) The aims of multicultural education should always be the same, regardless of the setting. However, the strategy points and methods may have to be contextualized.

(6) A multicultural curriculum can be taught with almost any materials if the teachers have the knowledge, skills, and attitudes needed to transform their thinking and consequently the school curriculum.

(7) Multicultural education is an inclusive and cementing movement . . . It attempts to bring various groups that have been on the margins of society to the center of society (pp. 23–27).

The implications of multicultural perspectives for general and special educators are that: (a) behaviors are influenced by culture; (b) learning and social interactions are inextricably connected and inseparable from cognition; and (c) both teacher and student are engaged in the process of constructing knowledge through shared social activities and dialogue. Therefore, general and special educators are challenged to: (a) interpret the social behaviors of learners from culturally diverse backgrounds; (b) distinguish academic and social behaviors from deficits; and (b) employ instructional strategies effective to help these learners maximize their schooling experiences and acquire the most productive interpersonal skills.

Providing a culturally appropriate education for multicultural learners with LD has become an imperative for general and special educators, service providers, and related professionals. Grossman (1995) noted that "because there is no legal definition of culturally appropriate education, there are many different approaches aimed at increasing respect for diversity, reducing prejudice, improving interethnic group relations, and resolving cultural incompatibilities between students' styles of learning and behavior and educators' styles of instruction" (p. 87). He recommended some broad approaches to address the educational difficulties of multicultural learners in schools, some of which include:

(1) Increasing respect for diversity, reducing prejudice, and improving interethnic group relations.

(2) Discussions of differences and similarities among different multicultural groups.
(3) The inclusion of students' cultures in the curriculum and classroom.
(4) Implementing a proactive anti-bias curriculum program.
(5) Eliminating teacher bias.
(6) Eliminating curriculum bias.
(7) Teaching about prejudice.
(8) Teaching an emancipatory and transformative curriculum to change biased discriminatory aspects of society (pp. 87–98).

CONCLUSION

In this chapter, we looked at innovative ways to work with multicultural learners with LD. In addition, we examined the concept of LD from three contemporary perspectives: sociocultural, transactional, and ecobehavioral analysis. Each contemporary paradigm has significant implications for assessing multicultural learners with LD. We strongly believe general and special educators must continue to challenge themselves and infuse educational perspectives to ensure that multicultural learners with LD are not misidentified, misassessed, misdiagnosed, miscategorized, misplaced, and misinstructed. Educators and service providers must be willing to shift their paradigm to maximize the learning potential of multicultural learners. The fields of general and special education can never be deemed reformed unless multicultural learners with and without disabilities are provided culturally and contextualized instruction in inclusive classroom settings.

REFERENCES

Adelman, H. S., & Taylor, L. (1993). *Learning problems & learning disabilities: Moving forward.* Pacific Grove, CA: Brooks/Cole.
Adler, S. (1993). *Multicultural communication skills in the classroom.* Needham Heights, MA: Allyn & Bacon.
Arreaga-Mayer, C. (1992). Ecobehavioral assessment of exceptional culturally and linguistically diverse students: Evaluating effective bilingual special education programs. Proceeding of the Third National Research Symposium on Limited English Proficient Student Issues: Focus on middle and high school issues. Washington, DC: Office of Bilingual Education and Minority Languages Affairs.
Arreaga-Mayer, C., Carta, J. J., & Tapia, Y. (1994). *Ecobehavioral assessment: A new methodology for evaluating instruction for exceptional culturally and linguistically diverse students*

(Monograph 1). Reston, VA: The Council for Exceptional Children, Division of Diverse Exceptional Learner.

Arreaga-Mayer, C., Utley, C. A., Perdomo-Rivera, C., & Greenwood (2003). Ecobehavioral assessment of instructional contexts in bilingual special education programs for English-Language Learners at risk for developmental disabilities. *Focus on Autism and Other Developmental Disabilities, 18*(1), Austin, TX: Pro-Ed.

Artiles, A. A., & Trent, S. C. (1994). Over-representation of minority students in special education: A continuing debate. *The Journal of Special Education, 27*, 410–437.

Bender, W. N. (1995). *Learning disabilities: Characteristics, identification, and teaching strategies* (2nd ed.). Needham Heights, MA: Allyn & Bacon.

Berninger, V. W., & Abbott, R. D. (1994). Redefining learning disabilities: Moving beyond aptitude-achievement discrepancies to failure to respond to validated treatment protocols. In: G. R. Lyon (Ed.), *Frames of Reference for the Assessment of Learning Disabilities: New Views on Measurement Issues* (pp. 163–184). Baltimore, MD: Brookes.

Blackhurst, A. E., & Berndine, W. H. (1993). *An introduction to special education* (3rd ed.). New York: Harper-Collins.

Bos, C. S., & Fletcher, T. V. (1997). Sociocultural considerations in learning disabilities inclusion research: Knowledge gaps and future directions. *Learning Disabilities Research & Practice, 12*(2), 92–99.

Bulgren, J. A., & Carta, J. J. (1993). Examining the instructional contexts of students with learning disabilities. *Exceptional Children, 59*(3), 182–191.

Byrd, H. B. (1995). Curricular and pedagogical procedures for African American learners with academic and cognitive disabilities. In: B. A. Ford, F. E. Obiakor & J. M. Patton (Eds), *Effective Education of African American Learners: New Perspectives* (pp. 123–150). Austin, TX: Pro-Ed.

Carta, J. J., Greenwood, C. R., & Atwater, J. (1985). *Ecobehavioral system for the complex assessment of preschool environments: ESCAPE.* Kansas City, KS: Juniper Gardens Children's Project, Bureau of Child Research, University of Kansas.

Carta, J. J., Greenwood, C. R., Schulte, D., Arreaga-Mayer, C., & Terry, B. (1987). *Code for the instructional structure and student academic response: Mainstream version (MS-CISSAR).* Kansas City, KS: Juniper Gardens Children's Project, Bureau of Child Research, University of Kansas.

Civil Rights Act of 1964, P.L. 88–352, 78 Stat. 241.

Cole, M., & Means, B. (1981). *Comparative studies of how people think: An introduction.* Cambridge, MA: Harvard University Press.

Collier, C. (1998a). *Assessing minority students with learning and behavior problems.* Lindale, TX: Hamilton Publications.

Collier, C. (1998b). Developing instructional plans and curriculum for bilingual special education students. In: L. M. Baca & H. T. Cervantes (Eds), *The Bilingual Special Education Interface* (3rd ed., pp. 28–35). Columbus, OH: Merrill.

Collier, C. (1998c). *Separating difference from disability: Assessing diverse learners.* Ferndale, WA: Cross-Cultural Developmental Education Services.

Council for Exceptional Children (2002). *No Child Left Behind Act of 2001: Reauthorization of the Elementary and Secondary Education Act.* Alexandria, VA: Author.

Craig, H. K. (1996). The challenges of conducting language research with African American children. In: A. G. Kamhi, K. E. Pollack & J. L. Harris (Eds), *Communication Development and Disorders in African American Children: Research, Assessment, and Intervention* (pp. 1–18). Baltimore, MD: Brookes.

Cunningham, J. L. (1998). Learning disabilities. In: J. Sandoval, C. L. Frisby, K. F. Geisinger, J.
    D. Scheueman & J. R. Grenier (Eds), *Test Interpretation and Diversity: Achieving Equity in
    Assessment* (pp. 317–347). Washington, DC: American Psychological Association.
Faas, L. A. (1980). *Children with learning problems: A handbook for teachers.* Boston, MA:
    Houghton-Mifflin.
Fuchs, D., Fuchs, L., Mathes, P. G., Lipsey, M. W., & Roberts, P. H. (2001). Is "learning disabilities
    just a fancy term for low achievement? A meta-analysis of reading differences between low
    achievers with and without the label. Paper presented at the Learning Disabilities Summit.
    Washington, DC.
Galagan, J. E. (1985). Psychoeducational testing: Turn out the lights, the party's over. *Exceptional
    Children, 52,* 244–265.
Garcia, S. B., & Dominguez, L. (1997). Cultural contexts that influence learning and academic
    performance. *Academic Difficulties, 6*(3), 621–655.
Garcia, S. B., & Malkin, D. H. (1993). Toward defining programs and services for culturally and
    linguistically diverse learners in special education. *Teaching Exceptional Children, 21*(1),
    52–58.
Garcia, S. B., & Ortiz, A. A. (1988). *Preventing inappropriate referrals of language minority students
    to special education.* (New Focus, No. 5). Washington, DC: National Clearinghouse for
    Bilingual Education.
Garcia, S. B., Wilkinson, C. Y., & Ortiz, A. A. (1997). Enhancing achievement for language minority
    students: Classroom, school, and family contexts. *Education and Urban Society, 27,* 441–462.
Gindis, B. (1995). The social implication of disability: Vygotsky's paradigm for special education.
    Educational Psychologist, 30(2), 77–81.
Gonzalez, V., Brusca-Vega, R., & Yawkey, T. (1997). *Assessment and instruction of culturally and
    linguistically diverse students with or at-risk of learning problems: From research to practice.*
    Needham Heights, MA: Allyn & Bacon.
Gottlieb, J., Alter, M., Gottlieb, B. W., & Wishner, J. (1994). Special education in urban America: It's
    not justifiable for many. *The Journal of Special Education, 27,* 453–465.
Grant, C. A., & Ladson-Billings, G. (1997). *Dictionary of multicultural education.* Phoenix, AZ: Oryx
    Press.
Greenwood, C. R. (1991). A longitudinal analysis of time to learn, engagement, and academic
    achievement in urban versus suburban schools. *Exceptional Children, 57,* 521–535.
Greenwood, C. R. (1996). The case for performance-based instructional models. *School Psychology
    Quarterly, 11,* 283–296.
Greenwood, C. R., Carta, J. J., & Atwater, J. (1991). Ecobehavioral analysis in the classroom. *Journal
    of Behavioral Education, 1,* 59–77.
Greenwood, C. R., Carta, J. J., Kamps, D., & Delquadri, J. C. (1997). *Ecobehavioral assessment
    systems software (EBASS version 3.0): Practitioner's manual.* Kansas City, KS: Juniper
    Gardens Children's Project, University of Kansas.
Greenwood, C. R., & Delquadri, J. C. (1988). Code for instructional structure and student academic
    response: CISSAR. In: M. Hersen & A. S. Bellack (Eds), *Dictionary of Behavioral Assessment
    Techniques* (pp. 120–122). New York: Pergamon.
Greenwood, C. R., Delquadri, J. C., & Hall, V. R. (1984). Opportunity to respond and student academic
    performance. In: W. Heward, T. Heron, D. Hill & J. Trap-Porter (Eds), *Behavior Analysis in
    Education* (pp. 58–88). Columbus, OH: Merrill.
Greenwood, C. R., Delquadri, J. C., & Hall, V. R. (1989). Longitudinal effects of classwide peer
    tutoring. *Journal of Educational Psychology, 81,* 371–383.

Greenwood, C. R., Hart, B., Walker, D., & Risley, T. (1994). The opportunity to respond and academic performance revisited: A behavioral theory of developmental retardation and its prevention. In: R. Gardner III, D. M. Sainato, J. O. Cooper, T. E. Heron, W. L. Heward, J. Eshleman & T. A. Grossi (Eds), *Behavior Analysis in Education: Focus on Measurably Superior Instruction* (pp. 213–224). Pacific Grove, CA: Brooks/Cole.

Gresham, F. (2001). Responsiveness to intervention: An alternative approach to the identification of learning disabilities. Paper presented at the Learning Disabilities Summit. Washington, DC.

Grossman, H. (1995). *Teaching in a diverse society.* Needham Heights, MA: Allyn & Bacon.

Hallahan, D. P., Kauffman, J. M., & Lloyd, J. W. (1999). *Introduction to learning disabilities.* Needham Heights, MA: Allyn & Bacon.

Hallahan, D. P., & Mercer, C. D. (2001). Learning disabilities: Historical perspectives. Paper presented at the Learning Disabilities Summit. Washington, DC.

Hamayan, E. V., & Damico, J. S. (1991). *Limiting bias in the assessment of bilingual students.* Austin, TX: Pro-Ed.

Hardman, M. L., Drew, C. J., & Egan, M. W. (1999). *Human exceptionality: Society, school and family* (6th ed.). Needham Heights, MA: Allyn & Bacon.

Harry, B. (1994). *The disproportionate representation of minority students in special education: Theories and recommendations.* Alexandria, VA: National Association of State Directors of Special Education.

Hebbeler, K., & Wagner, M. (2000). *The national early intervention longitudinal study (NEILS) design overview. SRI International.* Palo Alto, CA.

Hebbeler, K., & Wagner, M. (2001). *Representation of minorities and children of poverty among those receiving early intervention and special education services: Findings from two national longitudinal studies.* Menlo Park, CA: Stanford Research Institute.

Heller, K. A., Holtzman, W. H., & Messick, S. (1982). *Placing children in special education: A strategy for equity.* Washington, DC: National Academy Press.

Henley, M., Ramsey, R. S., & Algozzine, R. (1993). *Characteristics of and strategies for teaching students with mild disabilities.* Needham Heights, MA: Allyn & Bacon.

Individuals with Disabilities Education Act, 20 U.S.C. § 1400 et seq. 1997.

Kaufman, A. S. (1981). Assessment: The wechsler scales and learning disabilities. *Journal of Learning Disabilities, 16,* 616–620.

Kavale, K. (2001). Discrepancy models in the identification of learning disability. Paper presented at the Learning Disabilities Summit. Washington, DC.

Kavale, K. A., & Forness, S. R. (1998). The politics of learning disabilities. *Learning Disability Quarterly, 21*(4), 245–275.

Kea, C. D., & Utley, C. A. (1998). To teach me is to know me. *The Journal of Special Education, 32*(1), 44–47.

Keogh, B. K., Gallimore, R., & Weisner, T. (1997). A sociocultural perspective on learning and learning disabilities. *Learning Disabilities Research & Practice, 12*(2), 107–113.

Kretschmer, R. E. (1991). Exceptionality and the limited english proficient student: Historical and practical contexts. In: E. V. Hamayan & J. S. Damico (Eds), *Limiting Bias in the Assessment of Bilingual Students* (pp. 1–38). Austin, TX: Pro-Ed.

Lockwood, A. T. (1992). Education for freedom. *Focus in Change, 7*(Summer), 23–29.

Longstreet, W., (1978). *Aspects of ethnicity.* New York: Teachers College Press.

Losen, D. J., & Orfield, G. (2002). *Racial inequality in special education.* Cambridge, MA: Harvard Education Press.

Lyon, G. R. (1996). Learning disabilities. *The future of children: Special education for students with disabilities, 6*(1), 54–76.

MacMillan, D. L., & Reschly, D. J. (1997). Issues of definition and classification. In: W. E. MacLean, Jr. (Ed.), *Ellis' Handbook of Mental Deficiency, Psychological Theory, and Research* (3rd ed., pp. 47–74). Mahwah, NJ: Erlbaum.

MacMillan, D. L., & Siperstein, G. N. (2001). Learning disabilities as operationally defined by schools. Paper presented at the Learning Disabilities Summit. Washington, DC.

Manis, F. R. (1996). Current trends in dyslexia research. In: B. J. Cratty & R. L. (Eds), *Learning Disabilities: Contemporary Viewpoints* (pp. 27–42). Amsterdam, The Netherlands: Harwood Academic.

Massey, A. (1996). Cultural influences on language: Implications for assessing African American children. In: A. G. Kamhi, K. E. Pollack & J. L. Harris (Eds), *Communication Development and Disorders in African American Children: Research, Assessment, and Intervention* (pp. 285–306). Baltimore, MD: Brookes.

McIntosh, A. S. (2002). Categorization: Impact on African American learners with exceptionalities. In: F. E. Obiakor & B. A. Ford (Eds), *Creating Successful Learning Environments for African American Learners with Exceptionalities* (pp. 41–52). Thousand Oaks, CA: Corwin Press.

McKinney, J. D., & Feagans, L. (1981). The pattern of exceptionality across domains in learning disabled children. *Journal of Applied Developmental Psychology, 1*, 313–328.

Midgette, T. E. (1995). Assessment of African American exceptional learners: New strategies and perspectives. In: B. A. Ford, F. E. Obiakor & J. M. Patton (Eds), *Effective Education of African American Exceptional Learners: New Perspectives* (pp. 3–26). Austin, TX: Pro-Ed.

Mitchem, K. J., & Richards, A. (2003). Students with learning disabilities. In: F. E. Obiakor, C. A. Utley & A. Rotatori (Eds), *Effective Education for Learners with Exceptionalities* (Vol. 15, pp. 99–117). San Diego, CA: JAI Press.

Moll, L. C. (1992). Bilingual classroom studies and community analysis: Some recent trends. *Educational Researcher, 21*(2), 20–24.

Morris, E. K., & Midgley, B. D. (1990). Some historical and conceptual foundations of ecobehavioral analysis. In: S. R. Schroeder (Ed.), *Ecobehavioral Analysis and Developmental Disabilities: The Twenty-First Century* (pp. 1–32). New York: Springer-Verlag.

National Institute for Urban School Improvement (2001). *On the nexus of race, disability, and overrepresentation: What do we know? Where do we go?* Denver, CO: University of Colorado-Denver.

National Joint Committee on Learning Disabilities (1994). *Collective perspectives on issues affecting learning disabilities: Position papers and statements.* Austin, TX: Author.

National Research Council (2002). *Minority students in special and gifted education.* Washington, DC: Author.

Nazzaaro, J. N. (1981). *Culturally diverse exceptional children in school.* Alexandria, VA: ERIC 1–12.

Nieto, S. (2001). *Affirming diversity: The sociopolitical context of multicultural education* (3rd ed.). New York: Longman.

Obiakor, F. E. (1994). *The eight-step multicultural approach: Learning and teaching with a smile.* Dubuque, IA: Kendall/Hunt.

Obiakor, F. E. (1999). Teacher expectations of minority exceptional learners: Impact on "accuracy" of self-concepts. *Exceptional Children, 66*, 39–53.

Obiakor, F. E. (2001). *It even happens in "GOOD" schools: Responding to cultural diversity in today's classrooms.* Thousand Oaks: Corwin Press.

Obiakor, F. E., & Ford, B. A. (2002). *Creating successful learning environments for African American learners with exceptionalities.* Thousand Oaks, CA: Corwin Press.

Obiakor, F. E., Grant, P. A., & Dooley, E. A. (2002). *Educating all learners.* Springfield, IL: Charles C. Thomas.

Obiakor, F. E., Utley, C. A., & Rotatori, A. F. (2003). *Effective education for learners with exceptionalities. Advances in Special Education* (Vol. 15). San Diego, CA: JAI Press.

Olson, R. (1997, May). The genetics of LD: Twin studies. Paper presented at the Conference of Progress and Promise in Research and Education for Individuals with Learning Disabilities, Washington, DC.

Ortiz, A. A. (1997). Learning disabilities occurring concomitantly with linguistic differences. *Journal of Learning Disabilities, 30*(3), 321–342.

Osher, D., Woodruff, D., & Sims, A. (2002). Schools make a difference: The overrepresentation of African American youth in special education and the juvenile justice system. In: D. J. Losen & G. Orfield (Eds), *Racial Inequality in Special Education* (pp. 93–116). Cambridge, MA: Harvard Education Press.

Perkins-Gordon, R. (1996). Linguistic bias in the assessment of African Americans with learning disabilities. In: N. Gregg, R. S. Curtis & S. F. Schmidt (Eds), *African American Adolescents and Adults with Learning Disabilities: An Overview of Assessment Issues* (pp. 53–64). Athens, GA: University of Georgia.

Raymond, E. B. (2000). *Learners with mild disabilities: A characteristics approach.* Needham Heights, MA: Allyn & Bacon.

Rogoff, B., & Chavajay, P. (1995). What's become of research on the cultural bases of cognitive development? *American Psychologist, 50,* 859–877.

Roseberry-McKibbin, C. (1995). *Multicultural students with special language needs: Practical strategies for assessment and intervention.* Oceanside, CA: Academic Communication Associates.

Ruiz, N. T. (1995). The social construction of ability and disability: I. Profile types of Latino children identified as language learning disabled. *Journal of Learning Disabilities, 28*(8), 476–490.

Schmidt, S., Curtis, R., & Gregg, N. (1996). *Multiple factors impacting the assessment and instruction of African American adolescents and adults with learning disabilities.* Athens, GA: University of Georgia.

Seymour, H. N., & Bland, L. (1991). A minority perspective in the diagnosing of child language disorders. *Clinics in Communication Disorders, 1*(1), 39–50.

Seymour, H. N., Champion, T., & Jackson, J. (1995). The language of African American learners: Effective assessment and instructional programming for children with special needs. In: B. A. Ford, F. E. Obiakor & J. M. Patton (Eds), *Effective Education of African American Exceptional Learners: New Perspectives* (pp. 89–121). Austin, TX: Pro-Ed.

Sleeter, C. E. (1986). Learning disabilities: The social construction of a special education category. *Exceptional Children, 53*(1), 46–54.

Sleeter, C. E., & Hartney, C. (1992). Involving special educators in challenging injustice in education. In: C. Diaz (Ed.), *Multicultural Education for the 21st Century* (pp. 150–165). Washington, DC: National Education Association.

Smith, C. R. (1998). *Learning disabilities: The interaction of learner, task, and setting.* Needham Heights, MA: Allyn & Bacon.

Smith, E. C., Price, B. J., & Marsh, G. E. (1986). *Mildly handicapped children and adults.* St. Paul, MN: West.

Snow, C., Burns, M. S., & Griffin, P. (1998). *Preventing reading difficulties in young children.* Washington, DC: National Research Council.

Stanford Research Institute International (2002). *The national longitudinal transition study* (NLTS). Palo Alto, CA: Author.

Stanley, S. O., & Greenwood, C. R. (1981). *CISSAR: Code for instructional structure and student academic response: Observer's manual*. Kansas City, KS: Juniper Gardens Children's Project, Bureau of Child Research.

Taylor, O. L. (1986). *Nature of communication disorders in culturally and linguistically diverse populations*. Austin, TX: Pro-Ed.

Tomasi, S., & Weinberg, S. L. (1999). Classifying children as LD: An analysis of current practice in an urban setting. *Learning Disability Quarterly, 22*(1), 31–42.

Torgensen, J. K. (1998). Learning disabilities: An historical and conceptual overview. In: B. Y. L. Wong (Ed.), *Learning About Learning Disabilities* (pp. 3–34). San Diego, CA: Academic Press.

Torgenson, J. K. (2001). Empirical and theoretical support for direct diagnosis of learning disabilities by assessment of intrinsic processing weaknesses. Paper presented at the Learning Disabilities Summit. Washington, DC.

US Department of Education (1994). *The goals 2000: Educate America Act*. Washington, DC: Author.

US Department of Education (1995). *To assure the free appropriate public education of all children with disabilities. Eighteenth annual report to Congress on the implementation of the Individuals with Disabilities Act*. Washington, DC: U.S. Government Printing Office.

US Department of Education (1998). *To assure the free appropriate public education of all children with disabilities. Twentieth annual report to Congress on the implementation of the individuals with disabilities act*. Washington, DC: U.S. Government Printing Office.

US Department of Education (2001). *To assure the free appropriate public education of all children with disabilities. Twenty-third annual report to Congress on the implementation of the individuals with disabilities act*. Washington, DC: U.S. Government Printing Office.

US Department of Education, Office of Civil Rights (1997). *Annual report to Congress*. Washington, DC: Author.

Utley, C. A. (1993). Culturally and linguistically diverse students with mild disabilities. In: C. A. Grant (Ed.), *Educating for Diversity: An Anthology of Multicultural Voices* (pp. 301–324). Boston, MA: Allyn & Bacon.

Utley, C. A. (2002). Functionalizing assessment for African American learners in general and special education programs. In: F. E. Obiakor & B. A. Ford (Eds), *Creating Successful Learning Environments for African American Learners with Exceptionalities* (pp. 27–40). Thousand Oaks, CA: Corwin Press.

Utley, C. A., & Obiakor, F. E. (2001). *Special education, multicultural education, and school reform: Components of quality education for learners with mild disabilities*. Springfield, IL: Charles C Thomas.

Wertsch, J. V. (1991). *Voices of the mind: A sociocultural approach to mediated action*. Cambridge, MA: Harvard University Press.

NEUROLOGICAL AND NEUROPSYCHOLOGICAL ASPECTS OF LEARNING AND ATTENTION PROBLEMS

Roger Stefani

INTRODUCTION

For many years it has been speculated that some learning and attention problems in children are related to underlying problems in neurological functioning. In fact, the IDEA (1997) definition of learning disabilities utilizes terminology that specifically includes neurological processes and conditions:

> Specific learning disabilities means a disorder in one or more of the basic psychological processes involved in understanding or in using language, spoken or written, which may manifest itself in an imperfect ability to listen, think, speak, read, write, spell, or do mathematical calculations. The term includes such conditions as *perceptual handicaps, brain injury, minimal brain dysfunction, dyslexia,* and *developmental aphasia.* The term does not include children who have learning problems which are primarily the result of visual, hearing, or motor handicaps, of mental retardation, or of environmental, cultural, or economic disadvantage.

This chapter begins with a review of the role of *neuroimaging* in advancing an understanding of the basis and nature of learning and attention problems. The ever-increasing sophistication of neurodiagnostic technology has made it possible to obtain more precise information about neuroanatomical and neurophysiological

Current Perspectives on Learning Disabilities
Advances in Special Education, Volume 16, 65–93
Copyright © 2004 by Elsevier Ltd.
All rights of reproduction in any form reserved
ISSN: 0270-4013/doi:10.1016/S0270-4013(04)16004-2

bases of behavior, including learning and attention. Advances in technology have greatly increased the ability to study the functioning of the brain during the performance of relatively complex mental activities. With this advanced technology it is becoming increasingly possible to visualize normal and abnormal brain functioning, including important components of basic academic skills. The chapter includes a discussion of the recent evidence about the neurological basis of learning and attention problems.

The second portion of this chapter will provide a discussion of the *neuropsychological* aspects of learning and attentions problems. While neuroimaging technology has been instrumental in identifying the neurological structures and systems that underlie learning and attention problems, the field of neuropsychology has been instrumental in helping to define the component cognitive processing problems that result in learning and attention problems. Neuropsychology has also been helpful in identifying and describing patterns of cognitive strengths and weaknesses that are often associated with learning and attention problems, and the functional impact of these strengths and weaknesses. This section of the chapter will address subtypes of learning and attention problems that are based on differences in neuropsychological strengths and weaknesses.

Neuroimaging and Learning Disabilities

Researchers have used CT scan and MRI to investigate cerebral differences between individuals with reading problems and those without reading problems. Many of these studies have focused on the left hemisphere of the brain, due to the predilection of the left hemisphere to subserve language processing, and reading being viewed as a language process.

Rumsey (1996) provided a summary of the neuroimaging literature as is pertains to developmental dyslexia. Neuroimaging techniques such as CT scan and MRI have indicated that developmental dyslexia is not associated with large lesions of the kind that can be imaged with this kind of technology.

Neuroanatomical Differences in Dyslexia
The planum temporale is an area in the superior temporal region of the brain that lies deep in the Sylvian fissure. In most people the planum temporale is larger in the left hemisphere than it is in the right hemisphere, and this asymmetry in size is thought to be important in the left hemisphere dominance in language processing in most individuals. Using MRI, Larsen et al. (1992) found that adolescents with dyslexia displayed greater symmetry in the planum temporale than did normal readers.

Deficits in phonological decoding were strongly related to this symmetry. Kusch et al. (1993) examined the superior temporal plane in individuals ranging in age from 8 to 53 years. Individuals with dyslexia displayed increased symmetry in this area when the left and right hemispheres were compared, while normal readers displayed the normal leftward asymmetry. They also found that individuals with milder reading problems displayed more normal asymmetry in the superior temporal region.

Using MRI, Hynd et al. (1990) found bilaterally smaller and more symmetrical frontal lobe cortices in children with reading disability without attention deficit disorder. Several studies have examined the corpus callosum, which is a mass of fibers connecting the right and left hemispheres of the brain. Rumsey et al. (1996) examined 21 men with dyslexia. The only area of the corpus callosum that differed from normal was in the posterior third, which was larger in dyslexic men.

Post mortem neuropathological studies of individuals with dyslexia were performed by Galaburda and colleagues (Galaburda et al., 1985; Humphreys et al., 1990). These neuropathological studies were performed on the brains of four men and three women who had been diagnosed with dyslexia. Their findings indicated a few neuroanatomical differences between these brains, and more typical brains. For example, while the planum temporale is larger in the left hemisphere than it is in the right hemisphere for most people, all seven of the brains of the dyslexic individuals studied did not show this type of asymmetry, thus raising the possibility that this difference in brain structure may be a risk factor for reading problems. They also found small clusters of abnormally placed neurons and focal areas of distorted cortical architecture in the cerebral cortex of the dyslexic brains. These abnormalities were generally too small to be seen on MRI, and are likely prenatal in origin. Often, these anomalies were distributed in areas that are important to language function (e.g. left sylvian fissure), or in areas that have connections to language processing areas of the brain. Livingstone et al. (1991) studied the same seven brains discussed above, and in five of them they found anomalies in the lateral geniculate nucleus of the thalamus. This is an area of the brain that is important for the rapid processing of low-contrast visual information.

Neurophysiological Findings in Dyslexia
While many studies have investigated static neuroanatomical factors, advancements in neuroimaging have allowed for investigation of neurological structure and function based on measurement of physiological processes. These methods include positron emission tomagraphy (PET) and single photon emission computed tomography (SPECT). Both PET and SPECT rely on measurement of

radioactive isotopes that are either injected or breathed in by the individual. Some of the physiological processes that are measured include glucose utilization, oxygen utilization, and blood flow. The development of functional magnetic resonance imaging (fMRI) has allowed for the measurement of alterations in blood flow and blood volume in tissue, without exposure to radioactive materials. These techniques enable measurement of brain function.

Rumsey et al. (1987) performed a functional neuroimaging study using PET. They compared dyslexic men to control subjects in terms of brain activation while performing a semantic classification task or a line orientation task. The control subjects showed greater activation in the left hemisphere when performing the language based semantic classification task, and greater right hemisphere activation when performing the visually based line orientation task. The dyslexic men displayed exaggerated blood flow in the left hemisphere during the semantic classification task, and greater right hemisphere blood flow during the line orientation task. These findings were interpreted to indicate difficulties in the dyslexic subjects in terms of integrating the functions of the two hemispheres, or inefficient allocation of cognitive resources.

Gross-Glenn et al. (1991) used PET to examine glucose utilization in dyslexic men while performing a word reading task. The dyslexic men differed from normal subjects in that they displayed greater glucose utilization in portions of the occipital cortex, and greater symmetry of utilization in areas of the prefrontal and occipital cortices. These findings may also reflect inefficient processing, similar to that noted by Rumsey et al. (1992).

Hagman et al. (1992) compared dyslexic men to normal control subjects while performing a speech discrimination task. The dyslexic subjects showed higher metabolism in the medial temporal lobes in both the right and left hemispheres as compared to normal subjects. These findings may be another indication of the inefficient information processing that occurs in individuals with dyslexia, reflected in the increased metabolism and bilateral activation that occurred in the dyslexic subjects.

Rumsey et al. (1992, 1994) studied dyslexic men during performance of neuropsychological tasks designed to activate posterior and anterior language regions in the left hemisphere. Compared to normal subjects, the dyslexic men showed abnormal patterns of activation in the left posterior temporal region and in the left temporparietal region.

The development of fMRI has enabled the investigation of specific neural systems in the brain while specific cognitive tasks are being performed. This technology has also opened the door to the use of functional neuroimaging studies with children, as there is no exposure to radioactive isotopes, nor is the procedure invasive.

Shaywitz et al. (1996) reported on the use of fMRI technology for the investigation of the reading process, in order to isolate orthographic, phonological, and lexical-semantic processing areas. An investigation of the reading process with male and female normal readers provided information that indicated that aspects of the occipital region of the brain are important for the orthographic aspect of reading. A region in the inferior frontal lobe was found to be uniquely associated with phonological processing. Phonological processing was also found to be associated with activation in the superior and middle temporal lobe regions. However, this region was also important for lexical-semantic processing. When men and women were compared, men displayed lateralized activation of the left inferior frontal lobe during performance of the phonological processing task, while women displayed greater bilateral activation of the inferior frontal lobe while performing this task. This pattern of activation is consistent with the long held hypothesis that language functions are more likely to be highly lateralized to the left hemisphere in men, and more bilaterally represented in women.

Shaywitz and Shaywitz (2003) reported that converging evidence using fMRI indicates that dyslexic readers show a failure of posterior left hemisphere brain systems when performing reading tasks. In describing some findings from the research program at the Yale Center for the Study of Learning and Attention, Shaywitz and Shaywitz reported that fMRI findings with adult dyslexic subjects indicated that differences emerged between dyslexic readers and normal readers as tasks placed increasing demand on phonological analysis. The findings indicated a disruption in functioning in a posterior system involving the superior temporal gyrus, the angular gyrus, and the striate cortex. Similar findings were obtained when a group of children with reading disability were compared to normal readers. The differences in brain activation were most pronounced when children were engaged in tasks involving phonological analysis, and not during tasks involving visual perception.

Summary of Neuroimaging Findings
In summarizing the information that has been obtained with the use of neuroimaging technology, Shaywitz and Shaywitz (2003) stated that there is now "unassailable evidence that children with learning disabilities (LD) have a real disability, as real as a fractured arm or as pneumonia." Shaywitz and Shaywitz go on to say that "converging evidence from many laboratories implicate the left occipitotemporal region as a site for skilled automatic reading. Failure to activate this region by readers with dyslexia explains their lack of automaticity." Increased activation of right hemisphere frontal and posterior regions-ancillary systems for word decoding – provides an explanation for accurate but non-automatic reading.

"These secondary systems can decode the word but slowly and not with the degree of automaticity characteristic of left hemisphere linguistically structured brain regions" (Shaywitz & Shaywitz).

The information obtained with fMRI converges with the findings of other neuroimaging studies. In a summary of neurological correlates of reading disabilities, Miller et al. (2003) reported that there is an abundance of evidence that persistent differences exist in the patterns of brain symmetry and/or morphology for disabled readers. These differences consistently implicate the temporal-parietal region of the left hemisphere, in particular the planum temporale.

In conclusion, the rapid development of neuroimaging techniques, especially fMRI has yielded increasingly specific information about the neurological basis of reading and reading disorders. In the future these techniques may also prove valuable in identifying the kinds of neurological changes that occur with effective intervention, and they will likely be helpful in determining which interventions are likely to be beneficial.

Neuroimaging and Attention Problems

Some attention problems, like learning disabilities, have long been believed to be of a neurological/neurodevelopmental origin. Labels that have been used to describe this disorder over the last century reflect this belief. Some of these labels include *organic drivenness, minimal brain damage, and minimal brain dysfunction.* The belief in the neurological basis of these problems was based on the frequent presence of neurological "soft signs" in many children with the disorder, and the similarity in behavior to individuals with known neurological conditions and brain injury. Barkley (1997) suggests that the characteristics of ADHD symptoms, including early onset and a developmental course as well as their remediation in the presence of stimulant medication, support a suspicion of a neurodevelopmental etiology.

Attention Deficit Hyperactivity Disorder
In recent years, various neuroimaging techniques have been used to study the possible neuroanatomical and physiological factors that are related to attention problems. These studies have often focused on subjects who have been diagnosed with Attention Deficit Hyperactivity Disorder (ADHD) (American Psychiatric Association, 1994). As Ernst (1996) has noted, it is difficult to make comparisons among these studies because there is often different diagnostic criteria used for selecting subjects, as well as different experimental designs and methods of analysis. As will be discussed further, it is also the case that children with ADHD

may or may not display problems in the cognitive processes that are believed to comprise attention. Thus, there are many factors that make it difficult to identify the neuroanatomical and physiological factors that are related to problems in attention.

Hynd et al. (1990, 1991) performed the first studies of ADHD to use MRI. In comparing children with ADHD to typical children, these researchers found that the ADHD group had smaller frontal cortices bilaterally, especially on the right. The frontal lobe asymmetry that is normally observed, with the right frontal lobe larger than the left, was not found in the children with ADHD. Hynd et al. (1991) then looked at the corpus callosum, which is the band of fibers that connects the right and left hemispheres, and allows for much of the communication between the two sides of the brain. They found that the corpus callosum in children with ADHD was significantly smaller than in normal children. Other recent studies have indicated that only a portion of the corpus callosum is different, either the anterior region (Gedd et al., 1994) or the posterior region (Semrud-Clikeman et al., 1993). MRI studies of subcortical regions, that is the areas that are deeper in the brain, have demonstrated that the head of the caudate nucleus is smaller in subjects with ADHD, either on the left (Hynd et al., 1993) or the right (Castellanos et al., 1994). While there has been some variability in the findings of MRI studies, in general, the right frontal cortex, the corpus callosum and the head of the caudate nucleus have been found to be smaller in subjects with ADHD than in normal control subjects.

Several studies have utilized functional brain imaging to investigate ADHD and attention problems. Lou et al. (1984, 1989, 1990) investigated cerebral blood flow in children diagnosed with ADD or ADHD. The findings of these studies indicated relatively less blood flow in the frontal and striatal regions of the brain. These studies also produced findings that indicated some increase in cerebral blood flow to these regions after treatment with medication (i.e. Methylphenidate). The findings of these studies are generally consistent with the neuroanatomical differences that were identified in studies using MRI.

Zametkin et al. (1990) carefully screened adults with ADHD for inclusion in their study, and compared them to normal control subjects. All of the adults with ADHD had a childhood history of ADHD, met criteria of diagnosis of ADHD in adults, and had children who were diagnosed with ADHD. When brain glucose metabolic rates were measured, the adults with ADHD had reduced levels compared to normal control subjects. Reduced rates of glucose metabolism were primarily found in four subcortical areas (right thalamus, right caudate nucleus, right hippocampus, and cingulate), and bilaterally in superior cortical regions. These findings are generally consistent with other studies previously discussed.

NEUROPSYCHOLOGICAL ASPECTS OF
LEARNING AND ATTENTION PROBLEMS

The field of *neuropsychology*, particularly child neuropsychology, has provided important contributions to an understanding of the *brain-behavior* relationship, specifically the behavioral manifestation of neurologically based learning disabilities.

Over the last 30–40 years, there have been tremendous advances in the neurosciences, particularly evident in the area of neuroimaging. These advances have provided an increase in the detail and specificity of knowledge of the neurological basis of learning disabilities and attention problems. At the same time, there has been extensive progress emanating from a number of fields that has advanced knowledge and understanding of the *perceptual, cognitive, and academic features* of learning disabilities and attention problems.

Neuropsychology and Learning Disability

Lyon (1996) pointed out that, since the mid-1980s, neuropsychological principles have been increasingly applied to the understanding and treatment of learning disabilities, in part, due to the growing awareness that relatively subtle problems in learning and behavior are related to "intrinsic neurological differences in brain structures and functions that are responsible for linguistic processing, alertness, motor activity, and arousal level." The field of neuropsychology has made important contributions to understanding learning difficulties from the perspective of central processing problems, and in identifying increasingly specific subcomponents of broad processing problems. The valuable role of neuropsychology also is evident in the developmental models of brain-behavior relationships that have emerged from neuropsychological research.

These models help to provide a basis for integrating and understanding the voluminous information that is emerging in terms of the subtypes and subcomponents of learning disabilities. By utilizing a broad perspective in evaluation that emphasizes identification of processing strengths as well as weaknesses, neuropsychology has had an important role in identifying associated problems in central processing, academics, and social functioning, and in identifying strengths that may be utilized in the development of interventions.

Over the last several years *developmental* neuropsychology has developed as a subspecialty within neuropsychology. This subspecialty combines the study of the development of the brain with the study of the development of behavior, in order to better identify and understand the changing nature of brain-behavior relationships across childhood and adolescence (Lyon, 1996). To this end, it is important to understand neural development, and how this interacts with the development of sensory, motor, cognitive, linguistic, and perceptual systems throughout development.

Rourke (1996) provided an excellent description of the role of developmental/ child neuropsychology in the investigation of learning disabilities. The neuropsychological approach utilizes models of brain-behavior functioning to better understand problems in learning. This approach attempts to combine the study of the development of the brain with the study of behavior (abilities, learning, etc). It is a systematic approach to obtaining an understanding of brain-behavior relationships through increasingly detailed assessment of central processing abilities and deficits.

Developmental neuropsychological assessment models have provided important contributions to the study of learning disabilities for several years (Morris, 1996). One of the contributions of neuropsychology to the study of learning disabilities is that the field of neuropsychology has "focused considerably on the development of more sophisticated and predictive tests and measures than were available historically..." (Morris, 1996). These tests have provided tools for more clearly describing and defining normal and disordered central processing, including ever more specific components of broad processing abilities. The pattern of central processing abilities and deficits that emerges from the assessment can then be applied to developmentally based models of brain-behavior functioning, in order to make predictions about learning and social problems (Rourke, 1996).

Approaches to Neuropsychological Evaluation
While the Halstead-Reitan approach to clinical neuropsychology is relatively well known and well researched, it is certainly not the only, or even most frequently used methodology in the field. Lyon (1996) and Lezak (1995) provided overviews of various methods of neuropsychological evaluation. The Halstead-Reitan approach is often referred to as a *fixed battery approach*. In this approach the same set of tests is administered to each individual regardless of the referral question. The tests that comprise the battery are used to measure a broad set of functions and abilities. An advantage of the fixed battery approach is the breadth and depth of functions that are measured. A weakness of this approach is the lengthy nature of the evaluation, and the use of measures that may not have clear functional application.

Another approach is referred to as the *flexible battery approach*. In this approach, a core set of standardized tests is used, along with a selected set of tests that address specific referral questions. This approach often allows for evaluation of both broad dimensions of abilities and behaviors, as well as more focused evaluation of sub-components of abilities or symptoms.

A third approach to neuropsychological evaluation is the individualized approach, that is sometimes referred to as the *"hypothesis testing" approach*. The tests that are selected for use in the evaluation are based on the history and presenting symptoms as well as the individual's successful and failed performance on tests. This method of neuropsychological evaluation emerged from the work of Luria, a Russian psychologist, who evaluated soldiers wounded in World War I and World War II. This approach, more than the others, requires the clinician to have extensive clinical knowledge and expertise in understanding and evaluating the specific and the nonspecific effects of brain lesions on behavior and development. The information that is obtained may provide in depth understanding of the specific problems investigated, but may be lacking in the breadth of abilities evaluated.

Similar to adult neuropsychological evaluation, the child neuropsychological evaluation may follow a fixed battery approach, a flexible battery approach, or a "hypothesis testing" approach. Rourke (1996) and Morris (1996) emphasized the importance of a comprehensive approach to evaluation. Rourke (1996) pointed out that there are various subtypes of individuals with learning disabilities, and the components of these subtypes can only reliably be identified through a comprehensive assessment. A comprehensive assessment is also critical for identifying areas of strength, which may not be identified on an evaluation that focuses on problem identification. A comprehensive evaluation is described as one that measures "principle skills and abilities that are thought to be subserved by the brain" (Rourke, 1996). Neuropsychological evaluation of children often includes assessment of intelligence, basic academic skills, memory and learning (both verbal and nonverbal), attention, information processing speed, sensory/perceptual functioning (auditory, visual, tactile), linguistic abilities, visual-spatial processing, motor and psychomotor processing, concept formation, and novel reasoning and problem solving. Since learning difficulties can occur for reasons other than processing problems, and because children with learning disabilities often have associated social and emotional difficulties, it is important to include measures that assess social and emotional functioning.

Neuropsychological Aspects of Specific Learning Disabilities

While learning disabilities can conceivably occur in a variety of academic skill areas, much of the research in the field of learning disabilities has focused on problems in reading. The term dyslexia is frequently used as a label for specific reading problems. Reading is a complex cognitive ability that requires the integrated use many cognitive sub-components (Vellutino et al., 1996). One important component of reading is *phonological processing*. This is the process by which the phonemic or sound component of the printed word is identified. Phonological awareness is an important component of phonological processing. Phonological awareness refers to the explicit awareness of individual phonemes or speech sounds in words. This is a cognitive process that develops at the time that children are beginning to learn to read. Rhyming ability is a good indicator of emerging phonological awareness. Effective reading also requires orthographic processing. This is the process by which the visual characteristics of letters and letter clusters are identified. Finally, effective reading requires lexical-semantic processing. This is the process by which specific patterns/clusters of letters are identified as words, and are associated with word meaning.

Vellutino et al. (1996) indicated that deficits in phonological processing are very often the primary cognitive deficits in reading disability (especially problems in word decoding). The primary phonological processing problem is in the development of phonological awareness. Due to this processing deficiency it is difficult for children to learn that words have parts made up of sequential sounds. Children with phonological processing problems have trouble segmenting the sounds of words for the purpose of learning to read and write. Individuals with this basic deficiency within the language system experience predictable difficulties in upper level language processing. These upper level problems may be evident in word decoding, spelling, written expression, word naming and retrieval, speech perception, and speech production.

Another common processing problem in children with reading disabilities involves the ability to rapidly retrieve familiar names of objects from permanent memory. Several studies using the Rapid Automitized Naming test (Denckla & Rudel, 1976) have indicated that this test reliably distinguishes poor and normal readers (Vellutino et al., 1993; Wolf, 1991). This test entails rapid naming of colors, objects, or letters, and evaluates the speed with which this information is retrieved from memory.

Utilizing a neuropsychological model for integrating extensive research findings, Rourke (1996) proposed a classification system for subtypes of learning disabilities. He divided these subtypes into three major categories; learning disabilities primarily characterized by *linguistic processing problems*, by *disorders of nonverbal functioning*, or by *output disorders in all modalities*. Within the category characterized by linguistic processing problems, Rourke (1996) proposed subtypes characterized by the following: problems in basic phonological processing; problems in phoneme-grapheme matching; and problems in word finding.

Phonological Processing Deficits

On neuropsychological evaluation, children with learning disabilities characterized primarily by problems in basic phonological processing, display significant
deficits in phonemic hearing, segmenting, and blending. Impairments in auditory-
verbal attention and memory are also evident. They are likely to display poor
verbal reception, repetition and storage of information. Problems in verbal
associations and verbal output are also likely to be evident. This group of children
is likely to display strengths in tactile perceptual, visual-spatial-organizational
processing, psychomotor output, and nonverbal problem solving and concept
formation. These children display normal attention to tactile and visual input,
and have a normal ability to deal with novelty. Children with problems in basic
phonological processing will display problems in reading and spelling, and in
aspects of arithmetic that require reading and writing. The nonverbal aspects of
arithmetic and mathematics are not as likely to be affected. These children have
a very guarded prognosis for advancement in reading and spelling.

Phoneme-Grapheme Matching Deficits

Children with learning disability who display primary problems in phoneme-
grapheme matching demonstrate neuropsychological assets similar to those
displayed by children whose primary problems involve phonological processing.
In addition, the former group displays normal abilities in terms of phonemic
hearing, segmenting, and sound blending. In terms of deficiencies, the primary
difficulty involves phoneme-grapheme or grapheme-phoneme matching. These
children are likely to perform adequately in terms of sight word reading and
spelling, but to have significant difficulty decoding and spelling words that
are not known by sight. Performance in arithmetic and mathematics is usually
normal, especially if there is not significant demand for word reading ability,
or if the words involved are one's usually learned by "sight." The prognosis for
advancement in reading and spelling is much better than it is for the children with
primary problems in phonological processing.

Word-finding Deficits

Some learning disabled children display a primary problem in word finding
and verbal expression skills. These children display assets that are similar to
those displayed by children with basic phonological processing problems, and
children with phoneme-grapheme matching problems. In addition, their phoneme-
grapheme matching ability is in tact. The only outstanding neuropsychological
deficit is in terms of access to verbal associations. Academically, reading and
spelling performance is usually very poor in the early grades, but improves in
later grades. Arithmetic and mathematics skills are areas of strength.

Math Deficits

Another group of learning disabled children often present with primary problems in mathematics. As Fleischner (1996) has pointed out, there are many different possible reasons underlying poor math achievement. Some of these factors include attitude, interest, anxiety, home and school experiences, and individual differences in intelligence. However, for some children there may be underlying processing problems that account for these problems. Much of the research in the field of learning disabilities has focused on identifying and describing the underlying factors involved in reading and spelling disabilities. In the last 15–20 years there have been increasing efforts to describe the factors that underlie or are associated with mathematics learning disabilities. Much of the information that has been obtained regarding the neuropsychological aspects of math related learning disabilities has come from the research of Rourke and his colleagues. This work is described in detail in *The Syndrome of Nonverbal Learning Disorders: Neurodevelopmental Manifestations* (Rourke, 1995).

Non-Verbal Learning Disability

Children whose learning disability is primarily characterized by nonverbal disorders usually display strengths in auditory-verbal processing, including perception, attention, and memory. Good verbal reception, storage, and associations are often evident in the early grades. They display good phonological processing skills, and they usually perform well on tasks that can be learned by rote. These children are typically quite talkative, especially when interacting with adults. Children with nonverbal disorders demonstrate problems in tactile and visual perception, and these problems are often apparent early in development. Problems are evident in attention and memory for information in these modalities. Problems are evident in performance of complex psychomotor tasks. These children prefer familiar and routine situations, and have an aversion for novel experiences, and unstructured activities and situations. As a consequence of these difficulties, there is often reduction in exploratory behaviors. As these children get older, problems in concept formation and problem solving emerge. While basic verbal reception and expression are areas of strength, linguistic deficits are evident in terms of pragmatic skills. Academically, skills in word decoding and spelling are often highly developed. These children also display good verbatim memory, especially for auditory-verbal material. Weaknesses often emerge as these children progress through the elementary grades. These weaknesses are especially evident in reading comprehension, mechanical arithmetic, mathematics, and science. These weaknesses are especially apparent when reasoning, deduction, and complex problem solving are required. Significant problems in social competence and psychosocial adjustment often emerge, especially in later grades. Deficits in perception, judgement, problem solving, and reasoning lead to difficulty in perceiving and understanding social information, and result in diminished social success and acceptance. Due to these social difficulties, these children are at significant risk for development of emotional adjustment problems.

Output Deficits
A third major subtype of learning disability described by Rourke (1996) includes children who display a significant problem in output of information in all modalities. Neuropsychologically, these children are very similar to children with to children with word finding problems in terms of their strengths. Their weaknesses are also similar to children with word finding problems, except problems are evident in organizing, directing, and orchestrating expression in all modalities. In the early grades, these children display significant oral and written output problems. As they progress through school significant progress usually occurs in basic reading and reading comprehension. They continue to demonstrate significant problems in written expression, and in the ability to deliver complex verbal descriptions and responses.

CASE EXAMPLES

In order to help elucidate the role of neuropsychological evaluation in the diagnosis and treatment of learning disabilities, two case examples will be provided.

Case: MM

Reason for Referral
MM is a nine and one-half year old boy who was seen for a neuropsychological evaluation at the request of his parents. His mother is a special education teacher and she expressed concern about his slow rate of academic progress, problems related to attention and concentration, and problems in emotional and behavioral adjustment. He is in a regular third grade classroom in the public school, and he is not receiving any special education services.

Relevant Background Information
MM's early development progressed without any significant difficulty. Basic motor milestones were achieved at normal ages. He was somewhat slow to achieve language milestones, and he began to receive Early Childhood Special Education services at four years of age to address language development problems. He has

continued to receive speech/language therapy as part of his special education program up to the present time. MM experienced many ear infections between one and four years of age, and he has asthma. There are no other significant medical problems.

MM's parents described him as a loving and good-hearted child. Recently, he has started to display problems in his emotional and behavioral adjustment. He has become aware that the special education services (i.e. speech/language therapy) he receives are not provided to all students, and he is upset that he has to receive these services. He struggles academically, particularly in reading and math. He has started to talk about himself as being "stupid." He is teased by his peers because of the special services he receives, and because of some of his academic difficulties. He has not displayed any significant emotional or behavioral problems at school, but at home he is much more emotionally sensitive and reactive. Also, he is more resistant to doing his schoolwork. At school, his primary problems involve difficulty paying attention, and being disorganized.

Behavioral Observations and Test Results
MM was seen for a neuropsychological evaluation, which was performed over the course of full day. He was moderately anxious and socially awkward. He was soft spoken and he did not initiate much social interaction. His language expression often reflected difficulty in formulating words and responses. He was able to comprehend simple questions and comments, but he was somewhat slow to understand task directions. It was often necessary to repeat and restate information in order to facilitate his comprehension. He tended to process information slowly, and to perform tasks slowly. He often had difficulty focusing and maintaining his attention.

MM completed the WISC III in order to evaluate his intellectual abilities. He displayed verbal abilities in the low average range, with his performance falling at the 14th percentile for his age. His nonverbal abilities were solidly in the average range, falling at the 52nd percentile for his age. On subtests measuring freedom from distraction, MM performed at the 19th percentile, and he performed at the 1st percentile in terms of processing speed.

MM completed the WIAT II to evaluate his academic achievement skills. His performance indicated low average to borderline level difficulties in the areas of word reading, pseudoword reading, written spelling, and reading comprehension. His reading and spelling errors indicated significant problems in terms of phonetic analysis and decoding. He performed at a low average level in terms of listening comprehension and oral expression, and he displayed low average/average abilities in written arithmetic and math reasoning.

MM displayed mild to moderate deficits on tests measuring basic oral and written language abilities, and low average receptive and expressive word knowledge. He displayed significant problems in terms of basic auditory perception, and auditory analysis reflecting significant problems in phonological processing. He displayed average visual perceptual and visual-motor skills. He displayed moderate deficits in verbal memory and verbal learning, but he displayed average visual memory and learning abilities. MM displayed borderline level difficulties on tasks measuring sustained attention, and the ability to shift and divide his attention. He also displayed significant problems on tasks that required mental and behavioral control. His performance on these tasks indicated significant problems in impulse control.

MM's parents and teacher completed behavioral questionnaires to assist in evaluating his social, emotional, and behavioral adjustment. The responses of his parents indicated the presence of moderate problems related to ADHD, and mild to moderate problems in terms of anxiety, depression, and social functioning. The responses of his teacher indicated the presence of mild problems related to ADHD, and mild problems in social functioning.

The results of the evaluation indicated the presence of a language-based learning disability. MM's test performances indicated weaknesses in basic language processing (including phonological awareness), and in upper level verbal abilities. These findings were not unexpected given his history of slow language development. As he has progressed through school, these problems have had an increasingly negative impact on his acquisition of basic academic skills. MM also demonstrated difficulties in several aspects of attention. He had difficulty focusing and sustaining his attention, especially in situations in which there was ongoing presentation of information. He also displayed difficulty dividing his attention, shifting his attention, and filtering out distraction. His test performances indicated difficulty integrating and organizing information. The responses of his parents and teachers on behavioral questionnaires indicated the presence of problems consistent with mild to moderate ADHD. These findings, taken together with the various problems in attention that he displayed on testing indicated that MM was experiencing problems related to ADHD. The co-morbidity of learning disabilities and ADHD is quite high (Barkley, 1998), so it was not unexpected that MM was experiencing a combination of a language based learning disability and ADHD. The more recent onset of emotional problems was likely at least in part due to the significant difficulty MM was experiencing in meeting academic challenges as a result of his attention and learning problems.

Recommendations
Based on the findings of the evaluation, MM and his parents were referred to his pediatrician to consider medication treatment for ADHD. MM's special education

program was modified to address the problems that he was displaying in terms of language and learning disabilities. He was provided with increased individual assistance in reading, with an emphasis on development of phonological awareness, phonetic skills, and reading fluency. It was also recommended that he obtain private therapy services to address these problems. MM had a daily period of resource services added to his special education program. Within the context of this service, MM participated in educational activities that addressed development of his ability to plan and organize.

Case 2: JA

Reason for Referral

JA is an 11-year-old boy who as referred for a neuropsychological evaluation by his pediatrician. He had a history of learning problems involving reading comprehension, organization, and independent functioning. Concern was raised about a possible attention problem. An evaluation by a developmental optometrist had identified a visual perceptual deficiency. JA also displays significant problems in his social and emotional adjustment.

Relevant Background Information

JA experienced some complications at birth that included swallowing meconium and being "blue and yellow" in color. However, no lasting problems were noted and he was described as a happy baby. He was slow to achieve basic and upper level motor milestones, and his language development also progressed somewhat slowly. He received speech/language therapy from three to four years of age in order to facilitate language development. Although he achieved toilet training by three and one-half years of age, he was still having occasional problems with bedwetting at the time of the evaluation. Medically, JA experienced frequent ear infections from infancy to three years of age. He has several minor injuries due to falls, but there was no history of significant head trauma.

JA's parents reported that he seemed to have visual perceptual and visual spatial problems from a young age. He is a very friendly child with a "heart of gold," but he is often immature and inappropriate in his social behavior. He often antagonizes other children, lacks respect for personal space and boundaries, and he seeks attention with negative behavior. Sometimes he is resistant to complying with directives, and he often is stubborn in his behavior. He tends to become "stuck" on certain issues, and he has difficulty "letting go and moving on" when he is not able to have his way, or things do not go as expected.

At the time of the evaluation JA was enrolled in a parochial school, and he was in the fifth grade. He was participating in a tutoring program after school, and he was receiving private occupational therapy services to treat problems in visual perceptual and visual motor functioning. He was experiencing significant problems in school, especially on tasks such as book reports and projects. He was also displaying increasing problems related to his social and emotional adjustment.

Behavioral Observations and Test Results

JA was seen for a neuropsychological evaluation, which was performed over the course of a full day. His behavior was generally age appropriate, with a few exceptions. Although he was friendly and interactive, he often made comments or asked questions that were unrelated to the task or topic at hand, which contributed to awkwardness in his social interaction. He seemed to easily become disorganized in his performance, and it was necessary to provide him with additional support and structure in order to facilitate his performance.

JA was administered the WISC III to evaluate his intellectual abilities. His verbal abilities were solidly average, falling at the 50th percentile for his age, while his nonverbal intelligence fell below the 1st percentile. His test performances indicated that he consistently performed at an average level on tasks measuring verbal processing, including basic verbal expression and comprehension, verbal learning and memory, and in basic reading. His test performances consistently indicated weaknesses in visual processing, including basic visual perception, visual-spatial orientation, visual motor skills, visual construction, visual memory and learning, and nonverbal reasoning and problems solving. JA also had difficulty on tasks that required processing of relatively detailed verbal and nonverbal information, and that required development and execution of strategies. His best performances occurred on tasks that emphasized relatively rote processing, or use of overlearned knowledge and skills. Evaluation of basic sensory and motor abilities indicated processing problems involving the left side of his body. JA demonstrated average academic achievement skills in the areas of word reading, written spelling, listening comprehension, and oral expression. Significant weaknesses were evident in reading comprehension, written expression, and mathematics.

The results of the neuropsychological evaluation indicated that presence of processing problems that are typical of children with a nonverbal learning disability. Like many children with nonverbal learning disabilities, JA displayed significant problems in basic visual perceptual and visual motor functions, visual memory and learning, nonverbal reasoning and problems solving, and basic sensory and motor problems affecting the left side of his body. He also displayed many of the social and emotional problems that are frequently experienced by children with nonverbal learning disabilities. His nonverbal processing problems likely contributed to the difficulty he experienced in interpreting social information, and in producing appropriate social responses. Although JA had performed adequately in the early elementary grades, his school performance and his performances on academic achievement tests indicated increasing academic difficulty. These difficulties were particularly evident in subjects or on tasks that required higher-level reasoning and problem solving, and on tasks requiring planning, organization, and execution of multi-step strategies and tasks.

Recommendations
Based on the findings of the evaluation, JA's parents decided to enroll him in the public school. It was clear to them that the parochial school would not be able to provide adequate support in order to meet his educational needs. He was identified as being eligible for special education services as a student with a learning disability. A special education program was developed that provided him with a combination of mainstream and "pull-out" services. The "pull-out" services were provided on a daily basis in the form of a specialized study hall. Within this setting he was provided with opportunities to review subject matter and assignments with a special education teacher. He was also provided with instruction in basic organizational and study skills. Mainstream support was provided by both the special education teacher and an instructional aide. This support primarily focused on generalizing the knowledge and skills developed in the "pull-out" program, to daily functioning within the classroom. JA's program also included occupational therapy services to address treatment of his visual perceptual and visual motor skills, and to provide consultation to the educational team about methods for reducing task demands in the areas of visual perception and visual motor output. Social work services were included in his educational plan, in order to address development of social perception and problem solving and social skills. These services were primarily provided in a group format. In addition to school based services, JA's parents also obtained private psychotherapy services to address development of his social skills, and more appropriate and effective emotional coping skills, and to assist his parents in understanding the nature of his difficulties and developing effective behavior management skills.

NEUROPSYCHOLOGICAL ASPECTS OF ATTENTION PROBLEMS

Children with problems in attention and self-regulation comprise a substantial percentage of children who experience significant educational problems. These problems often cross academic subject areas due to the generalized effects that deficiencies in attention and self-regulation often produce. Children with significant problems in attention and self-regulation are often diagnosed with Attention Deficit Hyperactivity Disorder (ADHD). Estimates vary, but approximately 3–5% of school age children are believed to have ADHD (National Institutes of Health Consensus Statements, November 1998), which indicates that ADHD is the most commonly diagnosed behavioral disorder of childhood.

Children with ADHD may or may not experience problems in the cognitive processes known as *attention*. The *Inattention* problems that occur in ADHD may be due to problems in the cognitive processes discussed by Mirsky, Anthony, Duncan, Ahearn, and Lellam (1991) and Mirsky and Duncan (2000), but other factors may also cause or contribute to the *Inattention* behaviors that are often evident in individuals with ADHD. In discussing the subtypes of ADHD, Barkley (1998) reports that children with ADHD, Primarily Inattentive type are often more likely to display problems in the cognitive processes of attention, than children with ADHD, Combined Type or ADHD, Hyperactive-Impulsive Type. These children often present with problems such as daydreaming, and staring, forgetfulness, inconsistency in cognitive performance, "foggy" thinking, lethargy or hypoactivity, social reticence, and passivity.

Neuropsychological evaluation is not required to make a diagnosis of ADHD, but there are several potential benefits of neuropsychological evaluation for children with possible ADHD. Neuropsychological evaluation is helpful in assessing for possible co-morbid conditions, or in assessing for other conditions that may be presenting primarily as an ADHD related problem. Also, neuropsychological evaluation is helpful in defining the specific processing problems that are resulting in the appearance of problems in attention. Similar to neuropsychological evaluation of children with learning disabilities, neuropsychological evaluation of children with ADHD or attention problems also helps to identify areas of strength that may be utilized in helping children to compensate and cope with their condition. Whether the issue is possible ADHD, or other educational problems, assessment of attention in children with educational problems is important because problems in attention can contribute to a variety of educational and behavioral problems. Also, information about a child's attention abilities may be helpful in clarifying diagnostic issues, including the diagnosis of ADHD. Sometimes, observed problems in attention are due specifically to problems in some aspect of the cognitive process of attention, while at other times these suspected attention problems are due to some other etiology (e.g. anxiety; reading disability; language disorder).

Attention and Cognitive Processing

Mirsky et al. (1991) and Mirsky and Duncan (2000) reported on extensive research addressing the components of the cognitive process that is often referred to as attention. These researchers have described five elements of attention that are important to assess when evaluating attention.

Encode Element

One element is referred to as the Encode Element. This element entails the ability to briefly hold information in mind while performing some mental operation on the information. This element is sometimes referred to as *working memory*. Mirsky and Duncan (2000) propose that this element is supported by the brain structures that are in and around the amygdala. Some of the measures that are useful in evaluating this element are the Digit Span and Arithmetic tests of the Wechsler batteries. The Wechsler batteries describe this element with the term Freedom from Distraction (Wechsler, 1991).

Focus/Execute Element

A second element of attention described by Mirsky et al. (1991) and Mirsky and Duncan (2000) is the Focus/Execute element. This element entails the ability to focus on a task, in the presence of distracting information, and to quickly execute the responses required by the task. These researchers proposed that this element of attention is supported by structures in the inferior parietal lobule, the superior temporal gyrus, and parts of the corpus striatum. The Digit Symbol and Coding tasks of the Wechsler batteries are helpful in evaluating this element of attention. Other tests that are helpful in evaluating this element are The Letter Cancellation Test (Talland, 1965), the Stroop Color-Word Interference Test (Golden, 1978), and the Trailmaking Test (Reitan & Davidson, 1974). The Letter Cancellation Test requires the individual to rapidly scan rows of letters, and cross out specified targets. The Stroop Color-Word Test first requires the individual to read columns of color names, all printed in black. The second trial requires the individual to rapidly name colors that are printed in columns. The third trial requires the individual to identify the print color of color names that are printed in some other color. For example, the word *red*, may be printed in the color blue. The individual must inhibit reading the word, and instead identify the print color. On Part A of the Trailmaking Test, the individual is timed while they draw a line connecting numbers scattered on a page in an ascending sequence. On Part B, the individual is timed while they draw a line connecting numbers and letters scattered on a page in a sequential order, while shifting back and forth between numbers and letters (e.g. 1 to A to 2 to B, etc.).

Shift Element

The third element of attention described by Mirsky and Duncan (2000) is the Shift element. This element involves the capacity to shift the focus of attention from one aspect of a complex stimulus to another. It is believed that this element of attention is supported by structures in the dorsolateral region of the prefrontal cortex, and the anterior portion of the cingulate gyrus. The Wisconsin Card Sorting Test (WCST) (Heaton, 1981) is used to evaluate this component of attention. The WCST requires the individual to sort a pack of cards based on one of three stimulus characteristics (i.e. color, form, number), and to shift sorting strategies based on changing feedback from the examiner regarding the accuracy of the strategy in use.

Sustain Element

The fourth element of attention described by Mirsky and Duncan (2000) is the Sustain element. This element involves the ability to maintain attention, or vigilance over a relatively long period of time. This ability can be measured independently in both the visual or auditory modalities. It is believed that this element of attention is supported by the brainstem reticular activating formation and midline thalamic structures. The Sustain element is evaluated with the Continuous Performance Test (CPT) (Rosvold et al., 1956). Several different versions of the CPT have been developed. Usually these tasks require the subject to attend to continuously presented stimuli, such as letters or numbers. The individual activates a button when a particular target stimulus, or a combination of stimuli is presented.

Stabilize Element

The fifth element of attention described by Mirsky and Duncan (2000) is the Stabilize element. This element reflects the stability with which a person can respond to designated "target" stimuli. The Stabilize element is measured by determining the variation in response time, when correctly responding to targeted stimuli. This element of attention is also evaluated with continuous performance tests. The neurological basis for this element is not known, but it is believed to be the same structures that support the other elements of attention.

Kelly (2000) investigated the application of the model of attention described above in children ages 7–13 years. Children were administered specific tests to investigate the various components of this model. These tests included the Trailmaking Test, the Stroop Color-Word Test, the Wisconsin Card Sorting Test, a number cancellation test, the Continuous Performance Test, and the Symbol Search, Coding, and Digit Span subtests of the WISC III. A factor analysis of the subjects' performances on these tasks revealed four factors (Kelly, 2000). The factor analysis of the data indicated a three-factor model of child attention rather than a four or five factor model. The focus-execute and encode elements of the model of Mirsky and Duncan (2000) combined into a single factor, which Kelly (2000) labeled as "speed of response."

The application of the model of Mirsky and Duncan (2000) was investigated by Loss et al. (1998) with children with myelomeningocele. The same or similar tasks to those used by Kelly (2000) were used to investigate aspects of attention in these children. In addition, academic achievement was measured, as was behavioral adjustment. The performances of children with myelomeningocele were compared to their siblings. Children with myelomeningocele performed lower than their siblings on all four factors of attention. These findings suggest that children with myelomeningocele have a broad range of deficits in attention, including but not exclusively due to slow response speed. Children with myelomeningocele who had a history of shunting (indicating significant problems due to hydrocephalus) were different from normal siblings on all four factors of the attention model. Children with myelomeningocele, who had not required shunting, only differed from normal siblings in terms of encode and shift. Among children with myelomeningocele, deficits in the focus/execute components were most strongly related to behavior ratings. The encode component of the attention model was most predictive of academic achievement.

The neuropsychological conceptualization of attention problems proposed by Mirsky and Duncan (2000) is helpful in understanding some of the facets of the complex cognitive process of attention, and the impact of these facets on various functions such as academic achievement and behavioral adjustment. As this model indicates, attention is not a unitary cognitive process, but rather, it consists of a variety of mental processes that contribute to the ability to "pay attention." Defining the nature of children's abilities in these components of attention through neuropsychological evaluation can help to better understand these specific mental processes, and to better understand problems in other areas such as behavioral adjustment and academic achievement.

Subtypes of ADHD

While the model developed by Mirsky and Duncan (2000) may help to conceptualize the problems of children with ADHD, Primarily Inattentive Type, this model may not effectively explain the problems experienced by the other subtypes of ADHD. Barkley (1997) has developed a neuropsychological model based on extensive research with children with ADHD, which helps in the conceptualization of the kinds of problems children experience who are hyperactive and impulsive. In Barkley's (1997) model, the primary problem underlying the various difficulties that emerge throughout development is a failure to develop adequate inhibition. In normal development, children progressively develop the ability to inhibit responses, interrupt ongoing ineffective responses, and control responses to interfering or distracting input. Barkley (1997) theorizes that children with ADHD are deficient in the development of these inhibitory abilities. As a result of these problems in the development of behavioral inhibition, problems emerge later in development in several different neuropsychological processes. The combination of problems in inhibition and neuropsychological processing problems leads to many of the functional difficulties that are experienced by children and adults with ADHD.

Non-verbal Working Memory Deficits

Barkley (1997) proposed that one area in which neuropsychological difficulties emerge is in the development of nonverbal working memory. Children with problems of this nature have difficulty holding events in mind, and so, they are unable to manipulate or act on the events. There are also problems in imitation of complex sequences that occurs as a result of deficient nonverbal working memory. Children with deficits in nonverbal working memory are likely to be defective in hindsight and forethought. They are likely to have poor anticipation, a diminished sense of time, and limited self-awareness.

Barkley (1997) described research that has shown children with ADHD to have greater difficulty than do normal children on tasks such as the Rey Complex Figure Test, the Wisconsin Card Sorting Test, and the Tower of London/Tower of Hanoi tasks. These tasks require abilities such as holding detailed nonverbal information in mind (working memory), adjusting response strategies based on recently received feedback (hindsight), mental planning (forethought), and ongoing adjustment of strategies based on self judgements of success/failure (self-awareness/self monitoring).

Limited Verbal Working Memory

Another area of difficulty to emerge due to poor inhibition is limited verbal working memory, and delayed internalization of speech. Children with this difficulty are likely to be deficient in terms of reflection and rule governed behavior, as internalization of speech assists with the capacity to follow through on rules, instructions, and commands. They are also likely to be poor in problem solving, and in generating rules for organizing information. Problems in this area may negatively affect reading comprehension, and moral development. Deficits in verbal working memory are often evident when more complex and larger amounts of information must be held in mind, especially over a lengthy period of time. When strategies are required to assist with organizing the material in order to respond to it or remember it more effectively, those with ADHD are likely to be less proficient.

Verbal working memory is often evaluated with digit span tests, tasks requiring mental arithmetic, and memory tasks that require retention of information over a period of time. Barkley (1997) describes several studies that indicate that children with ADHD are less proficient on tests measuring these kinds of abilities.

Immature Self-Regulation

Barkley (1997) described a third area of difficulty to emerge from poor inhibition as being immature self-regulation of affect, motivation, and arousal. These difficulties are evident in limited emotional control, less objectivity in social perspective, and diminished self-regulation of drive and motivation. These difficulties are also evident in terms of poor regulation of arousal necessary for sustaining goal directed behavior.

Barkley (1997) reported that many studies have demonstrated that children with ADHD show greater variability in central and autonomic nervous system arousal patterns, and are under-reactive to stimulation. This information has been obtained in terms of electrophysiological activation, and when activation is measured with a PET scan and cerebral blood flow. Less drive, motivation, and effort have often been identified in children with ADHD when performing tasks that require repetitive responding with little or no reinforcement.

Impaired Reconstitution

A fourth area of difficulty described by Barkley (1997) is impaired reconstitution. This type of difficulty results in such problems as limitations in analysis and synthesis of behavior. Analysis involves the ability to take units of behavioral sequences, and break them down into smaller components, while synthesis refers to the assembling of behavioral units into increasingly complex sequences of behavior. Individuals with problems in reconstitution often display reduced verbal and behavioral fluency, less creativity in goal directed behavior, less frequent use of behavioral simulations, and immature syntax of behavior.

Barkley (1997) reported that problems in reconstitution are evident in the increased difficulty that children with ADHD have demonstrated on tests of basic verbal fluency, and tests of more complex language fluency and discourse organization. A lack of behavioral flexibility or fluency may be evident in the increased problems of children with ADHD on the Wisconsin Card Sorting Test. However, there may be other factors such as reduced verbal working memory and generation of rule-governed behavior that may also contribute to this difficulty.

CONCLUSION

Research into the neuropsychological aspects of learning disabilities and attention problems has been helpful in identifying underlying processing weaknesses that contribute to, or are associated with various subtypes of learning disabilities. This information is helpful in identifying appropriate targets for intervention that go beyond merely addressing an area of academic weakness. While treatment of academic skill deficiency is important for maintaining academic progress, treatment of the underlying processing deficiencies may prove to be critical for eventually remediating the skill deficit, as well as remediating less academically specific deficiencies. It is also important to understand the processing strengths that are associated with various learning disabilities. These strengths may be important areas to cultivate for the purpose of helping children develop alternative skills and competencies, and for use in developing compensatory strategies and skills.

REFERENCES

American Psychiatric Association (1994). *Diagnostic and statistical manual of mental disorders* (4th ed.). Washington, DC: Author.

Barkley, R. A. (1997). *ADHD and the nature of self-control*. New York: Guilford Press.

Barkley, R. A. (1998). *Attention deficit hyperactivity disorder: A handbook for diagnosis and treatment* (2nd ed.). New York: Guilford Press.

Castellanos, F. X., Giedd, J. N., Eckburg, P., Marsh, W. L., Vactuzis, C., Kaysen, D., Hamburger, S. D., & Rapoport, J. L. (1994). Qualitative morphology of the caudate nucleus in attention deficit hyperactivity disorder. *American Journal of Psychiatry, 151,* 1791–1796.

Denckla, M. B., & Rudel, R. G. (1976). Rapid "automatized" naming of pictured objects, colors, letters, and numbers by normal children. *Cortex, 10,* 186–202.

Diagnosis and Treatment of Attention Deficit Hyperactivity Disorder. National Institute of Health Consensus Development Conference Statement Online (1998), November 16–18: *16*(2), 1–37.

Ernst, M. (1996). Neuroimaging in attention deficit/hyperactivity disorder. In: G. R. Lyon & J. M. Rumsey (Eds), *Neuroimaging: A Window to the Neurological Foundations of Learning and Behavior* (pp. 95–117). Baltimore, MD: Paul H. Brookes.

Fleischner, J. E. (1996). Diagnosis and assessment of mathematics learning disabilities. In: G. R. Lyon (Ed.), *Frames of Reference for the Assessment of Learning Disabilities: New Views on Measurement Issues* (pp. 441–458). Baltimore, MD: Paul H. Brookes.

Galaburda, A. M., Sherman, G. F., Rosen, G. D., Aboitiz, F., & Geschwind, N. (1985). Developmental dyslexia: Four consecutive patients with cortical anomalies. *Annals of Neurology, 18*, 222–233.

Gedd, J. N., Castellanos, X., Casey, B. J., Kozuch, P., King, A. C., Hamburger, S. D., & Rapoport, J. L. (1994). Quantitative morphology of the corpus callosum in attention deficit hyperactivity disorder. *American Journal of Psychiatry, 151*, 665–669.

Golden, C. J. (1978). *Stroop Color and Word Test*. Chicago, IL: Stoelting.

Gross-Glenn, K., Duara, R., Barker, W. W., Loewenstein, D., Chang, J. Y., Yoshi, F., Apicella, A. M., Pascal, S., Boothe, T., Sevash, S., Jallad, B. J., Nova, L., & Lubs, H. A. (1991). Positron emission tomographic studies during serial word-reading by normal and dyslexic adults. *Journal of Clinical and Experimental Neuropsychology, 13*, 531–544.

Hagman, J. O., Wood, F., Buschbaum, M. S., Tallal, P., Flowers, L., & Katz, W. (1992). Cerebral brain metabolism in adult dyslexic subjects assessed with PET during performance of an auditory task. *Archives of Neurology, 49*, 734–739.

Heaton, R. K. (1981). *Wisconsin card sorting test (WCST)*. Odessa, FL: Psychological Assessment Resources.

Humphreys, P., Kaufman, W. E., & Galaburda, A. M. (1990). Developmental dyslexia in women: Neuropathological findings in three patients. *Annals of Neurology, 28*, 727–738.

Hynd, G. W., Marshall, R., & Gonzalez, J. J. (1993). Asymmetry of the caudate nucleus in ADHD: An exploratory study of gender and handedness effects. Paper Presented at the annual meeting of Society for Research in Child and Adolescent Psychopathology, Santa Fe, New Mexico.

Hynd, G. W., Semrud-Clikeman, M., Lorys, A. R., Novey, E. S., & Eliopulos, D. (1990). Brain morphology in developmental dyslexia and attention deficit disorder/hyperactivity. *Archives of Neurology, 47*, 919–926.

Hynd, G. W., Semrud-Clikeman, M., Lorys, A. R., Novey, E. S., Eliopulos, D., & Lyytinen, H. (1991). Corpus callosum morphology in attention deficit hyperactivity disorder: Morphometric analysis of MRI. *Journal of Learning Disabilities, 24*, 141–146.

Individuals with Disabilities Education, Pub L. 105–17, 111 Stat. 37 (1997) (codified at 20 U.S.C. (1499–1487).

Kelly, T. P. (2000). The clinical neuropsychology of attention in school-aged children. *Child Neuropsychology, 6*, 24–36.

Kusch, A., Gross-Glenn, K., Jallad, B., Lubs, H., Rabin, M., Feldman, E., & Duara, R. (1993). Temporal lobe surface area measurements on MRI in normal and dyslexic readers. *Neuropsychologia, 31*, 811–821.

Larsen, J. P., Hoien, T., & Odegaard, H. (1992). Magnetic resonance imaging of the corpus callosum in developmental dyslexia. *Cognitive Neuropsychology, 9*, 123–134.

Lezak, M. (1995). *Neuropsychological assessment* (3rd ed.). New York: Oxford University Press.

Livingstone, M. S., Rosen, C. D., Drislane, F. W., & Galaburda, A. M. (1991). Physiological and anatomical evidence for a magnocellular defect in developmental dyslexia. *Proceedings of the National Academy of Sciences of the United States of America, 88*, 7943–7947.

Loss, N., Owen-Yeates, K., & Enrile, B. G. (1998). Attention in children with myelomeningocele. *Child Neuropsychology, 4*, 7–20.

Lou, H. C., Henriksen, L., & Bruhn, P. (1984). Focal cerebral hypoperfusion in children with dysphasia and/or attention deficit disorder. *Archives of Neurology, 41*, 825–829.

Lou, H. C., Henriksen, L., & Bruhn, P. (1990). Focal cerebral dysfunction in developmental learning disabilities. *Lancet, 335*, 8–11.

Lou, H. C., Henriksen, L., Bruhn, P., Borner, H., & Nielsen, J. B. (1989). Striatal function in attention deficit and hyperkinetic disorder. *Archives of Neurology, 46*, 48–52.

Lyon, G. R. (1996). Neuroimaging in developmental dyslexia: A review and conceptualization. In: G. R. Lyon & J. M. Rumsey (Eds), *Neuroimaging: A Window to the Neurological Foundations of Learning and Behavior in Children* (pp. 3–23). Baltimore, MD: Paul H. Brookes.

Miller, C. J., Sanchez, J., & Hynd, G. W. (2003). Neurological correlates of reading disabilities. In: H. L. Swanson, K. R. Harris & S. Graham (Eds), *Handbook of Learning Disabilities* (pp. 242–255). New York: Guilford Press.

Mirsky, A. F., Anthony, B. J., Duncan, C. C., Ahearn, M. B., & Lellam, S. G. (1991). Analysis of the elements of attention: A neuropsychological approach. *Neuropsychological Review, 2*, 109–145.

Mirsky, A. F., & Duncan, C. C. (2000). A nosology of disorders of attention. In: J. Wasserstein, L. Wolff & F. F. LeFever (Eds), *Adult Attention Deficit Disorder: Brain Mechanisms and Life Outcomes* (pp. 60–70). Annals of the New York Academy of Sciences.

Morris, R. (1996). Multidimensional neuropsychological assessment models: Potential and problems. In: G. R. Lyon (Ed.), *Frames of Reference for the Assessment of Learning Disabilities: New Views on Measurement Issues* (pp. 515–521). Baltimore, MD: Paul H. Brookes.

Rosvold, H. E., Mirsky, A. F., Sarason, I., Bransome, E. D., & Beck, L. H. (1956). A continuous performance test of brain damage. *Journal of Consulting Psychology, 20*, 343–350.

Rourke, B. P. (1995). *The syndrome of nonverbal learning disabilities: Neurodevelopmental manifestations*. New York: Guilford Press.

Rourke, B. P. (1996). Neuropsychological assessment of children with learning disabilities. In: G. R. Lyon (Ed.), *Neuroimaging: A Window to the Neurological Foundations of Learning and Behavior in Children* (pp. 57–77). Baltimore, MD: Paul H. Brookes.

Rumsey, J. M. (1996). Neuroimaging in developmental dyslexia: A review and conceptualization. In: G. R. Lyon & J. M. Rumsey (Eds), *Neuroimaging: A Window to the Neurological Foundations of Learning and Behavior in Children* (pp. 57–77). Baltimore, MD: Paul H. Brookes.

Rumsey, J. M., Andreason, P., Zametkin, A. J., Aquino, T., King, A. C., Hamburger, S. D., Pikus, A., Rapoport, J. L., & Cohen, R. M. (1992). Failure to activate the left temporoparietal cortex in dyslexia. *Archives of Neurology, 49*, 527–534.

Rumsey, J. M., Andreason, P., Zametkin, A. J., King, A. C., Hamburger, S. D., Aquino, T., Hanahan, A. P., Pikus, A., & Cohen, R. M. (1994). Right frontotemporal activation by tonal memory in dyslexia, an O15 PET study. *Biological Psychiatry, 36*, 171–180.

Rumsey, J. M., Berman, K. F., Denckla, M. B., Hamburger, S. D., Kruesi, M. J., & Weinberger, D. R. (1987). Regional cerebral blood flow in severe developmental dyslexia. *Archives of Neurology, 44*, 1144–1150.

Rumsey, J. M., Casanova, M., Mannheim, G. B., Patronas, N., De Vaughn, N., Hamburger, S. D., & Aquino, T. (1996). Corpus callosum morphology, as measured with MRI in dyslexic men. *Biological Psychiatry, 39*, 769–775.

Rumsey, J. M., Zametkin, A. J., Andreason, P., Hanahan, A. P., Hamburger, S. D., Aquino, T., King, A. C., Pikus, A., & Cohen, R. M. (1994). Normal activation of frontotemporal language cortex in dyslexia, as measured with oxygen 15 positron emission tomography. *Archives of Neurology, 51*, 27–38.

Semrud-Clikeman, M., Filipek, P. A., Biederman, J., Steingard, R., Kennedy, D., Renshaw, P., & Bekken, K. (1993). Attention deficit disorder: Differences in the corpus callosum by MRI morphometric analysis. Paper Presented at the annual meeting of the Society for Research in Child and Adolescent Psychopathology, Santa Fe, New Mexico.

Shaywitz, S. E., & Shaywitz, B. A. (2003). Neurobiological indices of dyslexia. In: H. L. Swanson, K. R., Harris & S. Graham (Eds), *Handbook of Learning Disabilities* (pp. 514–531). New York: Guilford Press.

Shaywitz, S. E., Shaywitz, B. A., Pugh, K. P., Skudlowski, P., Fulbright, R. K., Constable, R. T., Bronen, R. A., Fletcher, J. M., Liberman, A. M., Shankweiler, D. P., Katz, L., Lacadie, C., Marchione, K. E., & Gore, J. C. (1996). In: G. R. Lyon & J. M. Rumsey (Eds), *Neuroimagning: A Window to the Neurological Foundations of Learning and Behavior in Children* (pp. 79–94). Baltimore, MD: Paul H. Brookes.

Talland, G. A. (1965). Three estimates of the word span and their stability over the adult years. *Quarterly Journal of Experimental Psychology, 17,* 301–307.

Vellutino, F. R., Scanlon, D. M., & Tanzman, M. S. (1996). Components of reading ability: Issues and problems in operationalizing word identification, phonological coding, and orthographic coding. In: G. R. Lyon (Ed.), *Frames of Reference for the Assessment of Learning Disabilities: New Views on Measurement Issues* (pp. 243–278). Baltimore, MD: Paul H. Brookes.

Wechsler, D. (1991). *Wechsler intelligence scale for children* (3rd ed). Psychological Corporation.

Wolf, M. (1991). Naming speed and reading: The contribution of the cognitive neurosciences. *Reading Research Quarterly, 26,* 123–141.

Zametkin, A. J., Nordahl, T. E., Gross, M., King, A. L., Semple, W. E., Rumsey, J., Hamburger, S., & Cohen, R. M. (1990). Cerebral glucose metabolism in adults with hyperactivity of childhood onset. *New England Journal of Medicine, 323,* 1361–1366.

CURRICULUM MODIFICATIONS FOR STUDENTS WITH LEARNING DISABILITIES

Ann Richards and Elizabeth Dooley

Throughout the educational literature, schools are often referred to as communities of learners (Liberman & Grolnick, 1999). The image conjured up by this idea is that all students work side-by-side toward the achievement of their academic goals, including students with disabilities. With the signing of the No Child Left Behind Act (NCLB) (2002), the United States government declared that it will "judge all schools by one measure and one measure alone: whether every boy and every girl is learning – regardless of race, family background, or disability status" (President's Commission on Excellence in Special Education, p. 4). One measure used to distinguish if students within general education are learning are curriculum goals and objectives outlined by either state departments of education or local education agencies. For students with learning disabilities (LD), their achievements have been determined by completions of goals and objectives stated within their individualized education plans (IEP) that often do not reflect the standards set forth in the general curriculum. As the shape, scope, sequence, and format of the general education curriculum and instruction are shaped by new content standards, more students will be expected to succeed (Jitendra et al., 2002). In the past, professionals within the field of special education as well as state regulatory bodies have focused on the idea of process compliance and not on student outcomes; this has resulted in a weak link between the two frames of thought (President's Commission of Excellence in Special Education, 2002).

Current Perspectives on Learning Disabilities
Advances in Special Education, Volume 16, 95–111
© 2004 Published by Elsevier Ltd.
ISSN: 0270-4013/doi:10.1016/S0270-4013(04)16005-4

NCLB and the Individuals with Disabilities Education Act (IDEA) (1997) support the belief that students with LD should have access to the generalized curriculum. Because of this belief and federal legislation, a large number of students with LD are being serviced within general education settings for a large percentage of the school day. The number of students with disabilities being served by public schools during the 1999–2000 school year was 5,666,415; over half of these (2,861,333) were being served under the disability category of specific learning disabilities – this number has grown by 300% since 1976 (President's Commission of Excellence in Special Education, 2002; U.S. Department of Education, 2001). Of these 2,861,333 students, 47.46% are educated outside the general classroom for less than 21% of the school day (U.S. Department of Education, 2001) implying that students with LD are largely educated within general education classrooms. Along with this is the assumption that students with LD should achieve at a level commensurate with their peers even when no consideration to modifying the curriculum is discussed.

Although a large number of students with LD are placed in the general education classroom, there is evidence that suggests that students with disabilities are not fairing well within the general education curriculum. The outcome of limited to no curriculum modifications has resulted in a 12–49 point range difference in the reading scores on standardized tests between students with disabilities and those without disabilities as well as a 13–42 point range in the area of mathematics as reported by National Assessment of Educational Progress (U.S. Department of Education, 2001) Another piece of evidence is the drop out rate of students with disabilities. The break down in students with disabilities achievement within the general education curriculum is further evidenced by 27.1% of students with LD dropping out of school while only 63.3% graduated with a standard diploma (U.S. Department of Education, 2001). Although these figures illustrate an increase in the graduation rate and a decrease in the school drop out rate, when compared to 1993–1994 data, there is serious concern over these figures. These results culminate in only 32% of people with disabilities ages 18–64 years, working full or part-time, compared to 81% of the nondisabled population resulting in a 49% gap (National Organization on Disabilities, 2000).

The dilemma of students with disabilities mastering the special education curriculum has been an issue for over a decade because special education services and programs are not aligned with that of the general education curriculum. For students with LD, general education goals and objectives apply as well as those stated in their IEP. Curriculum and IEPs are "important because they delineate the relationship between what is to be taught and the desired academic and social behaviors" (Gunter et al., 2000, p. 116). For this alignment to occur, education stakeholders should: (1) be more responsive to legislative actions by implementing programs that are in concert with the spirit of the law; (2) modify and adapt curriculum and instruction at its' broadest level; (3) implement effective instruction and modifications in every classroom; and (4) ensure that these changes take place now and in the future. From these perspectives, we write this chapter.

RESPONDING TO LEGISLATIVE ACTIONS

Past and current legislative actions have impacted why curriculum must be modified. At the time of writing this chapter, the IDEA 1997 is up for reauthorization. Concurrently, NCLB was signed into law followed by a report submitted to the President by the President's Commission on Excellence in Special Education. This Commission summarized its findings after communications with various stakeholders vested in the educational performance of students with disabilities. In the NCLB report and IDEA reauthorization debates, concerns over students with LD access to the general curriculum were highlighted. There are revelations that limited access to the general curriculum was synonymous with students with LD not participating in state assessments. The standards based reform movement has been anchored in the belief that students with disabilities should be included in state assessments, thus transforming the curriculum to meet all students' needs.

Standard Based Reform Movement

The standard based reform movement calls for greater efforts to improve the quality of education by establishing criteria by which all students would be assessed (Thurlow, 2002). The intent of this movement is to create an educational system where standards drive the content of the curriculum and subsequent assessments. While the standards based reform movement has merit, some have questioned whether it establishes provisions for students with disabilities (Thurlow et al., 1998). This question was raised because students with disabilities were typically excluded from participating in state assessments resulting in inconclusive documentation for accurately evaluating their educational progress. Because of the exclusion, there is little effort to include students with disabilities in the core curriculum, thereby limiting student access. One of the reasons cited for this exclusion was that local and state education agencies did not want to jeopardize local and or state assessment rankings by including students with disabilities scores within their reporting systems (U.S. Department of Education, 2001). It is surmised that each of these entities felt that the scores of students who had none to limited access to the general education curriculum would

perform poorly thus lowering the overall ranking. With the reauthorization of
IDEA in 1997, states are now required to report the extent to which students with
disabilities participate in the state assessments and to publish their results both
aggregated and disaggregated from students without disabilities.

To date, there continues to be a wide dispersion among states that report the
data and those who do not. According to the 23rd Annual Report to Congress
on IDEA, only 17 states reported disaggregated performance data for students
with disabilities (U.S. Department of Education, 2001). Authorities in the field of
special education believe failure to include students with disabilities in assessment
results provides an inaccurate view of the entire educational system (Thurlow et al.,
1998). The newest piece of education legislation, NCLB calls for an end to
limiting the access of the general education curriculum to a specific group of
students.

No Child Left Behind Act

NCLB is intended to ensure that all children including those with LD have
access to the general curriculum. NCLB "addresses *all* public elementary and
secondary school children, thus clearly including all children receiving (or
potentially receiving) the support of special education" (Council for Exceptional
Children, 2002, p. 5) are included in its statues. NCLB also addresses adequate
yearly progress and notes that "95% of each group of students are required to
participate in the assessments with accommodations, guidelines, and alternative
assessments in the same manner as those provided under IDEA" (Council for
Exceptional Children, 2002, p. 12). Adequate yearly progress is measured by
these assessments so that accountability at the state, local school district, and
local school levels can be measured. NCLB also requires that states report the
scores of students with disabilities as aggregated and disaggregated data.

NCLB supports provisions stipulated in IDEA 1997 that emphasize that effective
education systems now and in the future must:

(A) maintain high academic standards and clear performance goals for children
    with disabilities, consistent with the standards and expectations for all students
    in the educational system, and provide for appropriate and effective strategies
    and methods to ensure that students who are children with disabilities have
    maximum opportunities to achieve those standards and goals;
(B) create a system that fully addresses the needs of all students, including chil-
    dren with disabilities by addressing the needs of children with disabilities
    in carrying out educational reform activities. (Pub. L. No. 115–17, § 671,
    p. 101).

As disability legislation continue to mandate greater participation of students with disabilities in the general education curriculum, more efforts must be made to facilitate student access and success (Ford et al., 2001).

MODIFYING CURRICULUM AND INSTRUCTION

From figures reported earlier in this chapter about the high school completion, high school drop out rates, employment rates, and inclusion in statewide assessments of students with LD, it is easy to conclude that instruction must be altered to assist students in their academic development. Clearly, there is a relationship between academic experiences and students' access to postsecondary education, employment, and community living opportunities (U.S. Department of Education, 2001). The U.S. Department of Education stated that in order for students with LD to have access to the general curriculum: (a) high expectations for student achievement and learning must be promoted; (b) systematic and appropriate assessment and instructional accommodations must be used; and (c) access to a full range of secondary education curricula and programs must be ensured. The first step to assisting students with LD in achieving these goals is to assess what type of curriculum framework is being implemented within the student's individual school.

Using Subject-Centered or Learner-Centered Curriculum Frameworks

There are two basic curriculum frameworks: the subject-centered curriculum and the learner-centered curriculum. The subject-centered curriculum places emphasis on the content of the subject areas being taught rather the learner. This framework focuses on the cognitive development and student acquisition of knowledge, emphasizes group learning, and relies heavily on textbooks and curriculum guides as the only source of instruction. In contrast the learner-centered curriculum places emphasis on the learner, recognizes the individual needs of each learner, takes into account the social and personal issues confronting students and reinforces independence and self-determination within the context of instruction. In addition, the learner-centered curriculum allows for student input on the content to be taught. When selecting a curriculum model for students with learning disabilities, the learner-centered curriculum is most suitable for students with LD because it acknowledges individual differences. When considering the education of any child with a disability, it is critical that general and special educators address the individual needs of the child; this begins with the development of a student's IEP.

Making the Individual Education Plan a Reality

The President's Commission on Excellence in Special Education (2002) found that education stakeholders view IEPs as documents used for the legal protection and compliance of school districts with federal regulations and not as frameworks for a child's individualized education. It is stressed throughout this report that parents in light of the current legislations should "hold schools accountable for compliance with IDEA that generates improved results for children with disabilities" (p. 17). For the IEP to provide a framework for this to occur, it should reflect the student's entire educational program including statements in relation to: (a) a child's present level of educational performance; (b) how the disability affects the student's participation in the general education curriculum; (c) the extent of the student's participation in general education classrooms; (d) what modifications or accommodations the student is entitled to; and (e) a listing of services as they relate to the achievement of measurable annual outcomes. The results of the psychological evaluation input from general and special educators, parents, and the student should help in constructing the content of the IEP. "IEPs must preserve basic civil rights and promote achievement" (President's Commission on Excellence in Special Education, 2002, p. 17) within the general education curriculum. To assure that students with disabilities achieve within the general education curriculum, proactive efforts must be made to promote successful inclusion classrooms throughout all schools.

Facilitating Inclusive Classrooms

Inclusion for students with LD within general education classrooms allows them greater access to the general education curriculum. Work done by Mastropieri and Scruggs along with several colleagues (1998, 2001) outlined seven characteristics for successful inclusion classrooms. The first being administrative support at both the building and district level. Administrative support allows for positive attitudes for inclusion to grow as well as resources being allocated to these efforts. Second is the support from special education for general education personnel. Assistance with planning, instructional adaptations, co-teaching, and classroom assistance with paraprofessionals are all classified as support (Glang et al., 1994). Thirdly, teachers who had successful inclusionary classrooms provided an environment in which individual differences were accommodated. These classrooms also presented appropriate curriculum in a highly interactive context thus, defining the fourth dimension. The fifth, six, and seventh characteristics effective general teaching skills, peer assistance, and disability specific teaching skills respectively are no doubt the cornerstones of implementing effective instruction and modifying curriculum and classrooms for students with LD.

IMPLEMENTING EFFECTIVE INSTRUCTION AND MODIFICATIONS

"Effective instruction for students with LD appears to involve the strategic integration of research-based practices in assessment, instructional design, and instruction tailored to the unique needs of the student and situated in the context of school" (Mitchem & Richards, 2003, p. 111). Although there is extensive evidence in research-based practices there is also a large body of literature that discusses the obstacles facing the adoption and sustained use of such practices (e.g. Gersten & Dimino, 2001; Gersten et al., 1992; Wong, 1997). Andrews et al. (2000) suggested that research-based practices are not relied upon because teachers are not taught the scientific method in their professional training. For such practices to be implemented Gersten and Dimino (2001) noted that teachers must find a practice that they believe to be effective with their students. Andrews et al. (2000) added that teacher preparation programs must teach students to use "traditional research methods to formulate instructional practices that produce optimal outcomes for individuals with disabilities and identifying the conditions necessary for institutionalizing those best practices" (p. 259).

Effective Instruction

Vaughn et al. (2000) concluded that effective instructional approaches for students with LD consist of both visible and explicit components. This is supported by the earlier work of Larrivee (1985) who investigated 118 elementary inclusive classrooms and reported that students with LD made the greatest academic achievements when teachers: (a) made efficient use of time; (b) had good relationships with students; (c) provided substantial amounts of positive feedback; (d) maintained a high success rate; (e) provided supportive responses to students in general; and (f) offered supportive responses to low-ability students. Santos and Lignugaris/Kraft (1997) stated more specifically that "effective teachers plan their instruction, establish a learning set, present new material and provide guided practice, provide opportunities for independent practice, and evaluate children's performance" (p. 97). For students with LD, positive outcomes have been correlated with a focus on the general education curriculum with accommodations (Rea et al., 2002). Students with and without LD recognize and appreciate instructors that slow instruction down when needed, explain expectations clearly, and use different materials and techniques to assist everyone in learning (Klingner & Vaughn, 1999).

Classwide Peer Tutoring

As students with learning disabilities move from individualized academic to more inclusive settings the individualized techniques once used become inappropriate (Jenkins & Mayhall, 1976; Sindelar & Deno, 1979; Vadasy et al., 1997). "Faced with increasing student heterogeneity, teachers can be expected to increasingly value practices designed for classroom use – in particular, those that target basic skills instruction, to meet a wide range of instructional needs" (Vadasy et al., 1997, p. 144). Classwide peer tutoring (CWPT) is a research-based practice, developed by researchers at Juniper Gardens Children's Project (see Delquadri et al., 1983), that benefits students from all ability levels (Fuchs et al., 1993) that is also perceived by teachers to be concrete, practical, and usable within general education classrooms (Doyle & Ponder, 1977; Gersten et al., 1992). Within the instructional procedure of CWPT, all students within a classroom take on the role of tutor and tutee within one session (King-Sears & Bradley, 1995).

The first step at implementing CWPT is to prepare and select classroom materials. Before students begin learning their roles in CWPT, the teacher must decide what subject matter is going to be covered utilizing this strategy. Most often, math facts, spelling words, vocabulary words, and reading comprehension are the academic areas that are focused on (King-Sears & Bradley, 1995). Once this is done, teachers must assess the students' skill level so that pairings can be made. The pairing can be based on either random assignment or skill level. After this has been completed, teachers then prepare the materials to be used for CWPT. It is also important to note that "CWPT can be used with standardized, commercially prepared materials or teacher made materials" (Fulk & King, 2001, p. 49). The next step is to train students to begin utilizing CWPT. The first step within this process is to make students aware of the rationale and purpose of CWPT (Fulk & King, 2001). Next the teacher should model and discuss for students ways in which to give corrective feedback. This assists students in gaining appropriate social skills as well as preventing students from becoming demeaning to their partners. This is followed by allowing students to practice getting into their pairings with necessary materials in a timely and orderly fashion. Lastly instruction, modeling, and practice as the role of "tutor" is given. Within this step students learn how to ask questions and understand that time on task is an important aspect of this procedure. After sufficient practice is given implementation can occur.

Within the implementation stage students are reminded of the procedures before tutoring sessions begin. Tutoring sessions last from fifteen to thirty minutes depending on the content (Fulk & King, 2001). Pairings are kept for a week and then changed. During the first ten minutes of a tutoring session one student is the tutor while the other is the tutee. After the first ten minutes are up they reverse roles and for the final ten minutes students summarize what skills they have learned. Tutors reward points to tutees when correct responses are given. While the tutoring sessions are occurring the teacher moves about the room and assists teams while keeping track of time. Teachers may also take notes to use as feedback when tutoring sessions are over (King-Sears & Bradley, 1995). The final phase of CWPT is measuring progress. One measure of progress is to chart each pairs points earned. Pairs of students can earn points by: (a) correct responses; (b) practice after incorrect responses; or (c) bonus points assigned by the teacher (King-Sears & Bradley, 1995). These point totals are displayed on a classroom chart and weekly winners are announced. Due to pairs being switched each week opportunity to be part of a winning team is increased. Pre and post tests of the skills being targeted are given providing the best measure of individual student progress. "One of the most powerful reasons for teachers to take the time to implement CWPT is that all students show academic gains" (King-Sears & Bradley, 1995, p. 31). In a study done by Maheady and Harper (1991), students reported that others: (a) thought they were smarter; (b) liked them better; and (c) were more friendly to them after participating in CWPT sessions. Likewise Klingner and Vaughn (1999) reported in their synthesis on perceptions of inclusion classrooms that students with and without LD indicated a strong preference for classrooms that included peer tutoring. Teachers have also reported positive attitudes towards the implementation of CWPT with one stating:

> I really liked the results I was seeing in the class because I knew the students were on task the entire reading period. They were doing their work, it was not me standing and lecturing. And that is the way it should be, the students working as active learners. They were doing more with less of my influence, and less of my struggling with having to perform up there. So it was a good feeling to know that they were actually having time reading (Vadasy et al., 1997, p. 145).

Along with the positive outcomes, CWPT balances the need for individualized instruction with total student participation in today's diverse classrooms.

Cognitive Strategies

Cognitive strategies take into account a student's learning disability and assists him/her during the process of acquiring, processing, retrieving and manipulating information. "Cognitive strategies are cognitive processes that the learner intentionally performs to influence learning and cognition" (Mayer, 2001 p. 5). When using cognitive strategies, students with learning disabilities for the most part become active and successful learners (Duffy et al., 1987; Haller et al., 1998; Mayer, 2001; Palincsar & Brown, 1985). To be successful in the general education curriculum, students should be taught cognitive strategies while matriculating through the general education curriculum; the teacher should prompt student use. Examples of cognitive strategies include the use of rehearsal strategies to memorize lists of information, metacognitive strategies such as a student assessing whether he or she has comprehended a reading passage and other strategies that influence student learning. Prior to the lesson, the teacher should determine cognitive strategies most suitable or compatible with the content or skills to be learned. By making this determination prior to teaching, students can be equipped with necessary strategies that will lead to favorable outcomes. Also, when teaching cognitive strategies, it is very important that teachers model what is to be learned. For example, if the teacher is teaching a student how to chunk like concepts to aide memory and recall, the teacher should model how that is to be done. After modeling, the teacher should check for student understanding. This check can be done by asking the student to either demonstrate what has been learned or the student may be asked to verbalize what has been taught.

Rehearsal Strategies
Through teacher demonstration and student guided and controlled practice, students are taught how to rehearse lists first out loud until the student rehearses list and other repetitive information covertly (Belmont & Butterfield, 1971). Through teacher demonstration and guided and controlled student practice, students are taught how to develop acronyms, construct sentences (such as every good boy does fine to memorize the G Clef of a music score) to aid in memorizing.

Comprehension Strategies
Through teacher demonstration and student guided and controlled practice, students are taught how to ask appropriate questions, research definitions of unfamiliar words and/or terms, predict the ending of a reading passage, and provide summaries and conclusions of reading passages (Brown & Palinscar, 1989; Palincsar & Brown, 1985).

Content Enhancements Routines

Content enhancements routines are used by teachers to enhance the delivery of content information and to assist the learner in acquiring, retaining, and remembering key elements of what has been learned (Tralli, 1996). Content enhancement routines are defined "as a way of teaching an academically diverse group of students that meets both group and individual needs; maintains the integrity of the content; selects critical features of the content and transforms them in a manner that promotes learning and carries out instruction in partnership with students" (Lenz & Bulgren, 1996, p. 426). When enhancing the delivery of content, special and general education teachers may:

(1) Provide a detailed overview of the content that is to be learned.
(2) Present a graphic device to present key concepts.
(3) Select content suitable to the learners background.
(4) Provide students with word webs.
(5) Provide students with compare/contrast charts to help illustrate and compare difficult terms and/or concepts.
(6) Make complex information more meaningful by providing generalizations and concrete examples.
(7) Provide students with a Planning Pyramid developed by Schumm et al., in 1994 (cited in Bulgren & Lenz, 1996, p. 426).

The planning pyramid mentioned above was designed to help the teacher make curricular decisions when delivering instruction to students with LD. The pyramid encourages teachers to plan, and reflect on what to teach in an inclusive classroom setting with heterogeneous learners. When utilizing teachers should plan for instruction based on the following three levels explained by Bulgren and Lenz (1996):

> The first level, the base of the Planning Pyramid, represents the most important concepts to be taught. This level houses broad concepts and ideas that anchor the area to be taught. The guiding question here is: What do I want all students to learn? The middle level of the Planning Pyramid is the level of information considered next most important for understanding the information. It includes additional concepts and information that support the concepts listed in the base of the Planning Pyramid. The guiding question here is: What do I want most of my students to learn? The top level of the Planning Pyramid represents information that teachers consider to be of supplemental importance. It contains a list of information that teacher expects only a few students in the class to learn. The guiding question here is: What information might some students learn? By using this planning pyramid teachers become better able to teach all learners (pp. 426–427).

Teaching Devices

When using content enhancements, teachers may elect to use "teaching devices." These are used to optimize student learning. Teachers may use devices to help organize information, promote better student understanding, describe a story, enable the demonstration of a concept, and/or assist in promoting recall. The devices outlined by Bulgren and Lenz (1996) may be verbal or visual and may include:

(1) *Organizing*

The teacher may elect to use verbal devices by summarization, chunking; using advance organizers, post organizers, verbal cues about organization. When using visual devices, the teacher may elect to use outlines, webs, hierarchical graphic organizers, tables, grids, and/or flowcharts. All of these strategies allow students to arrange information into meaningful structures.

(2) *Promoting student understanding*

When promoting student understanding, the teacher may choose to use verbal devices by providing analogies, comparisons, synonyms, metaphors, antonyms, and/or similes. Visual devices in this category consist of the teacher providing symbols, concrete objects, pictures, models and/or diagrams.

(3) *Describing a story*

In this area, verbal devices consists of the teacher electing to provide students with information concerning current events, past events, fictional stories, hypothetical scenarios and or personal stories; visual devices consists of video, web casting, interactive video and/or power point presentations.

(4) *Demonstrating*

Teachers may elect to include role play or a dramatic portrayal as a verbal device and physical gestures or movements, movable objects, and/or demonstration as a visual device.

(5) *Promoting Recall*

When promoting recall, teachers may choose to use acronyms and or keywords as verbal devices and visual images, and/or sketches as visual devices.

Technology

Technology has proven to be a benefit to learners with LD. It has been used for academic skill building primarily in the areas of writing and math, social skill development and empowering children to become independent learners (Holzberg, 1994; Maccini et al., 2002; Ryba et al., 1995). As a skill builder, students are provided appropriate drill and practice exercises. In the area of social skill development, special lessons utilizing subject specific scenarios are placed on videodiscs and students are given the opportunity to participate in role-play situations where they become the actors and decision makers. The outcomes of the role play situations are reflective of the decisions made by the student.

Teachers have found that student use of computers (word processing software) during the writing process helps to alleviate student tension and stress thereby helping students become better writers (Holzberg, 1994; Ryba et al., 1995). MacArthur et al. (1991) found that text and graphics-based software may be best suitable for students with severe writing difficulties that exhibit poor organization skills, inability to shape one's own ideas and thoughts, and an inability to revise written work. Text and graphics based software increases the student's confidence and also serves as a motivator, and an enhancement for student participation in writing projects. Also, grammar, spellchecker, dictionaries and thesaurus programs along with word prediction software assist in alleviating the stress associated with writing sentences paragraphs and short stories. Word prediction software allows students to choose from several words.

In the area of math, Lewis (1993) discussed Math Word Problems software to assist students in sorting relevant information when computing word problems. The software allows the teacher to make program changes by determining the level of difficulty, and the amount of incorrect responses allowable. Research studies have proven that the use of computer-based instructional tools such as tutorials and computer study guides, videodisc lessons, and reading texts on computer-assisted instruction bring about an academically desirable benefit for students with LD (Maccini et al., 2002).

FUTURE DIRECTIONS

As Thurlow (2002) stated "the promise of standards based reform is still just that – a promise" (p. 201). With school districts incorporating the regulations set forth in NCLB, students with LD will become integral members of general education classrooms thus, gaining access to the general education curriculum and achieving the goal of the standards-based reform movement. For school districts, their effectiveness in this effort will be based on tenets from NCLB that impact IDEA and call for "accountability of results, flexibility, local solutions to local challenges, scientifically based programs and teaching methods, and full information and options for parents" (President's Commission on Excellence in Special Education, 2002, p. 5). Students with LD will be able to judge how effective the partnership between general and special education is to their learning due to their inclusion within general education classrooms (Klingner & Vaughn, 1998). The movement to more inclusive settings also changes the role of special education and the professionals involved in its objectives.

The President's Commission on Excellence in Special Education (2002) found that special education is "in need of fundamental re-thinking, a shift in priorities and a new commitment to individual needs" (p. 4). Andrews et al. (2000) supported this by asserting that special education can assist schools in seeing all students as important stakeholders while simultaneously implementing research-based practices thus, increasing the chances that students with LD will become successful members of society. For these outcomes to occur, general and special education teachers will have to work together to adapt curriculum and instruction based on individual students' needs (McLeskey et al., 1999). Special educators will have to educate themselves to the outcomes associated with the general education curriculum while general education teachers will have to learn how to incorporate different special teaching techniques into their everyday routine. Thus, answering the question, "What is the best way to teach the objective listed on the IEP and at the same time help the student fit in and be successful in the general education classroom?" (Klingner & Vaughn, 2002, p. 29).

"The intent of curriculum is to provide a road map that describes and directs the academic and social development of all students" while modifications help students with LD to attain similar results as those without disabilities (Gunter et al., 2000, p. 117). As Fisher and Frey (2001) pointed out, modifications and adaptations that meet the needs of students with LD in general education classrooms must focus on cooperative learning, partnership activities, learning centers, and individual instruction. Students with and without LD have reported that they like classrooms where they are allowed to support each other in achieving academic outcomes (Klingner & Vaughn, 1999). This pairing of accommodations in conjunction with the general education curriculum are seen as factors in positive student outcomes (Rea et al., 2002). By pairing students with and without LD in the achievement of academic objectives, teachers are actually able to create the community of learners.

REFERENCES

Andrews, J. E., Carnine, D. W., Coutinho, M. J., Edgar, E. B., Forness, S. R., Fuchs, L. S., Jordan, D., Kauffman, J. M., Patton, J. M., Paul, J., Rosell, J., Rueda, R., Schiller, E., Skrtic, T. M., & Wong, J. (2000). Bridging the special education divide. *Remedial and Special Education*, *21*(5), 258–260.

Belmont, J. M., & Butterfield, E. C. (1971). Learning strategies as determinants of memory deficiencies. *Cognitive Psychology*, *3*, 411–420.

Brown, A. L., & Palincsar, A. S. (1989). Guided, cooperative learning and individual knowledge acquisition. In: L. B. Resnick (Ed.), *Knowing, Learning, and Instruction* (pp. 393–451). Hillsdale, NJ: Lawrence Erlbaum.

Bulgren J., & Lenz, K. (1996). Strategic instruction in the content areas. In: K. Deshler, E. Ellis & K. Lenz (Eds), *Teaching adolescents with learning disabilities* (pp. 409–473). Denver, CO: Love.

Council for Exceptional Children (2002, September). *No Child Left Behind Act of 2001: Implications for special education policy and practice.* Arlington, VA: Author.

Delquadri, J. C., Greenwood, C. R., Stretton, K., & Hall, R. V. (1983). The peer tutoring spelling game: A classroom procedure for increasing opportunity to respond and spelling performance. *Education and Treatment of Children, 6*, 225–239.

Doyle, W., & Ponder, G. (1977). The practicality ethic in teacher decision-making. *Interchange, 8*, 1–12.

Duffy, G. G., Roehler, L. R., Sivan, E., Rackliffe, G., Book, C., Meloth, M., Vavrus, L. G., Wessleman, R., Putnam, J., & Bassiri, D. (1987). Effects of explaining the reasoning associated with using reading strategies. *Reading Quarterly, 22*, 347–368.

Fisher, D., & Frey, N. (2001). Access to the core curriculum: Critical ingredients for student success. *Remedial and Special Education, 22*(3), 148–157.

Ford, A., Davern, L., & Schnorr, R. (2001). Learners with significant disabilities. *Remedial& Special Education, 22*, 214–222.

Fuchs, D., Fuchs, L. S., & Mathes, P. G. (1993, April). Peer mediated learning strategies: Effects on learners at different points on the reading continuum. Paper presented at the annual meeting of the American Educational Research Association, Atlanta.

Fulk, B. M., & King, K. (2001). Classwide peer tutoring at work. *Teaching Exceptional Children, 34*(2), 49–53.

Gersten, R. M., & Dimino, J. (2001). The realities of translating research into classroom practice. *Learning Disabilities Research & Practice, 16*(2), 120–130.

Gersten, R. M., Woodward, J., & Morvant, M. (1992). The quest to translate research into classroom practice: Strategies for assisting classroom teachers' work with at-risk students and students with disabilities. In: D. Carnine & E. Kameenui (Eds), *Higher Cognitive Functioning for All Students* (pp. 201–218). Austin, TX: Pro-Ed.

Glang, A., Gersten, R., & Morvant, M. (1994). A directive approach toward the consultation process: A case study. *Learning Disabilities Research & Practice, 9*, 226–235.

Gunter, P. L., Denny, R. K., & Venn, M. L. (2000). Modification on instructional materials and procedures for curricular success of students with emotional and behavioral disorders. *Preventing School Failure, 44*(3), 116–121.

Haller, E. P., Child, D. A., & Walberg, H. J. (1998). Can comprehension be taught? A quantitative synthesis of "Metacognitive" studies. *Educational Researcher, 22*, 5–9.

Holzberg, C. (1994). Technology in special education. *Technology & Learning, 14*(7), 18–21.

Individual with Disabilities Education Act, Pub. L. No. 105–17, 111 Stat (1997).

Jenkins, J. R., & Mayhall, W. F. (1976). Development and evaluation of a resource teacher program: The resource specialist model. *Exceptional Children, 43*, 21–29.

Jitendra, A. K., Edwards, L. L., Choutka, C. M., & Treadway, P. S. (2002). A collaborative approach to planning in the content areas for students with learning disabilities: Accessing the general curriculum. *Learning Disabilities Research & Practice, 17*(4), 252–2677.

King-Sears, M. E., & Bradley, D. F. (1995). Classwide peer tutoring. *Preventing School Failure, 40*(1), 29–36.

Klingner, J. K., & Vaughn, S. (1998). Inclusion or pull-out: Which do students prefer? *Journal of Learning Disabilities, 31*(2), 148–159.

Klingner, J. K., & Vaughn, S. (1999). Students' perceptions of instruction in inclusion classrooms: Implications for students with learning disabilities. *Exceptional Children, 66*(1), 23–37.

Klingner, J. K., & Vaughn, S. (2002). The changing roles and responsibilities of an LD specialist. *Learning Disability Quarterly, 25*, 19–31.

Larrivee, B. (1985). *Effective teaching for effective mainstreaming*. New York: Longman.

Lenz, B. K. I., & Bulgren, J. A. (1996). Promoting learning in content classes. In: P. A. Cegelka & W. H. Berdine (Eds), *Effective Instruction for Students with Learning Problems* (pp. 385–427). Needham Heights, MA: Allyn & Bacon.

Lewis, R. B. (1993). *Special education technology. Classroom applications*. Pacific Grove, CA: Brooks/Cole Publishing Company.

Liberman, A., & Grolnick, M. (1999). Networks and reform in American Education. In: L. Darling-Hammond & G. Skyes (Eds), *Teaching as the Learning Profession: Handbook of Policy and Practice* (pp. 292–312). San Francisco: Jossey-Bass.

MacArthur, C. A., Graham, S., & Schwartz, S. (1991). A model for writing instruction: Integrating word processing and strategy instruction into a process approach to writing. *Learning Disabilities Research and Practice*, 6, 230–236.

Maccini, P., Gagnon, C., & Hughes, C. (2002). Technology-based practices for secondary students with learning disabilities. *Learning Disabilities Quarterly*, 25, 247–261.

Maheady, L., & Harper, G. F. (1991). Training and implementation requirements associated with the use of classwide peer tutoring system. *Education & Treatment of Children*, 14(3), 177–199.

Mastropieri, M. A., & Scruggs, T. E. (2001). Promoting inclusion in secondary classrooms. *Learning Disability Quarterly*, 24, 265–274.

Mastropieri, M. A., Scruggs, T. E., Mantzicopoulous, P. Y., Sturgeon, A., Goodwin, I., & Chung, S. (1998). A place where living things affect and depend on each other: Qualitative and quantitative outcomes associated with inclusive science teaching. *Science Education*, 82, 163–179.

Mayer, R. (2001). What good is educational psychology? The case of cognition and instruction. *Educational Psychologist*, 36, 83–88.

McLeskey, J., Henry, D., & Axelrod, M. I. (1999). Inclusion of students with learning disabilities: An examination of data from reports to congress. *Exceptional Children*, 66, 55–66.

Mitchem, K., & Richards, A. M. (2003). Students with learning disabilities. In: F. E. Obiakor, C. A. Utley & A. F. Rotatori (Eds), *Advances in Special Education: Psychology of Effective Education for Learners with Exceptionalities* (pp. 99–117). Stamford, CT: JAI Press.

National Organization on Disabilities (2000). *N.O.D./Harris survey of Americans with disabilities*. Washington, DC: Louis Harris & Associates.

Palincsar, A. S., & Brown, A. L. (1985). Reciprocal teaching of comprehension-fostering and comprehension-monitoring activities. *Cognition and Instruction*, 1, 117–175.

President's Commission on Excellence in Special Education (2002). *A new era: Revitalizing special education for children and their families (ED-02-PO-0791)*. Jessup, MD: Education Publication Center.

Rea, P. J., McLaughlin, V. L., & Walther-Thomas, C. (2002). Outcomes for students with learning disabilities in inclusive and pullout programs. *Exceptional Children*, 68(2), 203–222.

Ryba, K., Selby, L., & Nolan, P. (1995). Computers empower students with special needs. *Educational Leadership International*, 53, 82–85.

Santos, R. M., & Lignugaris/Kraft, B. (1997). Integrating research and effective instruction with instruction in the natural environment for young children with disabilities. *Exceptionality*, 7(2), 97–129.

Sindelar, P., & Deno, S. (1979). The effectiveness of research programming. *The Journal of Special Education*, 12, 17–28.

Thurlow, M. L. (2002). Positive educational results for all students: The promise if standards-based reform. *Remedial and Special Education*, 23(4), 195–201.

Thurlow, M. L., Elliott, J. L., & Ysseldyke, J. E. (1998). *Testing students with disabilities: Practical strategies for complying with district and state requirements.* Thousand Oaks, CA: Corwin Press.

Tralli, R. (1996). The strategies intervention model: A model for supported inclusion at the secondary level. *Remedial & Special Education, 17*(4), 204–216.

U.S. Department of Education, Office of Special Education Programs (2001). *To assure the free and appropriate public education of all children with disabilities: Twenty-third annual report to congress on the implementation of the individuals with disabilities education act.* Washington, DC: Author.

Vadasy, P. F., Jenkins, J. R., Antil, L. R., Phillips, N. B., & Pool, K. (1997). The research-to-practice ball game: Classwide peer tutoring and teacher interest, implementation, and modifications. *Remedial and Special Education, 18,* 143–156.

Vaughn, S., Gersten, R., & Chard, D. (2000). The underlying message in LD intervention research: Findings from research syntheses. *Exceptional Children, 67,* 99–114.

Wong, B. Y. (1997). Clearing hurdles in teacher adoption and sustained use of research-based practices. *Journal of Learning Disabilities, 30*(5), 482–485.

TECHNOLOGY RESOURCES FOR PERSONS WITH LEARNING DISABILITIES

Jeffrey P. Bakken and Brian W. Wojcik

Technology has made considerable advances in helping individuals with learning disabilities become productive and independent participants in work, classroom, and leisure settings. Recent laws mandating civil rights for those with learning disabilities implies that the implementation of technology is a significant opportunity for the provision of equal access. The forces of "equal access," "non-discrimination," and "reasonable accommodations" have created an environment that encourages the use of technology to help those with learning disabilities function on a more equal basis with their non-disabled peers. Section 504 of the Vocational Rehabilitation Act of 1973 (P.L. 93–112) and the Americans with Disabilities Act of 1990 (ADA)(P.L. 101–336) prohibit discrimination against all individuals with disabilities, requiring both the public and private sectors to provide accommodations and make programs accessible. The application of these mandates are legally interpreted to apply to the acquisition and modification of equipment and devices, such as adaptive hardware and software for computers. For instance, P.L. 93–112 requires that electronic office equipment purchased through federal procurement meet disability access guidelines. The Tech Act's 1994 amendments provide funding to establish programs that promote the provision of technology-related assistance. The National Literacy Act of 1991 (P.L. 102–73) strategically encourages the use of technology in literacy programs.

Current Perspectives on Learning Disabilities
Advances in Special Education, Volume 16, 113–132
Copyright © 2004 by Elsevier Ltd.
All rights of reproduction in any form reserved
ISSN: 0270-4013/doi:10.1016/S0270-4013(04)16006-6

When assessing possible technologies that could be implemented with students with learning disabilities, there are certain aspects of the assessment process that include: (a) identification of student needs; (b) collection of background information; (c) family and staff interviews; (d) student observations and interviews; (e) motor assessments; (f) cognitive and sensory assessments; (g) language assessments; (h) feature/match process (i.e. how features of the technology match the needed processes of the individual to enhance success); (i) trial runs and/or equipment mockups; and (j) assessment of results (Bierly & McCloskey-Dale, 1999). At present, many agree that computers and related technologies have great potential for enhancing the capabilities of children, adolescents, and adults with learning disabilities (Alliance for Technology Access, 1994; Lewis, 1993; Lindsey, 1993; Male, 1994). Assistive technologies also need to be considered. Assistive technologies have been implemented and have documented effectiveness in fostering academic success and independence for students with learning disabilities (Bryant, Bryant & Raskind, 1998; Bryant & Seay, 1998; Raskind & Higgins, 1998). It is important to note, however, that assistive technology is not a cure-all, when chosen (especially high tech devices), it must meet the user's needs. For example, Phillips (1991) and Scherer (1991) reported that nearly one-third of all purchased assistive technology devices are abandoned, most frequently during the first year after they are recommended. Reasons given for this lack of use were the devices (a) did not improve independent functioning, (b) were too difficult to use, (c) were unreliable, and (d) required too much assistance from another person (Phillips, 1992; Phillips & Zhao, 1993). As the world becomes more and more technologically advanced, educational technology and educational software should be a part of a student's specially designed instruction to prepare them for integration into society. This chapter reiterates this proposition and emphasizes technology resources for persons with learning disabilities.

TECHNOLOGY CONSIDERATIONS
FOR PERSONS WITH LD

Consideration can be defined as the process of giving careful thought to something. When an IEP team considers the instructional programming and related goals and objectives for a student identified eligible for special education services, the process gives careful attention to a multitude of factors from different perspectives that result in individualized instruction for that student. Similarly, when assistive technology is considered for students with certain learning characteristics, careful attention must be given to ensure that the recommended assistive technology is required for the student to be successful and reflects an appropriate match between him/her and the tools (Zabala, 1995, 1996). For example, given that prescription eyeglasses can be considered assistive technology, and that a certain degree of visual acuity is generally needed in order for an individual to visually access print, one can see the importance of ensuring that the prescription is indeed required for an individual to perform and is appropriately matched to the visual needs of the individual. If eyeglasses are arbitrarily assigned to an individual, they may serve as an obstacle for the individual to see properly, thus, hampering his/her overall performance.

There is much in the literature supporting using a team approach when considering the potential benefits of assistive technology for individuals (Brennan, 1998). A team approach is critical since no single individual will have all the necessary information to make decisions regarding appropriate assistant technology (Smith, Benge & Hall, 1994). Inge and Shepard (1995) indicated that persons on decision-making teams should have knowledge of the potential user of the assistive technology, his/her family, as well as a range of assistive technology devices that may be deemed appropriate. It is crucial that teams that are considering assistive technology for particular individuals be comprised of a variety of persons representing several aspects of the student (Brennan, 1998). Stakeholders in this consideration process may include the student (if at all feasible) for whom the assistive technology is being considered, the student's family, the general education teacher(s), the special education teacher(s), related services providers (Speech Language Pathologist, Occupational Therapist, Occupational Therapist Assistant, Physical Therapist, Physical Therapist Assistant, etc.), school administrators, medical personnel, and rehabilitation counselors (Brennan, 1998). The involvement of a variety of stakeholders allows the team to consider multiple aspects of the student's abilities and needs within multiple contexts ultimately resulting in an appropriate match between the student and the assistive technology and an ownership in the process of the consideration and implementation of the assistive technology amongst the team members. Factors related to the consideration of assistive technology can be grouped into the following domains: student, environment, tasks, and tools (Zabala, 1995). As this process is a student-centered one, it makes sense that the first area to consider is the student himself or herself. One goal of assistive technology is to capitalize on the ability of an individual to offset areas in which he/she has difficulties (Kelker & Holt, 2000). Therefore, it is necessary to determine strengths that a person brings to the table in addition to the limitations (Melichair & Blackhurst, 1993). For instance, if a student in fifth grade has a good recall for information presented auditorily but has difficulty recalling information presented visually, the team should note that auditory memory is a strength and, eventually, choose a tool that capitalizes on this strength. Questions, such as "what does the student need to do?", "what are the student's current abilities?", and "what are the students current needs?" (Zabala, 1995) should guide the assistive technology consideration process in respect to the student. The team should also consider the student's personal perceptions (i.e. preferences, expectations on the assistive technology, and perceived need for potential assistive technology) (Melichair & Blackhurst, 1993). How well the potential user of assistive technology "buys into" the consideration process and the potential assistive technology will have a large impact on whether or not the assistive technology will be successful (Rogers, 1995).

The second area in the consideration of assistive technology focuses on environmental factors. It can be said that one's ability to perform is greatly dependent on what the environment will allow him/her to do. An extreme example could be an individual's ability to access different levels in a building when the individual is a wheelchair user. If the building has an elevator or some other type of vertical access, then the individual is able to perform the task of moving well from floor to floor whereas if the building only has stairs, he/she might not be able to perform the task as well. Perhaps a less obvious example would be the case of a student with Attention Deficit Hyperactivity Disorder (ADHD). In a class that grouped all of the desks into islands, the student may be less attentive because he or she is distracted by peers than if the desks were arranged in an alternate fashion. Zabala (1995) noted that materials currently available to the student as well as potential supports need to be considered across environments when evaluating for assistive technology. In looking at current materials and supports available, the team can identify potential tools and interventions that, if deemed to be appropriate, are readily available, and may be easily implemented. Environmental factors not only span across school contexts but contexts outside of school as well. In some cases, students will need to use the same assistive technology in the home setting that they use in the school setting. For example, a student that has difficulty recalling mathematical facts may use a calculator to circumvent his or her learning difficulties. It is likely that the calculator would be used on math related problems within the school setting, as well as at home for homework assignments. Consequently, factors related to the home life of the student should also be considered (Parette & Angelo, 1996; Parette & Brotherson, 1996). The team needs to determine the nature and extent of supports the student has outside of the school setting. Information related to the family's expectations, openness, and concerns regarding potential assistive technology needs to be accumulated and discussed.

The third area of assistive technology consideration focuses on the tasks that the student is being asked to accomplish. This is first accomplished by surveying the activities that take place in the environment (Zabala, 1995). One could do this by observing the student, observing the student's peers, and interviewing the teacher to gain a picture of tasks that students are expected to perform. Then, one should determine which tasks are required of the student to progress towards mastery of an educational objective or for the student to be an active member of the class (Zabala, 2002). For example, let us look at a student who has visual perceptual difficulties in a 4th grade math class. In observing the student, the student's peers, and interviewing the teacher, the following tasks might be noted: timed multiplication (2 digit by 1 digit) tests, pre-printed worksheets, word problems, multiplication problem sets from the class text, multiplication practice at the board (problems are already written on the board and then the class discusses them), and flash card drill and practice. It is noted in this student's IEP that he has grade appropriate computation skills but has difficulty lining up columns and often makes mistakes because he cannot keep his columns straight. In fact, a goal in his IEP states that he will successfully set up and solve mathematical problems. In looking at tasks that are needed for this student to successfully complete the goal, a team may determine to address all of the tasks except the flash card drill and practice because all of the tasks require the student to either set up a mathematical problem and/or solve the problem while maintaining column order. In this way, tasks directly related to mastery of curricular and/or IEP goals are purposefully addressed.

Finally, identifying tools that can be of use to the student, across environments, to support the identified tasks needs to occur. This "phase" occurs in four parts: (1) the identification of possible tools; (2) the evaluation of the tool characteristics for best match; (3) the trial of the tools with the student; and (4) the acquisition of the tools for long term use (Bowser & Reed, 1995; Edyburn, 2000; Zabala, 1995, 1996). When identifying tools, it is important to consider tools across a continuum from "low tech" (tools that are readily available, require little training, and are relatively low cost) to "high tech" (tools that may not be readily available, require significant training, and are relatively expensive) (Zabala, 1995). Tools should be identified based on how they can augment a student's strengths counterbalancing any effects of the student's disability and/or how they can provide an alternate means of completing a task so as to circumnavigate the effects of the disability on the students' performance altogether (Lewis, 1993). Additionally, identification of tools should take into consideration previous tools either tried and discarded or tried and implemented (Bryant & Raskind, 1995).

The characteristics of the tools themselves are important in determining a best match between the tool and the student. King (1999) proposed four dimensions on which tool characteristics should be evaluated. The first dimension is the extent to which the tool places cognitive demands upon the student. Cognitive demands refer to the determination of the amount of thinking that is required to use a device. This may include sensing, remembering, discriminating, analyzing, and sequencing actions needed to operate the tool. The second dimension is the extent to which the tool places physical demands upon the student. Physical demands refer to the determination of the amount of muscle strength and movement required to initiate, pursue, and complete the task of using the tool. Third, linguistic demands refer to the determination of the amount of symbolic interpretation and processing that the user must invest in order to operate the tool. Finally, time factors related to whether or not the tool will aid in the completion of the task within an acceptable amount of time needs to be addressed. Other factors related to the characteristics of tools should include the tool's durability, dependability, lifespan, and maintenance costs/programs.

It is important to recognize the process of consideration of assistive technology that is ongoing and recursive (Bowser & Reed, 1995; Chambers, 1997; Melichair & Blackhurst, 1993; Zabala, 2002). Over time, it is conceivable that environments within which the student is expected to work will change. In addition, as a student becomes older, the student's abilities, needs, expectations, and preferences may change affecting, in turn, the match between the student, the tasks, and the tools (Melichair & Blackhurst, 1993). Furthermore, new technologies may become available that allow the student a greater degree of independence. Without periodic review, changes within the student, environment, tasks, and/or tools may be missed and the assistive technology system may be compromised.

USING TECHNOLOGY TO DEAL WITH LEARNING PROBLEMS

To fully address this section it is important to discuss specific aspects of learning problems (i.e. reading, writing, spelling, mathematics, and instruction).

Reading

Approximately 80% of students identified with learning disabilities have their primary difficulties in reading (Lerner, 2002). When it comes to reading instruction, the norm has been for children with disabilities to receive remedial reading instruction from special education professionals and paraprofessionals (Cunningham & Allington, 1999). The type of reading instruction that children with disabilities often receive is narrow in focus and lacking in contextualized direct instruction and other types of instructional approaches which research suggests struggling readers need in order to learn to read and write (Allington, 1994). Students with disabilities are many times not getting enough instructional time working on reading skills to help them benefit and be successful independently.

Computers provide a multisensory delivery system in which words can be manipulated, heard, color-coded, and automatically linked with graphic cues. When reading is integrated with writing, "computers can offer students unlimited opportunities for practice and the repetition necessary to build fluency with continuous corrective feedback (computer-assisted instruction) and build comprehension by providing strategic prompts as students are reading/listening to content (e.g. eReader or ultimate Reader)" (Male, 2003, p. 48). Multimedia software is a possible mechanism to provide additional practice or even another mode of instruction for students with learning disabilities. Poole (1997) described multimedia as including such items as entertaining graphics and animation, high quality digitized speech, and motion video. Specific principles behind multimedia as described by Wissick and Gardner (2000) are: (a) the source of human learning is modeled; (b) the learner control is increased; (c) the exploration is encouraged; (d) the creation of individual relationships is fostered; (e) the individual's active involvement is encouraged; (f) numerous choices for navigation are provided; (g) different levels of prior knowledge are available; and (h) learners are allowed to adapt materials to fit their needs. Multimedia reading software can include phonemic awareness and other emergent literacy issues, phonological decoding, reading comprehension, and "talking" storybooks (Ashton, 2000). This extra time working on reading could provide students with learning disabilities a little bit of extra time to practice skills and strategies learned in reading class and to possibly apply them to more real-life situations and work on them in more automatic ways. Reading deficits may also be improved through the use of a related technology, text-to-speech systems, including improved comprehension, fluency, and accuracy, as well as enhanced concentration (Leong, 1992; Lundberg & Olofsson, 1993). Olson and Wise (1992) found that children with word recognition difficulties who read stories with speech feedback made significant gains in word recognition over children where reading time was spent in regular instruction.

For reading and writing activities, individuals with learning disabilities will likely find voice output/text-to-speech systems effective compensatory tools. One such system, an optical character recognition (OCR) system, scans and converts written text into computer documents that can be read by a speech synthesis/screen review system. Books on tape are available on loan to students with learning disabilities. Finally, help in researching and information-gathering can be obtained from books on computer disc, CD-ROM discs, and entire texts that can be downloaded from on-line services. With the use of an OCR system with speech synthesis, an individual with poor reading skills, yet strong receptive oral language abilities is able to read and thus, comprehend with greater ease. OCR systems provide a means for directly inputting printed material into a computer and displaying it on the computer screen. The input is accomplished through a full-page scanner that scans an entire page at once or a hand-held scanner that the user moves across or down the page of material. Another option available is the use of a hand-held wand that scans single words or phrases at a time. An example of this system may include, the Quicktionary Pen (http://www.wizcomtech.com) which allows a user to scan in a word or phrase, the word or phrase is translated and read back to the user, and then the user may choose to also seek additional information about the word using the built-in dictionary. When the OCR system is used with voice output, the scanned material can be read back, thus creating what can be thought of as a "reading machine." WYNN (http://www.freedomscientific.com/WYNN/index.asp), Kurzweil 3000 (http://www.kurzweiledu.com/products_k3000win.asp), and Text Help! Read and Write Gold (http://www.texthelp.com) are examples of such integrated systems.

Basic tape-recorders are helpful for recording directives, messages, and materials that can be used as devices for learning through listening (reading skills can be strengthened if the learner follows along the material in the printed textbook while listening to the same taped version – multisensory). Tape recorders are necessary playback equipment for listening to taped books. Books on tape are provided by Recordings for the Blind and Dyslexic, Inc. (RFB&D http://www.rfbd.org/) and the National Library Service for the Blind and Physically Handicapped (NLS) (http://www.loc.gov/nls/), Library of Congress. Taped textbooks are available from RFB&D, while taped leisure- reading books and magazines can be obtained from NLS. Taped books from these sources are available on loan and must be played on specially designed tape-recorders that also can be borrowed. RFB&D also sells books on computer disc (E-Text) that are loaded onto the computer and can, with a voice synthesizer, be read to the user. While once thought of as special technology, screen readers (programs that use synthesized speech to "read" the contents of a computer display) have become readily available. Current operating systems and many current software programs have incorporated the use of synthesized screen reading capabilities. In addition, programs such as Help Read (http://www.helpread.com/) and Read Please (http://www.readplease.com/) offer free synthesized speech support to any text and/or web file. These kinds of assistive technologies help the reader with poor reading skills learn through listening. RFB&D specializes in producing academic and professional books on tape and requires a one-time registration fee, accompanied by formal documentation of a learning disability. RFB&D also recently has begun offering much of their collection on CD or in MP3 format. The NLS collection consists of popular novels, classical literature, poetry, biographies, and magazines that can be borrowed through a registration process. RFB&D's computer discs consist largely of reference materials and can be used on an individual's personal computer with most adaptive equipment, such as screen readers and speech synthesizers. It is important to also note that many popular trade books and literature curriculum series are now being offered in some kind of audio format as well.

For those whose reading deficits make conducting research a seemingly insurmountable challenge, use of CD-ROM discs (a means of providing large amounts of information on computer, such as a CD-ROM encyclopedia) and on-line services (sources of hundreds of electronic books and information texts) provide numerous resources. Speech synthesis, providing the user with auditory input, adds an additional support to the user of a CD-ROM resource. With these higher end types of assistive technology it must be noted that students need to be instructed on the benefits of each type of assistive technology as well as how to implement each of them independently.

Writing

Students with learning disabilities can experience problems in almost any area of written expression. Although they have ideas, they often have difficulty using written language to convey them (Johnson & Myklebust, 1967; Myklebust, 1973; Poplin, Gray, Larson, Banikowski & Mehring, 1980) or to generate stories (Barenbaum, Newcomer & Nodine, 1987). Overall production may also be impeded. Writers can often not write their ideas down fast enough (De La Paz & Graham, 1995) which may further interfere with content generation and remembering ideas or text already planned in their working memory. It has been noted that students many times do not have the strategy knowledge available to help them in the writing process (Bakken & Whedon, 2003). Graham (1990) also noted that fourth and sixth grade students with learning disabilities had difficulty with text production skills as the mechanic of writing interfered with both the quantity and quality of their writing. Some studies have shown that word processing may lead to increases in the quantity of text written (MacArthur & Schwartz, 1990; Outhred, 1987, 1989). "For individuals with learning disabilities, composing orally may allow them to circumvent transcription or text production problems (e.g. handwriting, spelling, and punctuation), which in turn may allow greater focus on higher-order concerns such as planning and content generation" (De La Paz, 1999, p. 173). It oftentimes is the actual act of writing that limits the writing and creativity of students with learning disabilities.

Word processing is a computer-based writing system that enables the user to write without having to be overly concerned about making errors. This freedom can release persons with written language deficits from concern about the mechanics of writing, allowing them to redirect their efforts toward the meaning of their writing. Using the computer and various features of assistive software for writing makes the writing process easier, allows more writing to take place, and can ultimately boost the user's self esteem (Raskind, 1994). A growing number of assistive computer software programs that go beyond basic word processing are available to the user to support the writing process. Many of these software features are available with voice output. Also available are spell checkers, dictionaries, and thesauruses, which are commonly features of word-processing programs, enabling the user to verify or correct spellings and access word definitions and synonyms. Grammar check and proofreading software programs are additionally available. These programs scan documents and alert the user to probable errors in grammar, word usage, structure, spelling, style, punctuation, and capitalization. Other software programs available to aid the individual is template-producing software which provides forms and applications to make writing tasks easier and facilitate brainstorming and outlining programs which enable the user to approach writing tasks by dumping information in an unstructured manner; this information can subsequently be placed into appropriate categories and ordered more easily (Raskind, 1994).

Related pre-writing programs, webbing or concept-mapping applications are beneficial to individuals with learning problems. These programs allow the user to diagram ideas and make connections between ideas. The idea map can be transformed into an outline, the outline into a draft and, finally, with revising-tool applications, the draft becomes a finished document. These approaches can be particularly helpful to those individuals who have difficulty getting started, organizing, categorizing, sequencing, and polishing writing assignments. In addition, they are useful in the workplace by providing fast, easy, and intuitive ways to create organization charts, flowcharts, and other diagrams (Raskind, 1994). Popular examples of these programs include Kidspiration and Inspiration (http:www.inspiration.com), as well as Draft:Builder (http://www.donjohnston.com). There are also programs available for poor spellers. Word prediction or word completion programs predict words on the basis of the first few letters typed, providing an excellent support tool to poor spellers. Word prediction programs typically come in two forms: split screen or cursor-activated window. In the split screen form (e.g. Co:Writer from http://www.donjohnston.com), the user types in one window with the word prediction support and then, periodically, "dump" the contents of the first window into the second window, which is typically a standard word processing program. The cursor-activated window form allows the user to type directly into a standard word processing application with a floating window that follows the cursor containing the word prediction support (e.g. WordQ from http://www.wordq.com/). Both types of word prediction typically allow the topic lists to be modified to include content words that students may need to access.

Abbreviation expansion programs are very useful programs for students with writing needs. These programs allow users to create their own abbreviations for frequently used words, phrases, or standard pieces of text, cutting down the number of keystrokes needed to complete sentences. Some programs offer a combination of abbreviation expansion with the word-completion feature. It is important to note that these programs can be an "add on" to existing software or may already be included in software such as in the case of Microsoft Word. A number of these software applications can be used with speech synthesis (Raskind, 1994). Other software writing programs can take the user, guided by easy-to-use on-screen prompts and reinforced by speech synthesis, through the writing process from beginning to end. Once the kind of writing has been identified (e.g. journal, personal story, one-act play, research paper, newspaper article, review, and letter), customized prompts take the user through the different stages of writing. Some programs enable the user to include graphics. Other programs take the user through the process of creating multimedia projects. For individuals with written-language problems related to lack of organization and difficulty staying focused, the opportunity to conduct research while sitting at the computer is available through the use of encyclopedias on computer via a CD-ROM disc, or through a link with an on-line service. Much information is available to the computer user who has connection to the Internet and the World Wide Web. The user is thus able to access reference materials without shutting down the word-processing program. Depending on the particular product, one can consider incorporating the use of speech synthesis and, as such, have the information read aloud. Stand-alone computers can be connected to larger systems, such as the Internet, through phone lines or high speed cable or fiber optic lines via a modem.

During classroom lectures, there are technologies that can aid students. Laptop computers, tape-recorders, and pressure-sensitive papers can be used for notetaking during lectures to support individuals with written language problems. The use of pre-writing and writing software programs can also aid students in the classroom. An individual with strong auditory skills might try dictating ideas onto a tape and listening as a pre-writing technique. Besides computer-related tools, there are also hand-held talking electronic devices: spell checkers, dictionaries, and thesauruses are available with speech synthesizers that provide voice output. As stated earlier, screen review systems with speech synthesis and highlighting are assistive technology tools that are particularly helpful to individuals with reading and written-language problems. This multisensory approach can be achieved for the individual with written-language deficits through text-to-speech/voice output systems and speech-to-text or voice input systems. Text-to-speech/voice output systems, also known as speech synthesis, screen review systems and talking word processors, highlight and read what has been keyed into the computer. As the user types in data on the computer, a voice synthesizer "speaks" what is being typed. At the same time the print is highlighted on the computer screen, or the entered text can be "read back" at a later time. In addition, materials produced by others (e.g. instructor and employer materials, books on disc, and CD-Rom discs) can be reviewed and read aloud to the user. Speech-to-text or voice input, also known as speech recognition, on the other hand, is technology that allows the user to operate the computer by speech. The user speaks into a headphone-mounted microphone; the system then converts the spoken words to electronic text displayed on the computer screen. This system is particularly useful for those adults whose oral language exceeds their written language abilities. These technologies provide support that capitalizes on strengths, while working around or circumventing the individual's written-language deficits (Raskind, 1994).

Current technology allows speech recognition systems to accept continuous speech by converting the writer's message into digitized signals, which are then transformed by the computer into word output (Milheim, 1993). This approach to composing may be especially advantageous for individuals with learning disabilities, as it allows them to focus on high-level concerns, such as planning and content generation, rather than on the mechanics of writing. This could be a powerful tool for students with learning disabilities since research has documented they make considerable more spelling, capitalization, and punctuation errors than their normally achieving classmates (MacArthur, Graham & Schwartz, 1991), and their handwriting is both quite slow and less legible (Graham & Weintraub, 1996). According to Scardamalia, Bereiter and Goelman (1982), having to switch their attention to the mechanical demands of the writing may lead the writer to forget already developed intentions and meanings. Apparently, there are many different types of software and assistive technologies available in the area of written language. It must be noted that simply getting or accessing assistive technology is not the only answer. The answer lies in actually teaching the student how to use the assistive technologies and to implement them independently. Other assistive technologies could include but are not limited to larger spaced paper, more time to complete tasks, the use of slant boards, tilted desktops, clipboards, alternative keyboards, trackballs, and trackpads.

Spelling

The intrinsic skill of spelling is essential in order for individuals to communicate in a written format which can be understood by others (Montgomery, Karlan & Coutinho, 2001). The effective use of spelling correction technologies such as dictionaries and personal word lists, however, are inhibited by not being able to spell correctly. Spelling instruction needs to address acquisition skills (remedial instruction) as well as compensation skills (write with accurate spelling). The word processor is one popular compensation tool for writing. Misspellings typical of students with learning disabilities are complex in several ways. First, misspellings have few similar phonetic characteristics of the target, which classifies them as severe phonetic mismatches (MacArthur, Graham, Haynes & De La Paz, 1996). Second, in comparison to students with dyslexia their spelling is similar which is often less mature and contains characteristics of younger children (Pennington et al., 1986). Third, students with learning disabilities experience a difficult time applying spelling rules to unknown words (Bailet, 1990; Bailet & Lyon, 1985; Carlisle, 1987).

Just as the fluency of writing has been helped by the word processing (Crealock & Sitko, 1990; Glazer & Curry, 1988; Kerchner & Kistinger, 1984; Outhred, 1989), spell checkers can influence the mechanics of writing. Gerlach, Johnson and Ouyang (1991) found that poor spellers have a difficult time identifying misspelled words. Many students with learning disabilities are poor spellers. Even with the addition of spell checkers, these students have been documented to only identify 63% of their errors (MacArthur et al., 1996). To be effective for these students, spell check algorithms for spell check functions need to generate the target word for misspellings of varying degrees of phonetic mismatch. Also, to be the most beneficial, the target word needs to be within the first three suggested replacements, preferably first or nearest the top of the list of choices (Montgomery et al., 2001). MacArthur and associates (1996) investigated the use of spell checkers of 27 students with learning disabilities. When the target word was presented first in the list of possibilities by the spell checker, students were able to correct 83.5% of their errors. This correction rate dropped to 71.6% when the target word was presented later in the list. Students were only able to correct 24.7% of the errors when no choice was presented. This research suggests that teachers need to make informed decisions when implementing spell checker programs for students with learning disabilities to find the most accurate program to be helpful to their students.

Mathematics

Technology may be helpful to students who struggle in math and have one or more of the following problems: (a) "they don't have a conceptual understanding of the mathematical principle they are studying, (b) they have problems with short- or long-term memory and fluency of math facts that would enable them to solve problems more efficiently and effectively (automaticity), (c) they struggle with the language of word problems, which interferes with their selection of an appropriate algorithm or operation to solve the problem, and (d) they have fine and gross motor problems that interfere with the organization of their work on paper" (Male, 2003, p. 55). Very often, teachers are urged to provide opportunities for students to apply mathematics in meaningful contexts. It is recommended that schools prepare students for the future by including in their programs ways to learn marketplace technology, opportunities for active learning, and time for real-world projects (NCTM, 1991; Uchida, Cetron & McKenzie, 1996). Finding ways to satisfy these recommendations when teaching secondary students with learning disabilities is difficult. At this time in their lives, these students are just tired and sick of mathematics, probably because of the large amount of time needed working on problems every day that have no bearing on problem situations they encounter in their daily lives. Even when approaches are found that may help students in general education classrooms they rarely help those with learning disabilities because of problems in social skills, higher order thinking, and motivation (Deshler & Schumaker, 1988; Reschly, 1987).

Individuals with learning disabilities may have difficulty in the academic area of mathematics. For example, they may have difficulties lining up the columns in a basic mathematical problem. They may not line up the numbers in a mathematical problem correctly and therefore when they try to solve the problem their calculations are affected and they get the incorrect solution. Assistive technologies that can help make mathematical tasks less complicated and less strenuous include color coding for maintaining columns, reduced number of problems per page, using graph paper to help students line up the numbers, basic hand-held calculators that can help a learner who has problems writing numbers in correct order, hand-held talking calculators that vocalize data and resulting calculations through speech synthesis and, thus, provide multisensory feedback (visual and audio), special-feature calculators that enable the user to select speech options to speak and simultaneously display numbers, functions, entire equations, and results, on-screen computer calculator programs with speech synthesis, large screen displays for calculators and adding machines, and big number buttons and large keypads (Bakken, 1999). Again, it must be noted that just providing the assistive technologies is not the answer, but the student must also know the benefits of each and how to appropriately implement each independently.

Instruction

Learning is an active process in which students construct meaning based upon their experiences (Bruner, 1961, 1990; Duffy & Jonassen, 1992). Cognitive science research indicates that many students learn best in environments that teach them to apply knowledge rather than viewing knowledge as an entity, attribute, or relationship that must be memorized (Glaser, Rieth, Kinzer, Colburn & Peter, 1999). Goldsworthy, Barab and Goldsworthy (2000) found that technology can be used to enhance social problem-solving skills and potentially increase social competence. They found that students in an interactive software (The STAR Project: multimedia-enhanced and regular VHS videos of socially problematic situations) condition performed at least as well as those in a therapist-directed condition when learning problem-solving skills in a social context. Multimedia materials that support the development of children's problem solving strategies can reach a much larger number of individuals at risk (see Goldsworthy et al., 2000).

Anchored instruction is an instructional technique that begins with a focal event or problem situation presented via a video segment or movie providing students with a mental model or an "anchor" to facilitate learning (Bransford, Kinzer, Risko, Rowe & Vye, 1989; Bransford, Sherwood, Hasselbring, Kinzer & Williams, 1990). A preferred method of delivering anchored instruction is through the use of contextualized video instruction via compact disc or videodisk. Multimedia anchors are useful tools for teachers to provide students with a common background on which to base classroom discussions and instruction. The visual format provides students with cues to aid them as they attempt to perceive concepts that are difficult to interpret in written form (Glaser et al., 1999). It helps students to create a visual representation that can be difficult to derive from written text. Research indicates that as students learn to use their existing knowledge as a tool to solve problems, they begin to gain confidence in their implicit knowledge and recognize its availability for unfamiliar tasks (Bransford et al., 1990). This will allow students to become conscious, creative problem solvers by learning to generate their own paths to solutions and beginning to understand alternative solutions and approaches.

FUTURE PERSPECTIVES

What does the future hold for technology and students with learning disabilities? Two primary "forces" are driving the future regarding the relationship of technology and students with learning disabilities. The first relates to technological advances themselves. There are general trends in technology to make technology better, faster, smaller, less expensive, and more individualized for the user (Hasselbring, 2001). As this happens, it is conceivable that technology tools, once difficult to obtain or implement due to cost or level of difficulty, would be readily available and easily integrated into the classroom. Hofstetter (2001) noted that computers and computing devices are becoming better able to handle individual user profiles, allowing a student to have specific preferences set relating to specific programs so that when he/she logs in, there is no need to readjust settings for him/her. Networking (Tinker, 2001) and technologies such as SmartCards (a kind of credit card containing personalized information) and JavaRings (a ring that stores information and programs and "plugs in" to a computer) may allow instantaneous transfer of a student's profile to a given computer. In addition, there is the advent of programming languages such as XML that would allow individualized web content presented in a format defined by the user (Hofstetter, 2001).

The second "force" driving the future relationships between technology and students with learning disabilities, at least in the school setting, is setting up classrooms for Universal Design. The basic premise behind Universal Design in the classroom is to proactively establish curricula and related materials that can be adjusted to meet needs of all learners, regardless of ability levels. Not long ago, the Center for Applied Special Technology (CAST) proposed four fundamental shifts in our ideas of teaching that serve as a basis for Universal Design classrooms namely: (1) students with disabilities fall along a continuum of learner differences, just as all students do; (2) teachers should make curricular, instructional, and material adjustments for all students, not just those with disabilities; (3) curriculum materials should be as varied and diverse as learning styles and needs in the classroom, rather than focusing on the textbook and related materials; and (4) the curriculum itself should be flexible to accommodate a range of student differences rather than a "one size fits all" approach (Center for Applied Special Technology, 2002). In the end Universal Design in the classroom supports the provision of a variety of tools that allow maximum adaptability across three dimensions: (1) multiple means of representation – this provides choices to support varied systems of recognition, (2) multiple means of expression and control – this provides choices for students to access different strategies to learn, and (3) multiple means for engagement – this provides choices for accessing different ways of holding the student's attention and motivating learning (Center for Applied Special Technology, 2002). These technological advances are helping us to shift our ways of teaching diverse students and finally will serve as bases for how classrooms of the future will look (Gardner & Edyburn, 2000).

REFERENCES

Alliance for Technology Access (1994). *Computer resources for people with disabilities*. Alameda, CA: Hunter House.

Allington, R. L. (1994). What's special about special programs for children who find learning to read difficult? *Journal of Reading Behavior, 26*, 1–21.

Ashton, T. M. (2000). Technology for students with learning disabilities in reading. *Journal of Special Education, 15*(2), 47–48.

Bailet, L. L. (1990). Spelling rule usage among students with learning disabilities and normally achieving students. *Journal of Learning Disabilities, 23*, 121–128.

Bailet, L. L., & Lyon, G. R. (1985). Deficient linguistic rule application in a learning disabled speller: A case study. *Journal of Learning Disabilities, 18*, 162–165.

Bakken, J. P. (1999). *Assistive technology: Competencies and skills for teachers. Book 7 – Technologies to complete academic tasks.* Normal, IL: Illinois State University.

Bakken, J. P., & Whedon, C. K. (2003). Giving students with learning disabilities the POWER to write: Improving the quality and quantity of written products. *LEARNING DISABILITIES: A Multidisciplinary Journal, 12*(1), 13–22.

Barenbaum, E., Newcomer, P., & Nodine, B. (1987). Children's ability to write stories as a function of variation in task, age, and developmental level. *Learning Disability Quarterly, 10*, 175–188.

Bierly, D. R., & McCloskey-Dale, S. R. (1999). The tasks, the tools: Needs assessment for meeting writing demands in the school curriculum. www.closingthegap.com/library.

Bowser, G., & Reed, P. (1995). Education TECH points for assistive technology planning. *Journal of Special Education Technology, 12*, 325–338.

Bransford, J., Kinzer, C., Risko, V., Rowe, D., & Vye, N. (1989). Designing invitations to thinking: Some initial thoughts. In: S. McCormick & J. Zutell (Eds), *Cognitive and Social Perspectives for Literacy Research and Instruction* (pp. 35–54). Chicago, IL: The National Reading Conference.

Bransford, J. D., Sherwood, R. D., Hasselbring, T. S., Kinzer, C. K., & Williams, S. M. (1990). Anchored instruction: Why we need it and how technology can help. In: D. Nix & R. Spiro (Eds), *Cognition, Education, and Multimedia: Exploring Ideas in High Technology* (pp. 115–141). Hillsdale, NJ: Lawrence Earlbaum Associates.

Brennan, J. K. (1998). Assistive technology: It takes a team. *The Delata Kappa Gamma Bulletin, 64*(2), 24–28.

Bruner, J. S. (1961). The act of discovery. *Harvard Educational Review, 31*(1), 21–32.

Bruner, J. S. (1990). *Acts of meaning.* Cambridge, MA: Harvard University Press.

Bryant, B. R., & Seay, P. C. (1998). The technology-related assistance to individuals with disabilities act: Relevance to individuals with learning disabilities and their advocates. *Journal of Learning Disabilities, 31*, 4–15.

Bryant, D. P., Bryant, B. R., & Raskind, M. H. (1998). Using assistive technology to enhance the skills of students with learning disabilities. *Intervention in School and Clinic, 34*, 53–58.

Carlisle, J. F. (1987). The use of morphological knowledge in spelling derived forms by learning-disabled and normal students. *Annals of Dyslexia, 37*, 90–108.

Center for Applied Special Technology (2002). Summary of universal design for summary concepts. http://www.cast.org/udl/index.cfm?i=7.

Chambers, A. C. (1997). *Has technology been considered: A guide for IEP teams.* Reston, VA: Council for Exceptional Children.

Crealock, C., & Sitko, M. (1990). Comparison between computer and handwriting technologies in writing training with learning disabled students. *International Journal of Special Education, 5*, 173–183.

Cunningham, P. M., & Allington, R. (1999). *Classrooms that work: They can all read and write* (2nd ed.). New York: Longman.

De La Paz, S. (1999). Composing via dictation and speech recognition systems: Compensatory technology for students with learning disabilities. *Learning Disability Quarterly, 22*(3), 173–182.

De La Paz, S., & Graham, S. (1995). Dictation: Applications to writing for students with learning disabilities. In: T. E. Scruggs & M. A. Mastropieri (Eds), *Advances in Learning and Behavioral Disabilities* (Vol. 9, pp. 227–247). Greenwich, CT: JAI Press.

Deshler, D., & Schumaker, B. (1988). An instructional model for teaching students how to learn. In: J. Graden, J. Zins & M. Curtis (Eds), *Alternative Educational Delivery Systems: Enhancing Instructional Options for All Students* (pp. 391–412). Washington, DC: National Association of School Psychologists.

Duffy, T. M., & Jonassen, D. H. (1992). Constructivism: New implications for instructional technology. In: T. M. Duffy & D. H. Jonassen (Eds), *Constructivism and the Technology of Instruction: A Conversation* (pp. 1–16). Hillsdale, NJ: Lawrence Erlbaum Associates.

Edyburn, D. L. (2000). 1999 in review: A synthesis of the special education technology literature. *Journal of Special Education Technology, 15*(1), 7–18.

Gardner, J. E., & Edyburn, D. L. (2000). Integrating technology to support effective instruction. In: J. D. Lindsey (Ed.) *Technology and Exceptional Individuals* (pp. 191–240). Austin, TX: Pro-Ed.

Gerlach, G. J., Johnson, J. R., & Ouyang, R. (1991). Using an electronic speller to correct misspelled words and verify correctly spelled words. *Reading Improvement, 28,* 188–194.

Glaser, C. W., Rieth, H. J., Kinzer, C. K., Colburn, L. K., & Peter, J. (1999). A description of the impact of multimedia anchored instruction on classroom interactions. *Journal of Special Education Technology, 14*(2), 27–43.

Glazer, S. M., & Curry, D. (1988). Word processing programs: Survival tools for children with writing problems. *Reading, Writing and Learning Disabilities, 4,* 291–306.

Goldsworthy, R. C., Barab, S. A., & Goldsworthy, E. L. (2000). The STAR project: Enhancing adolescents' social understanding through video-based, multimedia scenarios. *Journal of Special Education Technology, 15*(2), 13–26.

Graham, S. (1990). The role of production factors in learning disabled students' compositions. *Journal of Educational Psychology, 82,* 781–791.

Graham, S., & Weintraub, N. (1996). A review of handwriting research: Progress and prospects from 1980 to 1984. *Educational Psychology Review, 8,* 7–87.

Hasselbring, T. S. (2001). A possible future of special education technology. *Journal of Special Education Technology, 16*(4), 15–21.

Hofstetter, F. T. (2001). The future's future: Implication of emerging technology for special education program planning. *Journal of Special Education Technology, 16*(4), 7–13.

Inge, K. J., & Shepard, J. (1995). Assistive technology application and strategies for school system personnel. In: K. F. Flippo, K. J. Inge & J. M. Barcus (Eds), *Assistive Technology: A Resource for School, Work, and Community* (pp. 133–166). Baltimore, MD: Brookes.

Johnson, D., & Myklebust, H. (1967). *Learning disabilities: Educational principles and practices.* New York: Grune & Stratton.

Kelker, K. A., & Holt, R. (2000). *Family guide to assistive technology.* Cambridge, MA: Brookline Books.

Kerchner, L. B., & Kistinger, B. J. (1984). Language processing/word processing: Written expression, computers and learning disabled students. *Learning Disability Quarterly, 7,* 329–335.

King, T. W. (1999). *Assistive technology: Essential human factors.* Needham Heights, MA: Allyn & Bacon.

Leong, C. K. (1992). Enhancing reading comprehension with text-to-speech (DECtalk) computer system. *Reading and Writing: An Interdisciplinary Journal, 4,* 205–217.

Lerner, J. (2002). *Learning disabilities: Theories, diagnosis, and teaching strategies* (9th ed.). Boston: Houghton Mifflin.

Lewis, R. (1993). *Special education technology: Classroom applications.* Pacific Grove, CA: Brooks/Cole.

Lindsey, J. (Ed.) (1993). *Computers and exceptional individuals* (2nd ed.). Austin, TX: Pro-Ed.

Lundberg, I., & Olofsson, A. (1993). Can computer speech support reading comprehension? *Computers in Human Behavior, 9,* 282–293.

MacArthur, C. A., Graham, S., Haynes, J. B., & De La Paz, S. (1996). Spell checkers and students with learning disabilities: Performance comparisons and impact on spelling. *Journal of Special Education, 30,* 35–57.

MacArthur, C. A., Graham, S., & Schwartz, S. (1991). Knowledge of revision and revising behavior among learning disabled students. *Learning Disability Quarterly, 14,* 61–74.

MacArthur, C. A., & Schwartz, S. (1990). An integrated approach to writing instruction: The computers and writing instruction project. *LD Forum, 16*(1), 35–41.

Male, M. (1994). *Technology for inclusion. Meeting the special needs of all students* (2nd ed.). Boston: Allyn & Bacon.

Male, M. (2003). *Technology for inclusion. Meeting the special needs of all students* (4th ed.). Boston: Allyn & Bacon.

Melichair, J. F., & Blackhurst, A. E. (1993). *Introduction to a functional approach to assistive technology* [Training Module]. Lexington, KY: Department of Special Education and Rehabilitation Counseling, University of Kentucky.

Milheim, W. D. (1993). Computer-based recognition: Characteristics, applications, and guidelines for use. *Performance Improvement Quarterly, 6,* 14–25.

Montgomery, D. J., Karlan, G. R., & Coutinho, M. J. (2001). The effectiveness of word processor spell checker programs to produce target words for misspellings generated by students with learning disabilities. *Journal of Special Education Technology, 16*(2), 27–41.

Myklebust, H. (1973). *Development and disorders of written language: Studies of normal and exceptional children* (Vol. 2). New York: Grune & Stratton.

National Council of Teachers of Mathematics (1991). *Professional standards for teaching mathematics.* Reston, VA: Author.

Olson, R. K., & Wise, B. W. (1992). Reading on the computer with orthographic and speech feedback. *Reading and Writing: An Interdisciplinary Journal, 4,* 107–144.

Outhred, L. (1987). To write or not to write: Does using a word processor assist reluctant writers? *Australia and NewZealand Journal of Developmental Disabilities, 13,* 211–217.

Outhred, L. (1989). Word processing: Its impact on children's writing. *Journal of Learning Disabilities, 22,* 262–264.

Parette, H. P., & Angelo, D. H. (1996). Augmentative and alternative communication impact on families: Trends and future directions. *The Journal of Special Education, 30,* 77–98.

Parette, H. P., & Brotherson, M. J. (1996). Family participation in assistive technology assessment for young children with disabilities. *Education and Training in Mental Retardation and Developmental Disabilities, 31*(1), 29–43.

Pennington, B. F., McCabe, L. L., Smith, S. D., Lefly, D. L., Bookman, M. O., Kimberling, W. J., & Lubs, H. A. (1986). Spelling errors in adults with a form of familial dyslexia. *Child Development, 57,* 1001–1013.

Phillips, B. (1991). *Technology abandonment: From the consumer point of view*. Washington, DC: Request Publication.

Phillips, B. (1992). *Perspectives on assistive technology services in vocational rehabilitation: Clients and counselors*. Washington, DC: National Rehabilitation Hospital, Assistive Technology/Rehabilitation Engineering Program.

Phillips, B., & Zhao, H. (1993). Predictors of assistive technology abandonment. *Assistive Technology*, *5*, 35–45.

Poole, B. J. (1997). *Education for an information age*. New York: McGraw-Hill.

Poplin, M., Gray, R., Larson, S., Banikowski, A., & Mehring, T. (1980). A comparison of components of written expression abilities in learning disabled and non-learning disabled children at three grade levels. *Learning Disability Quarterly*, *3*, 46–53.

Raskind, M. (1994). Assistive technology for adults with mild disabilities: A rationale for use. In: P. Gerber & H. Reiff (Eds), *Learning Disabilities in Adulthood: Persisting Problems and Evolving Issues* (pp. 152–162). Austin, TX: Pro-Ed.

Raskind, M. H., & Higgins, E. L. (1998). Assistive technology for postsecondary students with learning disabilities: An overview. *Journal of Learning Disabilities*, *31*, 27–40.

Reschly, D. J. (1987). Learning characteristics of mildly handicapped students: Implications for classification, placement, and programming. In: M. C. Wang, M. C. Reynolds & H. J. Walberg (Eds), *Handbook of Special Education: Research and Practice* (Vol. 1, pp. 35–38). Elmsford, NY: Pergamon.

Rogers, E. M. (1995). *Diffusion of innovations* (4th ed.). New York: Free Press.

Scardamalia, M., Bereiter, C., & Goelman, H. (1982). The role of production factors in writitng ability. In: M. Nystrand (Ed.), *What Writers Know: The Language, Process, and Structure of Written Discourse* (pp. 173–210). New York: Academic Press.

Scherer, M. (1991). Assistive technology use, avoidance and abandonment: What we know so far. In: *Proceedings of the 6th Annual Technology and Persons with Disabilities Conference* (pp. 815–826). Los Angeles, CA: California State University Northridge.

Smith, R., Benge, M., & Hall, M. (1994). Technology for self care. In: C. Christionson (Ed.), *Ways of Living: Self Care Strategies for Special Needs* (pp. 379–422). Rockville, MD: American Occupational Therapy Association.

Tinker, R. (2001). Future technologies for special learners. *Journal of Special Education Technology*, *16*(4), 31–37.

Uchida, D., Cetron, M., & McKenzie, F. (1996). *Preparing students for the 21st century*. Arlington, VA: American Association of School Administrators.

Wissick, C. A., & Gardner, J. E. (2000). Mutimedia or not to multimedia? That is the question for students with learning disabilities. *Teaching Exceptional Children*, *32*(4), 34–43.

Zabala, J. (1995, March). The SETT framwork: Critical areas to consider when making informed assistive technology decisions. Paper presented at the Florida Assistive Technology Impact Conference and Technology and Medial Division of Council for Exceptional Children, Orlando, FL.

Zabala, J. (1996). SETTing the stage for success: Building success though effective selection and use of assistive technology systems. *Proceedings of the Southeast Augmentative Communication Conference* (pp. 1–11). Birmingham, AL: Southeast AC Conference.

Zabala, J. (2002). *Update of the SETT framework, 2002*. Retrieved from http://www.joyzabala.com on 11/11/02.

COMPREHENSIVE ASSESSMENT OF STUDENTS WITH LEARNING DISABILITIES

Anthony F. Rotatori and Tim Wahlberg

The comprehensive assessment of students with learning disabilities (LD) is critical in terms of correctly identifying students for special education eligibility, planning curriculum programs of instruction, evaluating academic intervention, and recertifying students with LD for special educational services. The assessment is influenced by the prevailing definition of LD that is held by diagnosticians carrying out the evaluation. This can create dilemmas due to the array of LD definitions currently available.

Hallahan and Kauffman (1997) pointed out that the array of definitions has steadily increased since the field's inception in the early 1960s. For example, Hammill (1990) discussed eleven definitions that have been given serious attention. Hallahan and Kauffman emphasized that four factors "each of which is included in some definitions, but not all have historically caused considerably controversy: (1) IQ-achievement discrepancy; (2) presumption of central nervous system dysfunction; (3) psychological processing disorders; and (4) learning problems not due to environmental disadvantage, mental retardation or emotional disturbance" (p. 165). Furthermore Flanagan et al. (2002) stressed that the ambiguity and inconsistency among these definitions interfere with the reliable and consistent identification of students with LD because assessment procedures will vary depending on the definition used. For example, public school educational diagnosticians generally employ procedures related to the United States Office

Current Perspectives on Learning Disabilities
Advances in Special Education, Volume 16, 133–155
Copyright © 2004 by Elsevier Ltd.
All rights of reproduction in any form reserved
ISSN: 0270-4013/doi:10.1016/S0270-4013(04)16007-8

of Education (1997) published LD evaluation guidelines in the Federal Register (Mitchem & Richards, 2003) and state specific regulations.

Unfortunately, these guidelines emphasis IQ-discrepancy factors. While there is considerable criticism of this approach, Flanagan et al., indicated that the federal and state guidelines do not provide an operational definition of LD which would allow practitioners to select specific assessment devices for the measurement of a student's cognitive and achievement abilities. With this dilemma in mind, this chapter will provide a model for LD assessment which emphasizes assessment data facets that allow practitioners to answer questions related to identification, instructional needs, effectiveness of intervention and recertification in a generic manner. Also, purposes and approaches to assessment and suggested devices to gather information on a student's abilities are delineated.

PURPOSES OF ASSESSMENT

The National Information Center for Children and Youths with Disabilities (NICHCY, 1999) listed five purposes of assessment: (1) screening; (2) evaluation; (3) eligibility and diagnosis; (4) IEP development; and (5) instructional planning. Screening is concerned with identifying students who are suspected of having a disability. In the area of LD, assessors would be evaluating children who are exhibiting learning difficulties or delays in acquiring academic skills. Data from the screening would point out the degree to which these students with suspected LD are approximating average academic growth patterns. Students with extremely deficient skills would be recommended for a full evaluation. This evaluation would delineate the student's strengths and weaknesses, and overall academic progress across the curriculum. Evaluation would encompass three areas, namely, pre-academic, academic, and learning style assessment. Pre-academic assessment provides information related to a student's status on prerequisite behaviors (e.g. attention to task) that need to be acquired before instruction in an academic domain (e.g. math) occurs. Academic assessment allows educators to: pinpoint deficit academic readiness skills; describe a student's overall skill performance level; identify academic skills necessary for learning a domain area; and delineate the steps of a learning task a student has mastered. Learning style assessment involves the identification of a student's individual learning pattern that she has acquired based on her learning and behavior assets and weaknesses (e.g. active vs. passive learner, auditory vs. visual learner).

Eligibility and diagnosis involves a determination as to whether a student's present academic skill level is sufficiently deficit to warrant special education services and to describe the specific nature of the student's LD. Even though IDEA

(1997) mandated that public schools employ more than one method to establish eligibility for LD services many school districts rely heavily on IQ-achievement discrepancy formulas to make the decision (Bailey, 2003). Criticism of the IQ-achievement discrepancy arises from three aspects, namely, differences in variance, methodology concerns and a "wait-to-fail" dilemma (Bailey, 2003). Bailey (2003) stressed that the issue of variance occurs because some states specify that the IQ-achievement discrepancy involve one standard deviation, whereas, other states require more than one standard deviation. Methodological concerns stem from the fact that test scores have problematic statistical properties (Sternberg, cited in Bailey, 2003). Lastly, a wait-to-fail approach requires that students perform at a deficit level for a few years before an IQ-achievement discrepancy will materialize.

As a correction for the above problems, the federal government is proposing text in the new version of IDEA for an alternative model of determining eligibility and diagnosis. The new model is called "Response to intervention" (RTI). According to Bailey (2003) in this model "Students progress through several levels of intervention before entering special education. The first level is the general classroom, where teachers and other school personnel regularly assess students to identify those who are struggling. These children are diverted into a secondary intervention, which is often intensive, small- grouped instruction that's tailored to the student's needs, while school staff continue to monitor their progress. Some RTI models include a tertiary intervention that's even more intensive. Once students have failed to respond to each of the intervention levels they are placed in special education" (p. 99).

A fourth purpose of assessment is to collect data to develop and implement an IEP and place the student. According to Heward (2003), the data should assist educators in writing an IEP that would include the following seven components: (1) a statement of the child's present levels of educational performance; (2) a statement of measurable annual goals including benchmarks or short-term objectives; (3) a statement of the special education and related services and supplementary aids and services to be provided to the child; (4) an explanation of the extent, if any, to which the child will not participate with nondisabled children in the regular class; (5) a statement of any individual modifications in the administration of State or district-wide-assessments of student achievement that are needed in order for the child to participate in such assessment; (6) the projected date for the beginning of the services and modifications and the anticipated frequency, location and duration of those services and modifications; and (7) a statement of how the child's progress toward the annual goals will be measured (p. 60).

A fifth purpose of assessment is to collect instructional planning data and launch instruction appropriate to the student's identified learning deficits. This data could include information related to a student's social, academic physical and behavioral management needs (Pierangelo & Giulianai, 2002). For example, behavioral characteristic assessment would identify problematic behavior (e.g. excessive out-of-seat, frequent noncompliance) which interfere with the acquisition of academic curriculum objectives. Similarly, data may be needed to plan for effective behavioral intervention to eliminate the problematic behavior. Such assessment may involve the identification of reinforcing stimuli to shape new responses or eliminate maladaptive behaviors.

Approaches to Assessing Students with LD

IDEA mandates that no one assessment procedure be used as the sole criterion for the identification or program planning of a child with a disability. As such a comprehensive assessment is recommended (see Bender, 2004; Cohen & Spenciner, 2003; Flanagan et al., 2003; Hunt & Marshall, 2002; Pierangelo & Giulianai, 2002). According to Pierangelo and Giuliani (2002) a comprehensive assessment of students with LD would include many of the following aspects:

- An individual psychological evaluation including general intelligence, instructional needs, learning strengths and weaknesses and social emotional dynamics.
- A through academic history with interviews or reports from past teachers.
- A physical examination including specific assessments that relate to vision, hearing, and health.
- A classroom observation of the student in his or her current educational setting.
- An appropriate educational evaluation specifically pinpointing the area of deficits or suspected disability including, but not limited to, educational achievement, academic needs, learning strengths and weaknesses, and vocational assessments.
- A functional behavioral assessment to describe the relationship between a skill or performance problem and variables that contribute to its occurrence.
- A bilingual assessment for students with limited English proficiency.
- Auditory and visual discrimination tests.
- Assessment of classroom performance.
- Speech and language evaluations when appropriate.
- Physical and/or occupational evaluations when indicated.
- Interviewing the student and significant others in his or her life.
- Examining school records and past evaluations results.
- Using information from checklists completed by parents, teachers, or the student.
- Evaluating curriculum requirements and options.
- Evaluating the student's type and rate of learning during trial teaching periods.

- Evaluating which skills have been and not been mastered, and in what order unmastered skills need to be taught.
- Collecting ratings on teacher attitude toward students with disabilities, peer acceptance, and classroom climate (pp. 9–10).

Popular assessment approaches to collect information on the above include the following: norm-referenced, criterion-referenced, curriculum-based, portfolio and authentic. The below sections delineate these approaches.

Norm-Referenced Assessment

A norm-referenced assessment involves the use of standardized tests which allow the assessor to compare the performance of the student to the performance of other students of a given ethnicity, socioeconomic status, age and/or grade (Pierangelo & Giulianai, 2002). Norm-referenced testing is most useful when the assessor is examining whether a discrepancy exists between a student's intellectual ability and her academic achievement level. Scores from a norm-referenced test allow an assessor to determine how a student's performance compares with that of other students who may be in a local, state or national groups (Rotatori et al., 1990). Cohen and Spenciner (2003) stress that "When assessing students with disabilities, evaluators should employ caution before making comparisons or interpretations stemming from norms" (p. 57).

Criterion-Referenced Assessment

A criterion-referenced assessment allows an assessor to compare a student's performance to a defined list of specified objectives in highly discrete skill areas related to instructional material (Rotatori et al., 1990). Information from a criterion-referenced test allows an assessor to determine whether a student has mastered a particular skill without comparing the student to other students. The test information generated is helpful in establishing IEP goals and objectives because the assessment data identify the specific skills a student has learned and the skills that require instruction (Heward, 2003).

Curriculum-Based Assessment

Hallahan and Kauffman (1997) defined curriculum-based assessment (CBA) as a "formative evaluation method to evaluate performance in the particular curriculum to which students are exposed" (p. 174). A CBA test is composed of sample items directly from the curriculum. It links instruction with assessment and has three purposes, namely, to: determine eligibility, develop the goals for instruction, and evaluate the student's progress in the curriculum (Cohen & Spenciner, 2003). Also, CBA allows schools to compare "the performance of students with disabilities to that of their peers in their own school or school district . . . a comparison with a local reference group is seen as more relevant than comparisons with national norming groups used in commercially developed standardized tests" (Hallahan & Kauffman, 1997, p. 175).

Portfolio Assessment

Portfolio assessment involves the analysis of a student's file (portfolio) or academic work over a period of time. The portfolio may include daily class worksheets, homework, permanent products, quizzes and formal and informal tests. Portfolio assessment allows the assessor to evaluate a student's progress more closely over time to ascertain his/her attainment of established IEP objectives and curriculum goals. Salvia and Ysseldyke (1998) caution that "the literature on portfolio assessment offers little practical guidance about: (1) the types of decisions teachers should be making; (2) the characteristics of the content used for specific decisions; and (3) the criteria to guide decision making about grading, identification of academic weaknesses, instructional improvement, eligibility for entitlement programs, assessing educational outcomes and educational reform" (p. 279).

Authentic Assessment

Authentic assessment is "a method that evaluates a student's critical-thinking and problem-solving ability in real-life situations in which he or she may work with or receive help from peers, teachers, parents or supervisors" (Hallahan & Kauffman, 1997, p. 175). Sometimes authentic assessment is referred to as naturalistic-based or performance-based assessment (Pierangelo & Giulianai, 2002). Common characteristics of authentic assessment include the following: students are requested to perform, create, produce or do something (Herman et al., 1992); the activities are public and involve an audience or panel (Cushman, 1990); the activities are essential, enabling, engaging, open-ended, and contextualized (Cushman, 1990); and tasks are used that represent meaningful instructional activities that invoke real-world applications (Herman et al., 1992). Bender (2004) concluded that "if children can conduct the types of authentic tasks described-tasks that are required of adults in a real-world arena such as ecological studies- then the student may be said to understand the concepts. In short, they have been 'assessed' in a much more authentic fashion than if given paper-and – pencil tests on the same topic in the school classroom" (p. 167).

COLLECTING DATA ASSESSMENT: DEVICES AND CONCERNS

Pre-Academic Skills Assessment

The identification of a student's mastery level on prerequisite academic behaviors is needed prior to formal instruction in academic areas. Pre-academic assessment data can delineate deficit behaviors that may interfere with the learning of a particular academic skill. Initially, students are screened for pre-academic deficits using brief, norm-referenced, reliable, inexpensive, valid, devices (Meisels & Wasik, 1990). Frequently used pre-academic devices include the following: AGS Early Screening Profiles (Harrison et al., 1990), Ages and Stages Questionnaire (ASQ) (Bricker & Squires, 1999), the Batelle Developmental Inventory (BDI) (Newborg et al., 1984).

Denver Developmental Screening Test II (DDST II) (Frankenburg et al., 1990), Developmental Indicators for the Assessment of Learning-Third Edition (DIAL-3) (Mardell-Czudnowski & Goldenberg, 1998), Early Screening Inventory-Revised (ESI-R) (Meisels et al., 1997), Kindergarten Readiness Test (KRT) (Larsen & Vitali, 1988), The Preschool Evaluation Scales (PES) (McCarney, 1992) and FirstSTEP (Miller, 1992). Summary information on these screening devices appears in Table 1.

The Dial-3 (Mardell-Czudnowski & Goldenberg, 1998) is a very popular screening device that has evidence of good validity and test-retest reliability, and adequate internal consistency. It was standardized on 1,560 English-speaking children who were stratified by age, geographic area, race or ethnic group and parent education level. The DIAL-3 is available in a Spanish edition, however, Cohen and Spenciner (2003) pointed out that "The DIAL-3 Spanish edition is not a direct translation but, rather test developers made efforts to adjust and validate the test to use in a different linguistic or cultural context" (p. 313).

Information on pre-academic screening devices may result in a referral for a more comprehensive pre-academic screening. Such an assessment would include the administration of more detailed norm-referenced or criterion-referenced tests. Information from these devices along with observations of the student's behavior

Table 1.   Pre-Academic Screening Devices.

Device	Age Range	Domain Areas
AGS early screening profiles	2 to 6–11 years	Cognitive, language, self-help, social, articulation, behavior, motor, home, and health
AGQ	4–60 months	Communication, gross and fine motor, problem solving and personal social
BDI	Birth to 8 years	Personal social, adaptive, motor, communication, and cognition
DDST II	Birth to 5–11 years	Gross and fine motor, language, personal social
DIAL-III	3 to 6–11 years	Conceptual abilities, language, and motor
ESI-R	3 to 4–6 years	Visual motor, gross motor, adaptive, language, and cognition
KRT	4–6 years	Awareness of one's environment, fine motor, reasoning, auditory attention, numerical awareness
PES	Birth to 6 years	Cognition, self-help, social/emotional, gross and fine motor, and expressive language
FirstSTEP	2–9 to 6–2 years	Cognition, communication, adaptive, and social-emotional

and a parent report are necessary to diagnose a preschool student with LD. The following are a list of popular comprehensive pre-academic devices: Assessment Evaluation and Programming System (AEPS) for Infants and Young Children (Bricker & Pretti-Frontczak, 1996); Bayley Scales of Infant Development II (BSID-II) (Bayley, 1993); Boehm Test of Basic Concepts, Third Edition-Preschool (Boehm-3 PS) (Boehm, 2001), Boehm Test of Basic Concepts, Third Edition (Boehm-3) (Boehm, 2000); Bracken Basic Concept Scale-Revised (BBCS-R) (Bracken, 1998); Brigance Inventory of Early Development-Revised (BIED-R) (Brigance, 1991); Developmental Assessment of Young Children (DAYC) (Voress & Maddox, 1998); Kaufman Survey of Early Academic Language Skills (K-SEALS) (Kaufman & Kaufman, 1993); Mullen Scales of Early Language (MSEL) (Mullen, 1995); and the McCarthy Scales of Children's Abilities (MSC-A) (McCarthy, 1972). Summary information on these comprehensive pre-academic devices appears in Table 2.

The Bracken Basic Concept Scales-Revised (Bracken, 1998) is a popular norm-referenced pre-academic device that has good internal consistency for its eleven subtests and total test as well as excellent test-retest reliability for the total test. "The manual reports solid content, concurrent and predictive validity. The test items are multiple choice and a student is shown four monochrome pictures and asked to identify the picture that depicts a particular concept" (Pierangelo & Giulianai, 2002, p. 258). A strength of this device is its' detailed and well-organized examiner's manual of basic pre-academic concepts (Pierangelo & Giulianai, 2002).

Table 2. Comprehensive Pre-academic Assessment Devices.

Device	Age Range	Domain Areas	Type of Device
AEPS	3 to 6 years	Fine and gross motor, adaptive, social-communication, cognitive, and social	Criterion-referenced
BSID-II	1 to 3–6 years	Mental and motor processing	Norm-referenced
Boehm-3 Preschool	3 to 5–11 years	Basic relational concepts	Norm-referenced
Boehm-3	5–8 years	Basic relational concepts	Norm-referenced
BBCS-R	2–6 to 7–11 years	Concepts related to color, letters, direction/position, shapes, time, self-social awareness, size, quantity, textures/materials, comparisons	Norm-referenced
BIED	Birth to 7 years	Fine and gross motor, receptive and expressive language, writing, comprehension, social-emotional, reading readiness, basic reading, math	Criterion-referenced
DAYC	Birth to 5–11 years	Communication, cognition, social-emotional, physical and adaptive	Norm-referenced
K-SEALS	3–6 years	Letters and word skills, numbers, expressive and receptive language	Norm-referenced
MSEL	Birth to 5–9 years	Gross and fine motor, visual reception, receptive and expressive language	Norm-referenced
MSCA	2–4 to 8–7 years	Verbal, perceptual performance, quantitative, memory, motor, and general cognitive	Norm-referenced

Cognitive Assessment

Cognitive assessment data provides the assessor a current level of the student's intellectual ability that is can be used to answer concerns related to potential IQ-achievement discrepancy. Intelligence tests used by assessors for this area require substantial training and practice. Typically, school psychologists, clinical psychologists or educational diagnosticians administer the devices. The following are frequently used devices that can be used to collect cognitive assessment data: Wechsler Intelligence Scale for Children-IV (WISC-IV) (Psychological Corporation, 2003); the Stanford-Binet Intelligence Scale, Fourth Edition (SBIS-4) (Thorndike et al., 1986); Kaufman Assessment Battery for Children (K-ABC) (Kaufman & Kaufman, 2004a, b); and the Woodcock-Johnson Tests of Cognitive Ability (WJ-III) (Woodcock et al., 2001). Table 3 summarizes age ranges, subtest areas and derived scores that are available from each device.

Table 3.   Cognitive Assessment Devices.

Device	Age Range	Scores	Domain Areas
K-ABC	2–6 to 12–6 years	Simultaneous, mental, and sequential processing, scores	Hand movements, number recall, word order, major windows, magic windows, face recognition, Gestalt closure, triangles, matrix analogies, spatial memory, and photo series
SBIS-4	2–23 years	Standard age scores and composite score	Verbal, quantitative, and abstract/visual reasoning and short-term memory
WISC-IV	6–6 to 16–6 years	Verbal, performance, and full scale IQ verbal comprehension, perceptual organization, freedom from distractibility, and processing speed index scores	Information, arithmetic, digit span, similarities, vocabulary, picture arrangement, picture completion, block designs, object assembly, coding, mazes, symbolic search
WJ-III	3–80	Age and grade scores composite scores	Memory for names, memory for sentences, visual matching, incomplete words, visual closure, picture completion, picture vocabulary, analysis-synthesis

The most widely use device for assessing the cognitive functioning level of students with LD is the WISC, which is now in its fourth edition. The WISC-III (Wechsler, 1991) manual reported a sample study in which 65 children with LD were administered the test. The children ranged in age from 6 to 14 years. This sample included 66% children with unspecified LD, 26% children with both writing and reading disorders, 5% children with primary arithmetic disorders, and 3% children with developmental writing disorders. Wechsler reported the following sample findings:

(1) The mean Verbal IQ (VIQ) was slightly less than the mean Performance IQ (PIQ).
(2) The difference between the Verbal Comprehension Index and the Perceptual Organization Index was even larger than the difference between the VIQ and the PIQ.
(3) The Distractibility Index and the Processing Speed Index scores were depressed.
(4) The ACID (Arithmetic, Coding, Information, and Digit Span) composite subtest score was depressed by one standard deviation.

Wechsler concluded that "The results suggest that when the ACID profile is present, the possibility of a learning disorder should be further investigated. When the ACID is absent, however, a learning disability can not be ruled out" (p. 213).

Support for the above findings comes from a variety of researchers (see Ackerman et al., 1976; Sandoval et al., 1988; Sattler, 1988; Wielkiewicz, 1990). However, there are a number of researchers (see Flanagan & Ortiz, 2001; Kavale & Forness, 2000; Siegel, 1998, 1999; Stanovich, 1999) who discuss the misconceptions that exist when applying the use of IQ as a discriminator for assessment of students with LD. Also, Flanagan et al. (2002) reported literature that intelligence testing results at times do not screen students with LD adequately from students without LD who are low achievers (see Aaron, 1997; Brackett & McPherson, 1996; Kavale & Forness, 2000; Siegel, 1998, 1999; Stanovich, 1999).

Academic Assessment

Rotatori and Mauser (1980) indicated that academic assessment assists educators in: "(1) pinpointing deficit academic readiness skills; (2) describing a student's overall academic skill performance level; (3) identifying deficit academic skills; (4) delineating the steps of a learning task that a student has mastered; and (5) establishing short-and-long range academic curriculum objectives in such areas as reading, spelling, and math" (p. 144). Devices that may elicit information to provide data to assist educators in the above are provided below.

Academic Readiness Skills
Academic readiness screening devices are helpful in identifying deficit academic skills of young school aged children with LD. Typically, these devices cover academic readiness areas in reading, language and math. The following are commonly administered devices that can elicit this information: The Metropolitan Readiness Tests-6 th Edition (MRT-6) (Nurss, 1995); Tests of Basic Experience 2 (TOBE-2) (Moss, 1979); Test of Early Reading Ability-Third Edition (TERA-3) (Reid et al., 2001); The Test of Early Mathematics Ability-Third Edition (TEMA-3) (Ginsburg & Barody, 2003); and the Basic School Skills Inventory-Third Edition (BSSI-3) (Hammill et al., 1998).

Overall Academic Skills
Norm-referenced, criterion-referenced and performance tests are administered to generate information about a student's overall academic skill level. Generally, these devices can be administered by a variety of professionals including teachers. According to Salvia and Ysseldyke (1998) "achievement tests can be classified along several dimensions; perhaps the most important one describes their specificity and density of content. Diagnostic achievement tests have dense content . . . to assess specific skills and concepts and allow finer analyses to pinpoint

Table 4.   Single and Multiple Skill Achievement Devices.

Name of Device	Single	Diagnostic	Multiple Skill	Referenced		Grade
				Norm	Criterion	
Basic academic skills individual screener (Sonnenchein, 1983) comprehensive			*	*	*	1–12
Mathematical abilities test (Hresko, Swain, Herron, Swain & Sherbenou, 2002)	*			*		1–8
Diagnostic achievement battery-third edition (Newcomer, 2001)		*	*	*		1–8
Durrel analysis of reading difficulty (Durrell & Catterson, 1980)	*	*		*		1–8
Gray oral reading test-4 (Wiederholt & Bryant, 2001)	*	*		*		1–12
Gates-McKillop-Horowitz reading diagnostic test (Gates, McKillop & Horowitz, 1981)	*	*		*		1–6
Formal reading inventory (Wiederholt, 1986)	*	*		*		1–12
Kaufman test of educational achievement (Kaufman & Kaufman, 2004a, b)			*	*		1–12
Kaufman assessment battery for children (Kaufman & Kaufman, 2004a, b)			*	*		K to 8
Key-math revised (Connolly, 1988)	*	*		*		1–8
Mini-battery of achievement (Woodcock, McGraw, & Werder, 1994)			*	*		1–12
Oral and written language scales (Carrow-Woolfolk, 1995)			*	*		1–12
Peabody individual achievement Test-revised (Markwardt, 1989)			*	*		K to 12
Stanford diagnostic reading test (Karlsen & Gardner, 1996)	*	*			*	1–12
Standardized reading (Newcomer, 1999)	*			*	*	1–8
Test of adolescent and adult language-third edition (Hammill, Brown, Larsen & Wiederholt, 1994)	*	*		*		1–12
Test of early written language-second edition (Hresko, Herron & Peak, 1996)	*	*		*		PK to 6

Table 4. (Continued)

Name of Device	Single	Diagnostic	Multiple Skill	Referenced		Grade
				Norm	Criterion	
Test of early mathematics ability-third edition (Ginsburg & Barody, 2003)	*	*		*		PK to 3
Test of language development-intermediate third edition (Hammill & Newcomer, 1997)	*	*		*		2–8
Test of mathematical abilities-second edition (Brown, Cronin & McEntire, 1994)	*	*		*		2–12
Test of reading comprehension-third edition (Brown, Hammill & Wierderholt, 1995)	*	*		*		1–4
Test of written language-third edition (Hammill & Larsen, 1996)	*	*		*		1–12
Test of written spelling fourth edition (Larsen, Hammill & Moats, 1999)	*	*		*		1–12
Wechsler individual achievement test-revised (Psychological Corporation, 2002)		*		*	*	K to 12

specific strengths and weaknesses in academic development" (p. 432). Salvia and Ysseldyke stressed that nondiagnostic achievement tests are used to assess a student's general achievement skill level and are not specific enough to generate information about a student's strengths and weaknesses in academic development. In general these devices can be broken down into single skill and multiple-skill batteries that are individually administered. Typically, multiple-skilled achievement tests cover the following areas: reading, spelling, mathematics and writing. In contrast single skilled tests cover only one area. Table 4 provides information on single and multiple-skilled tests.

A multiple-skilled achievement test, namely, the Wechsler Individual Achievement Test-Revised (WIAT-R) (Psychological Corporation, 2002) was conormed with the Wechsler Series of intelligence tests. This makes it very efficient for screening of students with LD. The subtests include the following: Basic Reading, Reading Comprehension, Mathematics Reasoning, Mathematics Calculation, Listening Comprehension, Oral Expression, and Written Expression. These subtests match up with the seven specified LD areas in IDEA. Salvia and Ysseldyke (1998) reported that this achievement test has "an adequate standardization sample and appears to be very reliable and valid. Two methods and statistical tables for computing ability-achievement discrepancies are provided along with a description of the limitations of each method" (p. 469).

Learning Style Assessment

Learning style assessment involves the identification of specific styles of learning that a student employs while engaged in learning and problem solving. The literature (see Bender, 2004; Pierangelo & Giulianai, 2002) indicates the following variables that have been called styles of learning: organization of information (e.g. field dependence vs. field independence); the speed of response (e.g. impulsive vs. reflective); brain hemisphere preference (e.g. right-language and sequential learning vs. right-spatial organization); type of problem solving strategy (e.g. trial and error vs. analyzing); environmental conditions of the classroom (e.g. temperature, and noise level); the student's reaction to instruction (e.g. cooperative vs. resistant); and the student's involvement in learning (e.g. active vs. lethargic). The goal of learning style assessment is to enable the instructor to match a student's learning style with a specific style of instructional presentation that will enhance the learning and problem solving of the student. Such matching will create a learning environment that allows the student to achieve in ways that compliment his/her natural learning style resulting in more efficient learning and problem solving (see Bender, 2004; Dunn & Dunn, 1979; Holland, 1983; Webb, 1983). The following are a few devices and procedures that may differentiate styles of learning: the Developmental Test of Visual-Motor Intergration-Fourth Edition (VMI-4) (Beery, 1997); Test of Gross-Motor Development-Second Edition (TGMD-2) (Ulrich, 2000); Bender Visual Motor Gestalt Test (BVMGT) (Bender, 1938); Developmental Test of Visual Perception-2 (DTVP-2) (Hammill et al., 1993); Motor-Free Perceptual Test-Third Edition (MVPT-3) (Colarusso & Hammill, 2002); Test of Auditory Perceptual Skills-Revised (TAPS-R) (Gardner, 1996b); Detroit Tests of Learning Aptitudes-Fourth Edition (DTLA-4) (Hammill, 1998); Illinois Test of Psycholinguistic Abilities-Third Edition (ITPA-3) (Hammill et al., 2001); Slingerland Screening Tests for Identifying Children with Specific Language Disability (Slingerland, 1993); Test of Visual Motor Integration (Hammill et al., 1996); and Test of Visual-Perception Skills-Revised (TVPS-R) (Gardner, 1996a). Another area of learning style assessment is concerned with how students interact with and responds to learning environments. According to Drummond (2000), these learning style assessment devices evaluate: environmental elements (e.g. sound, light, temperature, and design) that affect learning; emotional dimensions (e.g. motivation, persistence, responsibility, and structure); sociological dimensions (e.g. working-alone, with peers, in pairs, with adults); and

Table 5. Learning Style Assessment Devices.

Name	Domain Areas			
	Environment	Emotional	Sociological	Physical
Learning style inventory (Dunn, Dunn & Price, 1983)	*	*	*	*
Learning style profile (Keefe & Monk, 1988)	*	*		*
Canfield learning styles inventory (cited in Drummond, 2000)			*	*
Florida analysis of semantic traits (Bailey & Suidzinski, 1986)				*

the physical factors (e.g. intake of food, drink, time of day, and desire for mobility). Table 5 lists common learning style devices and dimensional areas that they cover.

Bender (2004) reported that the research literature on adjusting instructional intervention based on a student's learning style is not conclusive. Also, Drummond (2000) reported that "many of the learning style instruments used have questionable validity and reliability. Although these instruments have face validity, they have little concurrent or predictive validity" (p. 262). However, Bender stressed that the work from a number of investigations (see Carbo, 1983; Sousa, 2001; Webb, 1983) has provided some interesting information, which would allow teachers to adapt, they're instructional based on a student's learning style. For example, Bender listed the following points for teachers to consider when adapting instruction based on a student's learning style:

(1) In an attempt to respect the learning potential of the brain, all teachers should employ both visual and linguistic examples of problems in initial instruction, rather than merely rely on verbal explanations.
(2) Accommodate the diagnosed learning style of all learners in reading exercises. Schedule some short-duration assignments for those impulsive children who cannot persist in a long task.
(3) Use a variety of social and instructional groupings for reading and other assignments, and base these to a degree on the preferences of the child.
(4) Utilize holistic reading strategies that involve language-experience approaches and tactile-kinesthetic resources with "right-hemisphere-dominant" children.
(5) Structure some instructional activities for each learning style in an effort to broaden and strengthen both weak and strong learning style preferences.
(6) Learn to ignore impulsive answers while encouraging the child to reflect on other possible solutions and select another answer.
(7) Informally diagnose learning-style preferences repeatedly in an effort to remain cognizant of the instructional needs of the child.

(8) Recognize that you will tend to teach according to your own learning style, so
be sure to include techniques aimed at other learning styles also (p. 88).

Behavioral Characteristics Assessment

Rotatori and Mauser (1980) indicated that "behavioral characteristics assessment
is the identification of problematic behaviors (e.g. excessive out-of-seat behavior,
deficit compliance skills) which interfere with or are incompatible with the
acquisition of academic curriculum objectives" (p. 148). From this assessment,
teachers and counselors must determine to what extent the appearance of these
problematic behaviors elicit negative attitudes from parents, other teachers, or
peer in the environment. The most common problematic behaviors which are
exhibited by students with LD include the following: deficit task orientation,
disruptive behaviors, attention deficit hyperactivity (ADHD), social-emotional
difficulties, and poor motivation (see Bender, 2004; Cullinan, 2002; McLeskey,
1992; Pearl, 1992). When problematic behaviors like the above are not intervened
with, the student with LD can develop the following problems: a less than optimal
social interaction with peers and adults; a cumulative achievement deficit and
academic plateau; low self-esteem; a poor self-concept; and the development
of withdrawal, depression, anxiety, and suicide behavior. Assessors can gather
information on behavioral characteristics by administering behavioral rating
scales, having students complete self-reports, conducting interviews with parents
and teachers, carrying out in vivo observations of the student, performing a
behavioral analysis, or using situational measures (Salvia & Ysseldyke, 1998).
Table 6 provides a list of common behavioral characteristics assessment devices
and procedures.

Salvia and Ysselydke (1998) reported that the Systematic Screening for
Behavioral Disorders (SSBD) (Walker & Severson, 1992) is a valid and reliable
behavior characteristics assessment device that has been used in a research capacity. The SSBD has a three stage sequential screening system, which allows for the
collection of information on student's problematic behaviors. In Stage 1, a teacher
is instructed to rank order students enrolled in her classroom on both externalizing
and internalizing dimensions of problematic behaviors. Students who match a
specified behavioral profile for either the internalizing or externalizing dimension
are then assessed further by the teacher in Stage 2. During Stage 2, the teacher
rates the student on: (1) a 33 item critical events index to identify low-frequency
and/or high frequency events (e.g. stealing, fire setting, property damage); and
(2) a 12 item adaptive behavior section (e.g. follows established classroom rules,
initiates positive social interactions with peers).

Table 6.   Behavioral Characteristic Devices and Procedures.

Name	Behavior	Age Range	Type of Device
Attention-deficit disorders evaluation scale – second edition, school version (McCarney, 1995a, b)	ADHD	4–19 years	Behavior rating
Attention-deficit disorders evaluation scale – home version (McCarney & Leigh, 1990)	ADHD	4–19 years	Behavior rating
Behavioral assessment system for children (Reynolds & Kamphaus, 1992)	Social-emotional	3–20 years	Behavior rating
Behavior evaluation scale – 2 home version (McCarney, 1994)	Social-emotional	5–18 years	Behavior rating
Behavior and emotional rating scale (Epstein & Sharma, 1997)	Social-emotional	5 to 18–11 years	Behavior rating
Behavior rating profile – second edition (Brown & Hammill, 1990)	Social-emotional	6–6 to 18–6 years	Behavior rating
Child behavior checklist system (Achenbach & Rescorla, 2001)	Withdrawal, anxiety, depression	1–6 to 18 years	Behavior rating
Children's depression rating scale – revised edition (Pozansky & Mokros, 1996)	Depression	6–12 years	Behavior rating
Conners rating scale – revised (Connors, 1997)	ADHD	3–17 years	Behavior rating self-report
Culture free self-esteem inventories – third edition (Battle, 2002)	Self-esteem	6 to 18–11 years	Self-report
Depression and anxiety in youth scale (Newcomer, Barenbaum & Byrant, 1994)	Depression, anxiety	6–18 years	Behavior rating self-report
Internalizing symptoms scale for children (Merrell & Walters, 1998)	Depression, anxiety	8–13 years	Self-report
Multidimensional self concept scale (Bracken, 1992)	Self-concept	9–19 years	Self-report
Piers-Harris childrens self-concept scale – second edition (Piers, Harris & Herzberg, 2002)	Self-concept	7–18 years	Self-report
Preschool and kindergarten behavior scales – second edition (Merrell, 2003)	Social-emotional	3–6 years	Behavior rating
Scale for assessing emotional disturbance (Epstein & Cullinan, 1998)	Social-emotional	5–18 years	Behavior rating

Table 6. (Continued)

Name	Behavior	Age Range	Type of Device
Scales for diagnosing attention deficit/hyperactivitydisorder (Ryser & McConnell, 2002)	ADHD	5–18 years	Behavior rating
Social skills rating system (Gresham & Elliot, 1990)	Social-emotional	4–18 years	Behavior rating
Systematic screening for behavior disorders (Walker & Severson, 1992)	Social-emotional Observational	6–12 years	Behavior rating

In Stage 3, identified students from Stage 2 are then observed by a trainer who evaluates the teachers concerns about the identified problematic behaviors. Salvia and Ysselydke stressed that the SSBD authors provide "Systematic evidence of the SSBD scales' ability to differentiate between students exhibiting internalizing or externalizing problem behaviors...The essential strength of the SSBD is the conceptual framework of multiple gating procedures, which serves to organize and standardize what teachers and practitioners have been doing informally for years" (p. 649).

SUMMARY

This chapter has presented information on assessment procedures and devices for students with LD. Assessment of students with LD requires a comprehensive examination to gather information to answer concerns related to identification, classification, instructional intervention, IEP development and eligibility recertification. As such multiple data facet areas were delineated along with purposes and approaches to gathering information. To assist assessors, a detailed list of devices were provided along with general information concerned with age or grade levels and major content area(s). More inclusive information on an individual device can be gained from Cohen and Spenciner (2003), Maddox (2003), Pierangelo and Giuliani (2002), Salvia and Ysseldyke (2001) or Sattler (2001).

REFERENCES

Aaron, P. G. (1997). The impending demise of the discrepancy formula. *Review of Educational Research, 67*, 461–500.

Achenbach, T. M., & Rescorla, L. A. (2001). *Manual for the ASEBA school-age forms and profiles.* Burlington, VT: ASEBA.

Ackerman, P. T., Dykman, R. A., & Peters, J. E. (1976). Hierarchical factor patterns on the WISC as related to areas of learning deficit. *Perceptual and Motor Skills, 42,* 538–615.

Bailey, D. S. (2003). Who is learning disabled? *Monitor, 34,* 58–60.

Bailey, R. C., & Suidzinski, R. M. (1986). *The FAST profile instruction and reference manual: The Florida analysis of semantic traits profile.* Dallas, TX: BALI Screening Company.

Battle, J. (2002). *Culture free self-esteem inventories* (3rd ed.). Austin, TX: Pro-Ed.

Bayley. N. (1993). *Bayley scales of infant development* (2nd ed.). San Antonio, TX: The Psychological Corporation.

Beery, K. E. (1997). *Developmental test of visual-motor integration* (4th ed.). Austin, TX: Pro-Ed.

Bender, L. (1938). *Bender visual motor gestalt test.* New York: Grune & Stratton.

Bender, W. N. (2004). *Learning disabilities: Characteristics, identification, and teaching strategies* (5th ed.). Boston: Allyn & Bacon.

Boehm, A. (2000). *Boehm test of basic concepts* (3rd ed.). San Antonio, TX: The Psychological Corporation.

Boehm, A. (2001). *Boehm test of basic concepts, third edition – preschool.* San Antonio, TX: Psychological Corporation.

Bracken, B. A. (1992). *Multidimensional self concept scale.* Austin, TX: Pro-Ed.

Bracken, B. A. (1998). *Bracken basic concept scale-revised.* San Antonio, TX: Psychological Corporation.

Brackett, J., & McPherson, A. (1996). Learning disabilities diagnosis in postsecondary students: A comparison of discrepancy-based diagnostic models. In: N. Gregg, C. Hoy & A. F. Gay (Eds), *Adults with Learning Disabilities: Theoretical and Practical Perspectives* (pp. 68–84). New York: Guilford.

Bricker, D., & Pretti-Frontczak, K. (1996). *Assessment, evaluation, and programming system (AEPS) for infants and children.* Baltimore, MD: Paul H. Brookes.

Bricker, D., & Squires, J. (1999). *Ages and stages questionnaire (ASQ).* Baltimore, MD: Paul H. Brookes.

Brigance, A. H. (1991). *BRIGANCE inventory of early development – revised.* Billericia, MA: Curriculum.

Brown, V. L., Cronin, M. E., & McEntire, E. (1994). *Test of mathematical abilities* (2nd ed.). Austin, TX: Pro-Ed.

Brown, V. L., & Hammill, D. D. (1990). *Behavior rating profile* (2nd ed.). Austin, TX: Pro-Ed.

Brown, V. L., Hammill, D. D., & Wierderholt, J. L. (1995). *Test of reading comprehension* (3rd ed.). Austin, TX: Pro-Ed.

Carbo, M. (1983). Research in reading and learning style: Implications for exceptional children. *Exceptional Children, 49,* 486–494.

Cohen, L. G., & Spenciner, L. J. (2003). *Assessment of children and youth with special needs* (2nd ed.). Boston: Allyn & Bacon.

Colarusso, R. P., & Hammill, D. D. (2002). *Motor-free visual perception test* (3rd ed.). Austin, TX: Pro-Ed.

Connolly, A. (1988). *KeyMath-revised: A diagnostic inventory of essential mathematics.* Circle Pines, MN: American Guidance Services.

Connors, C. K. (1997). *Connors rating scales-revised.* Austin, TX: Pro-Ed.

Cullinan, D. (2002). *Students with emotional and behavioral disabilities: An introduction for teachers and others helping professionals.* Upper Saddle River, NJ: Merrill/Prentice-Hall.

Cushman, P. (1990). Performance and exhibitions: The demonstration of mastery. *Horace, 6*, 17–24.

Dunn, R. S., & Dunn, K. J. (1979). Learning styles/teaching styles: Should they...Can they be matched? *Educational Leadership, 33*, 238–247.

Dunn, R., Dunn, K., & Price, G. E. (1983). *Learning style inventory.* Lawerence, KS: Price Systems.

Epstein, M. H., & Cullinan, D. (1998). *Scale for assessing emotional disturbance.* Austin, TX: Pro-Ed.

Epstein, M. H., & Sharma, J. M. (1997). *Behavioral and emotional rating scale.* Austin, TX: Pro-Ed.

Flanagan, D. P., & Ortiz, S. O. (2001). *Essentials of cross-battery assessment.* New York: Wiley.

Flanagan, D. P., Ortiz, S. O., & Mascolo, J. T. (2002). *The achievement test desk reference: Comprehensive assessment and learning disabilities.* Boston: Allyn & Bacon.

Frankenburg, W. K., Dobbs, J., Archer, P., & Shapiro, M. (1990). *Denver developmental screening test II.* Denver, CO: Denver Developmental Materials.

Gardner, M. F. (1996a). *Test of visual-perceptual skills (non-motor) – revised.* Austin, TX: Pro-Ed.

Gardner, M. F. (1996b). *Test of auditory-perceptual skills – revised.* Austin, TX: Pro-Ed.

Ginsburg, H. P., & Barody, A. (2003). *Test of early mathematics ability* (3rd ed.). Austin, TX: Pro-Ed.

Gresham, F. M., & Elliot, S. N. (1990). *Social skills rating system.* Circle Pines, MN: American Guidance Service.

Hallahan, D. P., & Kauffman, J. M. (1997). *Exceptional learners: Introduction to special education* (7th ed.). Boston: Allyn & Bacon.

Hammill, D. D. (1990). On defining learning disabilities: An emerging consensus. *Journal of Learning Disabilities, 23*, 74–84.

Hammill, D. D. (1998). *Detroit tests of learning aptitude* (4th ed.). Austin, TX: Pro-Ed.

Hammill, D. D., Brown, V. L., Larsen, S. C., & Wiederholt, J. L. (1994). *Test of adolescent and adult language* (3rd ed.). Austin, TX: Pro-Ed.

Hammill, D. D., & Larsen, S. C. (1996). *Test of written language* (3rd ed.). Austin, TX: Pro-Ed.

Hammill, D. D., Leigh, J. E., Pearson, N. A., & Maddox, T. (1998). *Basic school skills inventory* (3rd ed.). Austin, TX: Pro-Ed.

Hammill, D. D., Mather, N., & Roberts, R. (2001). *The Illinois test of psycholinguistic abilities* (3rd ed.). Austin, TX: Pro-Ed.

Hammill, D. D., & Newcomer, P. L. (1997). *Test of language development intermediate* (3rd ed.). Austin, TX: Pro-Ed.

Hammill, D. D., Pearson, N. A., & Voress, J. K. (1993). *Developmental test of visual perception* (2nd ed.). Austin, TX: Pro-Ed.

Hammill, D. D., Pearson, N. A., & Voress, J. K. (1996). *Test of visual-motor integration.* Austin, TX: Pro-Ed.

Harrison, P. L., Kaufman, A. S., Kaufman, N. L., Bruininks, R. H., Reynolds, J., Illmer, S., Sparrow, S. S., & Cicchetti, D. V. (1990). Circle Pines, MN: American Guidance Service.

Herman, J., Ashbacher, P., & Winters, L. (1992). *A practical guide to alternative assessments.* Alexandria, VA: Association for Supervision and Curriculum Development.

Heward, W. L. (2003). *Exceptional children: A introduction to special education* (2nd ed.). Upper Saddle River, NJ: Merrill/Prentice-Hall.

Holland, R. P. (1983). Learning characteristics and learner performance: Implications for instructional placement decisions. *Journal of Special Education, 16*, 7–20.

Hresko, W. P., Herron, S. R., & Peak, P. K. (1996). *Test of early written language* (2nd ed.). Austin, TX: Pro-Ed.

Hresko, W. P., Schlieve, P. L., Herron, D. R., Swain, C., & Sherbenou, R. J. (2002). *Comprehensive mathematical abilities test.* Austin, TX: Pro-Ed.

Hunt, N., & Marshall, K. (2002). *Exceptional children and youth* (3rd ed.). Boston: Houghton Mifflin.

Karlsen, B., & Gardner, E. F. (1996). *Directions for administering the Stanford diagnostic reading tests*. San Antonio, TX: Harcourt Educational Measurement.

Kaufman, A., & Kaufman, N. (1993). *Kaufman survey of early academic skills*. Circle Pines, MN: American Guidance Service.

Kaufman, A., & Kaufman, N. (2004a). *Kaufman test of educational achievement*. Circle Pines, MN: American Guidance Service.

Kaufman, A., & Kaufman, N. (2004b). *Kaufman assessment battery for children*. Circle Pines, MN: American Guidance Service.

Kavale, K. A., & Forness, S. R. (2000). What definitions of learning disability say and don't say: A critical analysis. *Journal of Learning Disability, 33*, 239–256.

Keefe, J. W., & Monk, J. S. (1988). *Manual to learning style profile*. Reston, VA: National Association of Secondary School Principals.

Larsen, S. C., Hammill, D. D., & Moats, L. (1999). *Test of written spelling* (4th ed.). Austin, TX: Pro-Ed.

Larsen, S. L., & Vitali, G. C. (1988). *Kindergarten readiness test*. East Aurora, NY: Slosson Educational Publication.

Maddox, T. (2003). *Tests* (5th ed.). Austin, TX: Pro-Ed.

Mardell-Czudnowski, C., & Goldenberg, D. S. (1998). *Developmental indicators for the assessment of learning* (3rd ed.). Circle Pines, MN: American Guidance Service.

McCarney, J. (1994). *The behavior evaluation scale – 2, home version: Technical manual*. Columbia, MO: Hawthorne Educational Services.

McCarney, J. (1995a). *Attention-deficit disorder evaluation scale, home version – second edition: Technical manual*. Columbia, MO: Hawthorne Educational Services.

McCarney, J. (1995b). *Attention-deficit disorders evaluation scale, school version – Second edition: Technical manual*. Columbia, MO: Hawthorne Educational Services.

McCarney, S. B. (1992). *The preschool evaluation scales*. Columbia, MO: Hawthorne Educational Services.

McCarney, S. B., & Leigh, J. E. (1990). *Behavior evaluation scale – 2*. Columbia, MO: Hawthorne Educational Services.

McCarthy, D. (1972). *McCarthy scales of children's abilities*. San Antonio, TX: Psychological Corporation.

McLeskey, J. (1992). Students with learning disabilities at primary, intermediate, and secondary grade levels: Identification and characteristics. *Learning Disability Quarterly, 15*, 13–19.

Meisels, S. J., Mardsen, D. B., Wiske, M. S., & Henderson, L. W. (1997). *Early screening inventory – revised*. Ann Arbor, MI: Rebus.

Meisels, S. J., & Wasik, B. A. (1990). Who should be served? Identifying children in need of early intervention. In: S. J. Meisels & J. P. Shonkoff (Eds), *Handbook of Early Childhood Intervention* (pp. 605–632). Cambridge: Cambridge University Press.

Merrell, K. W. (2003). *Preschool and kindergarten behavioral scale* (2nd ed.). Austin, TX: Pro-Ed.

Merrell, K. W., & Walters, A. S. (1998). *Internalizing symptoms scale for children*. Austin, TX: Pro-Ed.

Miller, L. J. (1992). *FirstSTEP: Screening test for evaluating preschoolers*. San Antonio, TX: Psychological Corporation.

Mitchem, K. J., & Richards, A. (2003). Students with learning disabilities. In: F. E. Obiakor, C. A. Utley & A. F. Rotatori (Eds), *Effective Education for Learners with Exceptionalities* (Vol. 15, pp. 99–118). Amsterdam: JAI Press.

Moss, M. (1979). *Test of basic experience 2: Norms and technical data book*. Monterey, CA: CTB/McGraw-Hill.

Mullen, E. M. (1995). *Mullen scales of early learning*. Circle Pines, MN: American Guidance Service.

National Information Center for Children and Youth with Disabilities (NICHCY) (1999). Questions and answers about IDEA. *www.nichey.org/pubs/newsdig/nd21txt.htm.*

Newborg, J., Stock, J. R., & Wnek, J. (1984). *The Batelle developmental inventory.* Itasca, IL: Riverside Publishing.

Newcomer, P. L. (1999). *Standardized reading inventory* (2nd ed.). Austin, TX: Pro-Ed.

Newcomer, P. L., Barenbaum, E. M., & Bryant, B. R. (1994). *Depression and anxiety in youth scale.* Austin, TX: Pro-Ed.

Nurss, J. R. (1995). *Metropolitan readiness test* (6th ed.). San Antonio, TX: Psychological Corporation.

Pearl, R. (1992). Psychological characteristics of learning disabled students. In: N. N. Singh & I. L. Beale (Eds), *Current Perspectives in Learning Disabilities: Nature, Theory, and Treatment* (pp. 96–125). New York: Springer-Verlag.

Pierangelo, R., & Giulianai, G. A. (2002). *Assessment in special education: A practical approach.* Boston: Allyn & Bacon.

Piers, E. V., Harris, D. B., & Herzberg, D. S. (2002). *Piers-Harris children's self-concept scale* (2nd ed.). Austin, TX: Pro-Ed.

Pozansky, E. O., & Mokros, H. B. (1996). *Children's depression rating scale* (2nd ed.). Austin, TX: Pro-Ed.

Psychological Corporation (2002). *Wechsler individual achievement test – Revised.* San Antonio, TX: Psychological Corporation.

Psychological Corporation (2003). *Wechsler intelligence scale for children – IV.* San Antonio, TX: Psychological Corporation.

Reid, D. K., Hresko, W., & Hammill, D. D. (2001). *Test of early reading ability* (3rd ed.). Austin, TX: Pro-Ed.

Reynolds, C., & Kamphaus, R. (1992). *Behavior assessment system for children.* Circle Pines, MN: American Guidance Service.

Rotatori, A. F., Fox, R. A., Sexton, D., & Miller, J. (1990). *Comprehensive assessment. in special education: Approaches, procedures, and concerns.* Springfield, IL: Charles C Thomas.

Rotatori, A. F., & Mauser, A. J. (1980). IEP assessment for LD students. *Academic Therapy, 16,* 141–153.

Ryser, G., & McConnell, K. (2002). *Scales for diagnosing attention-deficit/hyperactivity disorders.* Austin, TX: Pro-Ed.

Salvia, J., & Ysseldyke, J. E. (1998). *Assessment* (7th ed.). Boston: Houghton Mifflin.

Salvia, J., & Ysseldyke, J. E. (2001). *Assessment* (8th ed.). Boston: Houghton Mifflin.

Sandoval, J., Sassenrath, J., & Penaloza, M. (1988). Similarity of WISC-R and WAIS-R scores at age 16. *Psychology in the Schools, 25,* 373–379.

Sattler, J. M. (1988). *Assessment of children* (3rd ed.). San Diego: Jerome M. Sattler.

Sattler, J. M. (2001). *Assessment of children* (4th ed.). La Mesa, CA: Jerome M. Sattler.

Siegel, L. S. (1998). The discrepancy formula: Its use and abuse. In: B. K. Shapiro, P. J. Accardo & A. J. Capute (Eds), *Specific Reading Disability: A View of the Spectrum* (pp. 123–136). Timonium, MD: York Press.

Siegel, L. S. (1999). Issues in the definition and diagnosis of learning disabilities: A perspective on Guckenberger v. Boston University. *Journal of Learning Disabilities, 32,* 304–319.

Slingerland, B. H. (1993). *Slingerland screening tests for identifying children with specific language disability.* Cambridge, MA: Educational Publishing Service.

Sousa, D. (2001). *How the special needs brain learns.* Thousand Oaks, CA: Corwin Press.

Stanovich, K. E. (1999). The sociopsychometrics of learning disability. *Journal of Learning Disability, 32,* 350–361.

Thorndike, R. L., Hagen, E., & Sattler, J. (1986). *Technical manual – the Stanford Binet intelligence scale* (4th ed.). Itasca, IL: Riverside publishing.

Ulrich, D. A. (2000). *Test of gross motor development* (2nd ed.). Austin, TX: Pro-Ed.

Voress, J. K., & Maddox, T. (1998). *Developmental assessment of young children.* Austin, TX: Pro-Ed.

Walker, H. M., & Severson, H. H. (1992). *Systematic screening for behavior disorders* (2nd ed.). Longmont, CO: Sopris West.

Webb, G. M. (1983). Left/right brains, teammates in learning. *Exceptional Children, 49,* 508–515.

Wechsler, D. (1991). *Wechsler intelligence scale for children – III.* San Antonio, TX: Psychological Corporation.

Wielkiewicz, R. M. (1990). Interrupting low scores on the WISC-R third factor: It's more than distractibility. *Journal of Consulting and Clinical Psychology, 2,* 91–97.

Woodcock, R., McGrew, K. S., & Mather, N. (2001). *Woodcock-Johnson III tests of cognitive ability.* Itasca, IL: Riverside Publish.

CAREER DEVELOPMENT FOR PERSONS WITH LEARNING DISABILITIES

Pamela Castellanos and Dale Septeowski

The transition from adolescence to adulthood is a challenging one for most youth. Developmental tasks such as selecting a college or vocational program, living independently, seeking a career and employment, and developing social and interpersonal relationships are benchmarks of adult accomplishments that most youth must address at this time. The ability of any adult to work and function independently is a universal concern (Dowdy et al., 1990). The lifelong process of career development, however, poses special challenges for people with learning disabilities (LD) (Kerka, 2002). Although individuals with LD may be classified as mildly disabled or may be more able to hide their disability, they are not exempt from challenges associated with their disability. It is generally accepted that deficiencies in academic, social and career domains do not end with adolescence, but will continue into adulthood.

In addition to coming to an understanding about the nature of one's own disability, individuals must confront myths and stereotypes about learning disabilities that may lead to discrimination in the classroom and in the workplace (see Hallahan & Kauffman, 2000). Discriminatory practices, in addition to the effect of the disability itself, may pose barriers to successfully meeting the challenges of developmental tasks common to adolescence. One of the most pervasive and damaging assumptions a person with LD may face at school or at work is that LD are linked to low intelligence. Key individuals such as parents, teachers,

Current Perspectives on Learning Disabilities
Advances in Special Education, Volume 16, 157–181
Copyright © 2004 by Elsevier Ltd.
All rights of reproduction in any form reserved
ISSN: 0270-4013/doi:10.1016/S0270-4013(04)16008-X

counselors, and eventually employers, may impede the personal, academic, and career development of persons with LD, if the nature and impact of the learning disability are not understood. Many may not be aware that most individuals with LD have average to above-average intelligence, some are gifted, and that all learning disabilities are not the same (Hughes & Smith, 1990; Sattler, 2001).

Given the diversity of specific types of LD and the social, psychological, academic and career implications for those individuals who are affected by LD, it is useful to examine the factors that have contributed to positive outcomes in career development. For adolescents who are making an important transition to adult lives, what factors have enhanced career awareness, knowledge and opportunities, and what might continue to contribute to their career development in the future?

The current chapter considers three major phases of career counseling for persons with LD: elementary and secondary school, college and employment. The role of school counseling programs for students with LD, the concept of *career maturity*, overviews of model secondary school approaches, and issues pertaining to adolescent career and vocational choices are defined and discussed. Transitional planning as an element of career counseling is addressed along with college support services and accommodations for students with disabilities as well as career development services and activities for college students are enumerated. The impact of the Americans with Disabilities Act on college students is considered. Lastly, employment issues for persons with LD and counselor strategies are presented. The chapter concludes with models for successful career intervention for persons with LD.

DEVELOPMENTAL AND COMPREHENSIVE SCHOOL COUNSELING PROGRAMS

For a number of years, the American School Counselor Association has been working to identify and clarify the role and function of school counselors within Developmental and Comprehensive School Counseling programs. The terms "Developmental" and "Comprehensive" mean that school counseling programs establish goals for their programs that are developmentally appropriate to the age and needs of students and that current and future goals build upon previous goal achievement. Thus, school counseling programs should be in place throughout students' entire K-12 academic experience.

Within Developmental and Comprehensive programs, four specific components identify the job description of the counselor. They are:

(1) Responsive Services: The counselor provides short- term help to children and youth with problems related to growing up that are experienced at school and home.

(2) Individual Planning: Counselors help students identify coursework for years ahead based upon future academic and career goals. Counselors also help students identify their strengths and weaknesses, interests, values, and other variables that relate to careers and to future educational routes to careers.
(3) System support: Counselors plan and organize counseling programs.
(4) Curriculum: The Counseling office advances its own curriculum (similar to Math, English, or other subject areas) that is designed to provide students with knowledge, skills, and attitudes that are developmentally appropriate and comprehensive in delivery.

Through these components, school counselors work to provide education and support for the academic, personal, social, and career needs of all students K-12. It is likely most students can benefit from Developmental and Comprehensive School Counseling programs. However, students with LD stand to gain even more than those without LD, as deficiencies in these key areas are frequently the source of poor career maturity and a lifetime of difficulties and unhappiness with employment and work adjustment.

THE IMPORTANCE OF CAREER MATURITY

Career maturity is a construct developed by Super (1957) to describe a given point reached on the continuum of vocational development beginning with the stage of exploration (ages 15–24 years) and continuing through decline (age 65 years). Career maturity during adolescence then is the "state of readiness" to make educational and career decisions (Super & Thompson, 1979). Problems experienced by youth with LD in making successful transitions to postsecondary education and to work do not appear to be just a problem of learning or of education itself, but also how the disability affects their own career development and career maturation. Concepts such as career ambition, career decision-making, the ability to relate traits of self to factors of education and the world of work have often been combined within the concept of career maturity.

Research on career maturity of individuals with LD, although relatively limited, has suggested they lag behind their non-disabled counterparts in career maturity. Herr and Cramer (1996) indicated that measures of career maturity in the adolescent stage predict later career adjustment better than other traditional assessment tools such as academic test scores and grades. Unfortunately, Ohler et al. (1995) pointed out that individuals with LD may suffer impairment in this developmental process, leaving them poorly prepared to deal with career choices.

Research, then, suggests that counselors must assess the unique career-related needs of these young adults with LD so that they may provide support services to help them find employment and make necessary adjustments in the world of work. If those with more severe LD experience less career maturity, they may be at the greatest risk of unemployment or underemployment. Counselor strategies that address issues of career maturity can be summarized as follows: (a) responsible assessment of intellectual ability, academic skills, personality traits, interests, and career maturity; (b) exploratory career activities, including job shadowing, internships, and job simulation; (c) individual academic and career counseling to develop a plan of study congruent to the student's goals and abilities; (d) experiential learning such as part-time or summer jobs, volunteer work, and internships; (e) social skills training in interpersonal communication and self-awareness; (f) monitoring of career needs and progress by counselors, school and/or rehabilitation personnel, and the student; (g) placement assistance including promotion of transition to the world of work; and (h) faculty consultation about the effect of the learning disability upon vocational potential (Ohler et al., 1996).

Career maturity is linked to academic achievement and previous work experience as well as to the number of accommodations a student with LD has received. However, greater use of accommodations in school has been shown to correlate with lower levels of career maturity (Ohler et al., 1996). This suggests that students with more severe LD are developmentally delayed and need additional assistance, since they are less able to benefit from the cognitive and attitudinal tasks that are related to career development. Another possibility is that those with LD develop a dependency to rely upon the system that provides accommodations, requesting and receiving more assistance than those who have not developed the same level of dependency. They may be passive in their approaches to gaining part-time employment or involvement in extra-curricular activities that promote career maturity (Ohler et al., 1996). Secondary schools may foster greater autonomy and career maturity by encouraging work and career-related experiences that enhance career decision-making skills. Colleges may target students with LD in secondary school that have received more accommodations and provide them with appropriate interventions, support and career counseling.

Modifications to the goals of Developmental and Comprehensive School Counseling programs and the methods of intervention are necessary to meet the individual needs of students with LD. A critical area related to career maturity is transition planning. Recognizing that students with LD pose more unique career problems than their non-disabled classmates, Public Law 101–476 requires a student's Individual Education Plan (IEP) to address the issue of transition, and that transition planning begin by age 16 years (Levinson & Ohler, 1998). Although this effort to make a purposeful plan for a transition is commendable, the process of educational and career planning and transitioning must begin early in the educational experience of the student.

Developmental and Comprehensive School Counseling programs emphasize development of self-awareness, self-esteem, basic academic skills, interpersonal relationships and career awareness during early school years. These early life experiences begin to lay the foundation of interests, abilities, values, ambitions and other career-related areas, a learning process that may be particularly difficult for the child with LD. Levinson and Ohler (1998) suggest that the establishment of work routines, which can be demonstrated in play and observed by parents and family, is a factor of career maturity. Some children with LD have difficulty establishing routines of any kind, which may serve to delay their career development. Children with LD have also been found to have difficulty processing information (Bender, 2004). This difficulty interferes with the ability to learn about self and to gain information about the world of work, whether through daily experiences or purposeful classroom instruction. It also interferes with development of a healthy concept of self which is important for occupational decision-making.

The establishment of realistic self-concepts and positive self-esteem, critical for career maturation and effective decision-making, is strongly related to academic success. School counselors, regular classroom teachers, and special education teachers and consultants need to work together to develop strategies that allow students with LD to be academically successful and to promote career maturity through greater self-understanding and occupational awareness.

SCHOOL COUNSELING PROGRAMS IN SECONDARY SCHOOLS

At the high school level, career counseling within a Developmental and Comprehensive School Counseling program includes further identification of strengths and interests, academic planning for transition from high school, as well as the development of a plan and timetable for postsecondary endeavors. Researchers have identified a number of special needs or weaknesses of youths with LD. For example, Hitchings and Retish (2000) state that many youth with LD lack a clear understanding of their disability and its impact on career choices and ability to perform a job. Biller and Horn (1991) found that those with LD lack career maturity and an awareness of their own abilities. Korterling and Braziel (2000) found that many youth with LD had unrealistic career ambitions or no ambitions and that those with realistic ambitions seldom acquired appropriate education or training that would prepare them for a job.

These needs and weaknesses result in poor career maturity. However, adolescents with LD who experience effective Developmental and Comprehensive School Counseling programs should demonstrate improved career maturity.

Since many adolescents with and without disabilities do not experience quality Developmental and Comprehensive School Counseling programs, the best approach to assisting those with LD may be to develop, implement, and assess special strategies and programs designed to meet their particular needs.

FOUR PHASE CAREER GUIDANCE MODEL

Biller and Horn (1991) outline a four-phase career guidance model for adolescents with LD that reframes the primary goal found in a more traditional model. While traditional models focus upon the imperative of career choice, Biller and Horn's model focuses on development and prevention. In this model, Phase 1 involves the collecting of preliminary and biographical data. Parents and the student are interviewed and both are consulted on the types of additional assessment that will be used. The inclusion of parents serves to generate "buy-in" and support for student and parents alike.

Phase 2 emphasizes assessment of career maturity and work importance, rather than prominent emphasis upon assessment of interests and abilities used in the traditional model. Super (1983) suggests that the use of computerized career guidance systems may be more useful in this phase than interest inventories and aptitude batteries. Phase 3 discusses occupations that match the student's profile; however, if career maturity is found to be below average, a plan to address this deficiency may be developed and included in the student's IEP. This model introduces the concept of career development as an aspect of career counseling. It assumes, however, that opportunities and experiences are available to students in school and outside school to fulfill IEP recommendations. Therefore, the model may work most successfully in schools that already use Developmental and Comprehensive School Counseling and Career programs. Phase 4 provides follow-up which is focused on the particular needs and problems experienced by those with LD.

THE PATHWAYS PROGRAM: A MODEL
SCHOOL COUNSELING PROGRAM

Secondary schools have emphasized academic remediation for students with LD for a number of years. In so doing, emphasis has been placed upon overcoming weaknesses. A different approach is the focus on post-school environments and the knowledge and skills needed to become employable. One such program is Pathways (Hutchinson & Freeman, 1994). Pathways is a course taken by students with LD that addresses five career-related areas: (a) awareness of self and careers;

(b) employment writing; (c) interview skills; (d) problem solving on the job; and (e) anger management. According to Conger, 1997, "Pathways uses cognitive instruction in which problem-solving and other complex thinking have central place." (p. 9). In cognitive instruction, students are taught to make sense of the new knowledge and to make meaning from the new learning. Through a process that incorporates teacher modeling, student-guided practice, and independent practices to enhance the student's competence and confidence, students also learn knowledge, skills, and attitudes in the five program areas (Conger, 1997).

Research on Pathway's impact on students reveals marked improvement in all five areas taught (see Hutchinson et al., 1993). In addition to the noted success of the program, two vital points must be made. The first point is the inclusion of a career counseling class that the counseling office provides. The second point is that teachers and counselors must adapt instructional methodology to the learning needs and modes of the students.

CAREER AND VOCATIONAL COUNSELING FOR ADOLESCENTS

Two key developmental areas for adolescents who are making the transition to adult roles and lives are the selection of appropriate education or training as preparation for future goals and the pursuit of employment. In both areas career and vocational counseling is essential for all young adults. However, it is even more complex and significant and can have a greater positive influence for the young adult with LD (Rosenthal, 1985).

The successful transition of students with all types of disabilities from school to adult life is a national priority, according to the Office of Special Education and Rehabilitative Services (Haring et al., 1990). Moreover, legislation of the last few decades has brought considerable attention to the needs and rights of persons with disabilities, bringing changes in perceptions and in programs to help them transition to the work world and independent living. Rojewski (1999) argues ". . . despite the tremendous strides made in recent years, adolescents with learning disabilities still struggle in preparing for and successfully completing the transition from high school to postsecondary education or work and ultimately adult life" (p. 533). While students with LD are often categorized as having mild impairment, the problems and needs associated with being disabled apply to them.

Even with milder forms of LD, students may suffer from lower self-esteem, stigmatization from labeling, barriers to competitive employment, and a limited view of higher education and career opportunities. Selecting a career, gaining training or education to enter a particular field, and pursuing employment require significant planning and preparation (see Benz et al., 2000; Johnson et al., 2002; Lindstrom & Benz, 2002; Mull et al., 2001). These career-related tasks provide a yardstick to measure oneself against adult standards. They may contribute to or detract from one's self-esteem. For students with LD who are handicapped by a "hidden disability," the transitional experience from school to employment may bring about feelings of hopelessness and fear of not meeting peer and family expectations (Fourqurean et al., 1991).

DEVELOPMENT OF A VOCATIONAL SELF-CONCEPT

The vocational self-concept is an important aspect of one's whole self-concept and evolves as individuals experience physical and mental growth, become exposed to work experiences, begin to identify with working adults, and learn to assess their strengths and weaknesses. Super (1983) stressed the importance of self-concept, which is related to career development. As youth mature into adulthood and their experience with work expands, they develop a more sophisticated vocational self-concept through assimilation of differences and similarities between themselves and others. An understanding of the compatibility or contrast of their interests and skills with working adults evolves, thereby helping them narrow the range of suitable occupations. Identification with individuals who share similar interests and skills, along with an increasing awareness of self, help adolescents focus upon employment that fits them. The degree to which one can find appropriate and adequate expression of their skills, needs, and values in a career has direct bearing upon work and life satisfaction.

Thus choosing an occupation is a means of implementing a self-concept. The development of a vocational self-concept may propel an individual into a career pattern that may be followed throughout a lifetime (Super, 1969). Building self-esteem is particularly critical in the career development process of students with LD. If individuals with LD have poor self-esteem, the effects are likely to transfer from the school to the employment arena. Low self-esteem and a lack of self-understanding will seriously impede the development of mature career attitudes, whereas high self-esteem can contribute to mature career attitudes and thus to work achievement.

Interventions with students should emphasize development of self-esteem to foster adoption of more mature career attitudes that ultimately translate into greater success and satisfaction in career (Ohler et al., 1995). Adelman and Vogel (1990) note that successful employment of individuals with LD coincides with finding the right match between career demands and personal strengths, and that lack of recognition of that relationship can lead to frustration and disappointment in the career domain. Expectations of self may be unrealistically high or low, leading to feelings of despair and learned helplessness, and resulting in their becoming passive in both learning and doing (Rosenthal, 1985). Students who lack self-insight are more likely to succumb to parental pressures or peer influences when making career decisions, rather than trust their ability to make choices for themselves. This may be related to an external locus of control that young adults often develop, resulting from a history of academic difficulties and frustrations. The belief that consequences are contingent upon the behavior of others, rather than one's self is another contributing factor to low career maturity (Ohler et al., 1995).

What is clear, according to the National Longitudinal Transition Study of Special Education Students (NTLS), prepared for the U.S. Department of Education, is that choices that are made by youth with disabilities or by significant others on their behalf during their secondary school years play a significant role in the pathways pursued in early adulthood (Wagner et al., 1993). For many individuals with LD in the period of late adolescence, secondary education programs have supported and prepared them for this transition by providing opportunities in vocational education, work experience, transition planning, and special curricula designed to foster academic persistence and success. For others, gaps in budget or lack of qualified teachers and counselors, appropriate programs, or commitment to provide the best possible life and educational preparation for this special population may have left individuals without the academic, interpersonal, or decision-making skills to navigate early, important post-secondary years. It may be assumed that the degree to which students with LD experience success upon exiting high school in important domains of adult living, including pursuit of vocational or postsecondary education, competitive employment and wages, and independent living, may be related to experiences in secondary education (see Lehmann et al., 2000).

Studies examining the relationship between post-secondary programs and adult adjustment provide evidence that many students leaving school lack the skills necessary to live independently or fully realize their potential in the world of work (Haring et al., 1990; Lock & Layton, 2001). Vocational education's most significant contribution for students enrolled in special education programs may be a slightly reduced drop-out rate; however, it is still estimated that approximately one-third of students enrolled in special education programs discontinue their education prior to having earned a diploma (see Scanlon & Mellard, 2002; Wagner et al., 1993). This finding implies that programs designed to meet the needs of students with LD may be of limited value even during the actual secondary school experience.

ADDRESSING TRANSITION NEEDS

The transition of individuals with LD to the world of work is a broad mix of experiences. Blackorby and Wagner (1997) state, "There is no single story to tell about the outcomes of students with disabilities" (p. 58). Many people with LD have been very successful in the workplace, obtaining advanced degrees and jobs of high status and income (Kerka, 2002). Studies also indicate significant problems experienced by those with LD in finding "good work," securing fulltime positions, and achieving academic success (see Dickinson & Verbeek, 2002). Using data from the National Longitudinal Transitions Study of Special Education Students from 1987, Wagner and Blackorby (1996) identified the high drop out rate of students with disabilities placed only two other groups at higher risk for dropping out, those with mental retardation and those with emotional disturbances. Wagner and Blackorby also noted that only 30.5% of students with LD had postsecondary enrollment three to five years out of high school compared to 68.3% of the general population of youth and 26.7% of all youth with disabilities.

On a more positive note, youth with LD approximated the general population of youth who were competitively employed three to five years out of high school at 70.8%. Many youth with LD, however, were under-employed. Researchers noted that the high percentage of youth with LD competitively employed was related to a high school curriculum allowing for a concentration of vocational and technical courses (see Bender, 2004). Data appear to support the findings of Wagner and Blackorby (1996) and continue to suggest that students with LD find the transition from high school to postsecondary school or to work to be difficult (Rojewski, 1996, 1999). Also, despite the increased enrollment of students with LD in postsecondary education, the educational and occupational attainment continues to be lower for youth with LD than for non-LD youth (Blackorby & Wagner, 1997; Janiga & Costenbader, 2002; Madans et al., 2002; Rojewski, 1993).

Transition planning in secondary school is essential and should include exploration of career options that take into account the student's strengths and weaknesses in academic and vocational domains. As adolescents often have limited knowledge and unrealistic expectations about the world of work, guidance counselors and teachers must be prepared to share occupational information, foster good self-knowledge and self-concept, and teach decision making skills that can help them transition smoothly from secondary school to college, vocational training, or employment. While these activities are important for all students, they may be considered even more critical when working with youth with LD.

These students may also need to develop better reality testing and more effective use of their personal history, as these areas are often notable weaknesses in the decision-making process (Rosenthal, 1985).

A model transition program aimed at prospective first-year students with LD at University of Wisconsin-Whitewater (UW-W) entitled Project ASSIST begins in the senior year of high school (Dalke & Schmitt, 1987). The rationale for this program is based upon an understanding of the many changes that occur between high school and college that compound an already difficult transition for students with LD. These changes include the following: (1) a decrease in teacher-student contact; (2) an increase in academic competition; (3) changes in personal support network; and (4) a change from environment of individual guidance and instruction to expectations of self-motivation and achievement.

Project Assist provides a post-high school, pre-college transition support experience aimed at preparing students with LD for college through a five week, non-credit summer program. This program provides comprehensive diagnostic and instructional support services for UW-W students with LD. The program aims to facilitate LD students' abilities to cope with issues that confront them during the transition period in the following ways: providing an opportunity to deal with emotional factors such as loss of support; offering an educational experience similar to college; by familiarizing students with the campus and surrounding community; helping them understand college procedures and functions; identifying helpful services; enhancing academic skills; and, providing direct instruction in important academic support skills such as study skills, time management and note-taking skills. Academic reinforcement over summer vacation is also a goal, as students are prone to forget previously learned concepts in math, reading and language (Dalke & Schmitt, 1987). Response to this program has been extremely positive. In addition to high overall ratings for the program, freshmen that attended the summer program had significantly higher grade point averages in their first semester than those who did not attend the summer program (Dalke & Schmitt, 1987). Given changes and adjustments that students with LD face when making the transition to college, support services are crucial to success. Dalke and Schmitt (1987) argue, "It is naïve to assume that, once students with learning disabilities graduate from high school, the need for support services suddenly dissipates. It is unrealistic to think that, after years of individual help and guidance in a structured, extrinsically controlled supportive environment, these students can suddenly adjust to an unstructured, intrinsically controlled setting without some assistance" (p. 180). Programs such as Project Assist are designed to address the needs of students with LD and enhance their opportunity for adjustment and persistence in college.

THE ROLE OF COLLEGE SUPPORT SERVICES, ACCOMMODATIONS, AND CAREER COUNSELING

Despite perceived and real difficulties in school, students with LD are choosing to pursue postsecondary education in community colleges and at four-year universities in greater numbers (see Murray et al., 2000). Many universities have made the admissions process easier for individuals with LD; however, easier access to higher education does not insure student persistence among this population. Although college may be a difficult goal to attain for students with LD, it is the responsibility of the admitting school to provide accommodations and support that can foster academic success.

Ruhl et al. (1990) identify five factors at the postsecondary level that distinguish students with LD from the non-LD students relative to difficulties with university courses. These include: (a) poor comprehension; (b) short attention span; (c) difficulties understanding and remembering information in lecture format; (d) problems with listening to lectures and taking notes; and (e) inadequacies in social situations. Some students are required to take additional non-credit courses necessary to remediate academic deficiencies that slows progress towards completion of a four-year degree. Success may ultimately rest upon the effects and outcomes of the services, support, accommodations, advising and career counseling that the college provides.

Adelman and Vogel (1990) found that support services in college have a significant long-term benefit, not only in college, but also later in the job market. College graduates with LD acknowledge that their disabilities affect their work. Common problems include difficulty with retaining information, needing extra time to complete work assignments, and perception problems with numbers and letters. Students who availed themselves of college support services that helped them understand their learning disabilities and develop compensatory strategies were able to successfully transfer that knowledge from the academic to the employment setting. Primarily, they developed compensatory strategies such as spending more time to finish work, asking for additional help, and carefully monitoring for errors.

Helping college students gain a sense of mastery and control over the career decision-making process is a critical task, particularly for those with LD. Courses in career development and decision-making may offer the college student with LD an opportunity to find order, personal meaning, and a locus of control within themselves as they search for their place in the world of work. They may also provide a venue to teach students to systematically gather career information and make rational, mature career decisions (Rosenthal, 1985). For students who are undecided in their career plans, a college career-planning class is strongly recommended, followed by individual counseling designed to formulate a plan of study that is consistent with the student's interests, abilities, and values (Ohler et al., 1995).

CAREER DEVELOPMENT SERVICES AND ACTIVITIES

One important avenue of support for college students with LD is career development activities. Specialized advising may be available for students to discuss their disability, explore career opportunities, get assistance with resume writing and interviewing, and examine the issue of disclosure of disability in the job search process. Recruitment programs designed to assist college students with disabilities find employment with Federal agencies, as well as listings of disability-friendly employers, may also be explored in many college career centers. Other benefits that may be acquired through Career Services include: (a) special hiring programs through State and Federal Government; (b) employment agencies who assist individuals in securing jobs consistent with their qualifications and career goals; (c) information about financial aid resources; and (d) most recently, well-designed websites. Career and guidance counselors may be especially skilled and suited to assisting youth with LD in navigating career pathways. They may serve as mentors, advocates, and job coaches, helping students better understand themselves and the work domain. They can also assist by providing accurate information about job requirements and opportunities and how they mesh with the student's skills, interests, and values about work.

Friehe et al. (1996) specifically sought to determine whether students used campus career-related services and if they were satisfied with them, and whether students were prepared to address disability issues that related to employment. A total of 213 students with various disabilities from two Midwestern universities completed the survey, with nearly one-fourth of the respondents identifying themselves as having LD. The most common services used were resources in the center (15%), followed by individual counseling (11%), and job listings (11%). On the lower end of student participation were interest testing (8%), career fairs (5%), workshops (4%), and campus interviews (3%).

Overall, students with disabilities in the Friehe et al. (1996) study rated career and student employment services positively, with one-fourth rating them very good to excellent. Yet few students with disabilities used certain services, such as on campus interviews, which could provide valuable training in learning and practicing interviewing skills. When students were asked to identify reasons for not availing themselves of career-related services, the results were as follows:

(a) they believed they did not need the service (61%); (b) they did not know about the service (23%); and (c) they did not think the service would be helpful (15%). Insofar as about 75% of students who did not use career services apparently knew about them, but made a choice not to use them, other means of getting information to students should be explored and service providers need to make decisions about who should offer career information, what the format should be, and what should be included. However, if students with disabilities are reluctant to use career services even when they know about them, the first step may be finding ways to influence students to use the services in the first place (Friehe et al., 1996).

FEDERAL AND STATE PROGRAMS AND AGENCIES FOR INDIVIDUALS WITH DISABILITIES

Students with LD can also enhance their career opportunities enormously by being knowledgeable about federal and state programs and agencies that can help them with employment preparation, job development, and placement. *The Federal Employment of People with Disabilities* website, for example, contains information about Selective Placement Program Coordinators who assist agency management with recruitment, hiring, and accommodations for people with disabilities. The *Federal Work Force Recruitment Program for College Students with Disabilities (WRP)* assists students in gaining employment with Federal agencies. Coordinated by the *Office of Disability Employment Policy* and a consortium of Federal agencies and private sector employers, this program sends recruiters to college campuses across the country. (*http://career.berkeley.edu/Disabilities*).

The *National Business & Disability Council* provides an employer membership list on their website and maintains a resume database for companies with a demonstrated commitment to hiring people with disabilities. Similarly, *Job Links*, provided by the *Office of Disability Employment Policy*, identifies employers with an interest in recruiting and hiring qualified individuals with disabilities. States and local communities also offer assistance to those with disabilities. For example, the *California Business Leadership Network (CABLN)* is an alliance of California companies who are working together to improve employment for persons with disabilities. This alliance also maintains an Online Recruiting Service for college students (*http://career.berkeley.edu/Disabilities*). This is by no means an exhaustive list; however, it exemplifies the range of services and assistance that is available to students with disabilities. All included above may be accessed through the Internet.

COLLEGE STUDENTS AND THE ADA

Students with LD should understand the significance of the Americans With Disabilities Act (ADA), which became law in 1991. The ADA requires that special accommodations and modification of policies, practices and procedures be made so equal access cannot be denied in various areas, including employment and education. It prohibits discrimination in employment practices including hiring, firing, advancement, compensation and training. While employers have the right to choose the most qualified applicant irrespective of disability, the decision on whom to hire must be based upon job performance needs (Zunker, 2002).

Furthermore, the ADA protects the rights of students with disabilities in seeking and maintaining employment, but only when the disability is disclosed. Thus, job applicants must make decisions about whether, when, and how to disclose their disabilities to employers, and whether or not accommodations in the workplace are needed or should be requested (Friehe et al., 1996). These considerations must be confronted by students with any type of disability, adding yet another dimension to the complex process of career training and development. Even after they are successfully employed, Blalock (1981) points out that individuals with LD put forth great effort in hiding their disability from employers by taking work home so they can receive assistance from friends or spouses without the knowledge of supervisors or colleagues.

College students with disabilities, however, are often not conversant with the ADA, lacking the necessary knowledge and skills to understand how the ADA may benefit them in the job search or how guidelines for disclosure may help or hinder them in getting a job offer (Thompson & Dooley-Dickey, 1994). Moreover, students with disabilities are often not prepared to arrange for the job accommodations for which they are eligible. Fearing stereotyping or tokenism, college students with disabilities often do not request job accommodations (Altschul & Michaels, 1994). According to the ADA "reasonable accommodations" must be provided for persons with disabilities so long as "undue hardship" on business operations is not imposed. This provision is intended to assist persons with disabilities in meeting job requirements and expectations. However, a survey of college graduates with learning disabilities conducted by Adelman and Vogel (1990) revealed that 86% of respondents compensated for their disability by taking extra time to complete tasks and monitor their own work, and did not ask employers for accommodations. This suggests that students with LD may not be effectively using ADA guidelines that could potentially provide them with the assistance needed to be fully competent in job tasks and responsibilities and be competitively employed.

THE ROLE OF VOCATIONAL
TRAINING OF EMPLOYMENT

The role of vocational training on the transition to work for individuals with LD is inconclusive. Some studies reveal that high school vocational training has been limited for most adults with LD (see Adelman & Vogel, 1993). For example, one survey of former high school students with LD, who had completed mainstream vocational/technical programs, indicated that 61% reported that they were not qualified for jobs in the vocational areas in which they had received training (Adelman & Vogel, 1993).

Fourqurean et al. (1991) assert that the number of semesters of vocational courses taken in high school did not relate to employment success. Since no distinction was made among various vocational courses that were completed, these findings should be viewed cautiously. Of the subjects employed, twelve were working in occupations that provided the necessary training in high school, particularly auto mechanics and cosmetology. It may be assumed that without this training these young adults might have been unemployed or underemployed.

Adelman and Vogel (1993) report that studies do not focus on the *quality* of vocational programs treatment as it relates to outcomes. Thus, evidence may suggest that high school vocational training is often unavailable or ineffective for individuals with LD (see Wagner et al., 1993). The conflicting results on the effect of high school vocational training may be due to a discrepancy between the quality of individual programs compared with the overall objective or goals of vocational training as a whole. Thus an evaluation of *educational experiences* within vocational training programs might yield more reliable results when considering the relationship between programs and occupational success.

Rosenthal (1989) suggests the benefit of experience-based education, which emphasizes the benefits of internships for students with LD. Work-related activities such as internships, allow individuals to observe, practice and adjust to the demands of the workplace, while promoting appropriate career choice. Another recommendation is the availability of a Comprehensive and Developmental School Counseling program to address the special academic, career, and employment needs of students with LD throughout their school experience.

THE IMPACT OF LD IN EMPLOYMENT

Once adults with LD do secure employment, what are the effects of their particular type of learning disability on the job? Both high school and college graduates report that their disabilities do, in fact, affect their work (Adleman & Vogel, 1990).

Also, problems with interpretation of non-verbal skills may create obstacles to success for students with LD. Studies have focused on problems with social skills and non-social interaction skills. A comparison of high school students with LD and those without LD showed significant differences. Mathews et al. (1982) concluded that non-LD students demonstrate better social skills and verbal communication skills with employers, co-workers, and supervisors. Non-LD students also performed better than students with LD on nonsocial interaction skills, such as letter writing or completing forms. An individual's ability to perceive and interpret reactions may be hindered due to the type of LD. LD that interferes in accurate perception of nonverbal cues such as facial expression and body language can be a serious barrier to understanding the intended messages in the workplace.

The good news is that employer awareness about LD and their effect on employees appears to be increasing according to Adelman and Vogel (1993). These authors reported that most employers would be willing to accommodate employees with LD by giving more time for training or project completion, helping employees with disabilities find the right job, or providing more detailed directions. Also, they reported a willingness to support employees as long as they were competently carrying out their job duties. Lastly, employers said they were not willing to become involved in the personal life of their employees, however.

Generalization about vocational development is difficult, given the wide range of abilities and limitations that adults with LD exhibit. Individuals also develop compensatory skills that allow them to function competently in various vocational areas despite their particular type of LD. Also, they may seek employment in positions that call for their strengths, rather than their deficiencies. Nonetheless, LD very likely continue to affect career development and decision-making, as well as successful work adjustment throughout adulthood (see Gerber, 1997; Price & Gerber, 2001).

Hershenson's (1984) model of vocational development is useful in identifying factors that may impede successful work adjustment and advancement for adults with LD. This model includes three interactive domains: *work personality, work competencies, and work goals.* The first domain, work personality, is the emergence of the individual's self-concept as a worker, which usually develops during youth through experiences and observations in the home. The second domain is work competencies, including work habits (e.g. promptness, reliability) and skills demanded in the work environment. These skills and habits are usually formed during the school years. The third domain is the formulation of clear, appropriate work goals. This develops as individuals are planning to leave school and enter the world of work. Each domain affects and is affected by prior ones.

Hershenson (1984) explains that domains continue to develop and interact over a lifetime, although less dramatically as time passes. Changes in one domain may prompt changes in the other two. For example, a positive work personality (self-concept as a worker) may become negative if a learning disability interferes with success in school or later on, in one's employment. Likewise, work competencies may be insufficient to meet the demands of a particular job, thus negatively impacting work goals. Hershenson suggests that any area of work competence, in fact, may be adversely affected by LD. Low self-concept and a distorted sense of work motivation and aspiration may also occur due to an inability to meet the skills needed to successfully accomplish one's job. Finally, work goals may be unrealistic, inappropriate, and poorly defined as a result of interaction between the work personality and work competencies. This model strongly supports the need for vocational counseling for individuals with LD given the complexity of the dynamics between and among domains.

Regardless of abilities, vocational counseling must concentrate on an individual's strengths and limitations. Little intervention may be required if career goals and job tasks are congruent with one's assets and abilities. However, this may not be the case with individuals with LD. More likely the impact of the LD on the individual's career development is severe. Hershenson (1984) suggests "... the relationship between the extent of the impairment and the relevant assets determines the amount of special intervention required..." (p. 42). Thus individuals needing the highest level of intervention are likely to be those with both severe learning disabilities and minimal career-related personal assets. To be effective with clients with LD, the counselor must understand how clients are impeded and help them conceptualize a plan. This requires an understanding of assessment and its application to those with learning disabilities.

COUNSELOR BEHAVIOR AND STRATEGIES

Providing feedback to clients is an important counselor behavior that may require special consideration and strategies when working with clients with LD. Insofar as clients with LD often have difficulty with interpersonal skills, it is important for the counselor to ascertain that his or her message has been understood and to be aware that difficulties encountered in reading, writing and spoken communication will probably occur with employers and co-workers as well. Deficiencies that can potentially make employment difficult to get and keep must be addressed with the client so that strategies may be developed (Hershenson, 1984). It is also crucial that the counselor do appropriate follow-up with the client, as work adjustment may be particularly difficult for the individual with LD. Monitoring client progress is important, as there may be disconnects between the individual and his or her strengths, limitations, and skills, job training, and the reality of the job itself.

Counselors must also help clients with self-exploration, as individuals with LD often have unrealistic ideas or inaccurate perceptions about job requirements, career/educational preparation and their own abilities as they coincide with a particular type of employment or profession. Paramount in this strategy is conveying to the client understanding and support. Also crucial is a specific, structured plan that the client must help construct and be responsible for implementing. The client must be invested in the plan and understand his or her role as the architect of it. Imposed by the counselor, a plan is likely doomed to failure. The role of the counselor will likely become increasingly supportive as issues and strategies have been identified and addressed. As time progresses, the client should assume more and more responsibility for self-monitoring, and the counselor should be assisting him or her move to greater independence. Thus the counselor must also be teaching the client how to approach problem solving, decision-making, planning, and evaluating so the client has the life and career skills necessary to be successful in the real world.

Ultimately, counselors must be able to establish a realistic evaluation of the person's competencies, limitations, and personal and career goals. A supportive environment must be fostered where the young adult can start working in his or her chosen career. Counselors must assist young adults with LD in addressing areas of concern that may range from basic (filling out the job application) to complex (when or if to disclose information regarding the disability). The counselor should also help the student become a self-advocate, which may require developing appropriate skills in assertiveness and methods of proactively seeking information and feedback from teachers, peers, and employers (see Kling, 2001).

AWARENESS OF VOCATIONAL REHABILITATION SERVICES

While vocational rehabilitation (VR) provides much needed assistance to clients with LD, research reveals that knowledge about federal laws and services among individuals qualified to use them is very limited (Smith, 1992; Wolinsky & Whelan, 1999). Until 1981 individuals with LD were not eligible for VR services unless another disabling condition was also present. While that has changed, eligibility is not automatically granted and must be sought by the individual, family or other advocates. Yet many individuals who would qualify simply do not apply for services. Questions arise as to whether individuals with LD have the information or resources necessary to negotiate the system that could provide them with much need assistance and services.

LD clients who have poor employment status may be more severely disabled or have more limited social skills than a more capable client with LD. They may also lack an understanding of their disability or be poorly matched to their job or place of employment. Lack of transition services on the secondary level, limited goals, and poor interagency cooperation between the public school and VR can also contribute to poor employment outcomes. Poor employer attitudes towards clients with LD can be a problem. Conversely, persons dissatisfied with menial jobs and wages could have unrealistic expectations about their own abilities, aptitudes and skills.

What seems clear, however, is that many people with LD could benefit from services and that an effort must be made to reach them. Better linkages must be made between educators and service providers so students leaving schools can continue to receive the services they need as they transition to adult roles as workers. Secondary students must prepare for navigating adult settings. An individualized education program (IEP) is essential in early high school. Vocational and career counselors need more training in working with individuals with LD, including understanding their characteristics, appropriate assessment techniques, and interventions. This may be achieved through consulting with special educators and other professionals with expertise who can offer seminars and training to counselors.

While most of the research on career development of individuals with LD has focused on weaknesses, delayed career maturation, and special needs, some studies have examined factors that contribute to the success of adults with LD. Despite the obvious challenges, many adults with LD achieve high levels of success and satisfaction in employment. For example, in research conducted by Ginsberg et al. (1994), highly successful and moderately successful adults were compared in terms of income level, job classification, educational level, prominence in their field, and job satisfaction. The single most important principle that applied to those who were successful was the ability to take control of their lives. The researchers defined control as making conscious decisions to take charge of one's life (internal decisions), and adapting oneself to move ahead (external manifestations). Adults with LD had spent their lives learning to control their existence and, in the workplace, their physical environment. Those who were the most successful as adults expressed the greatest need to be controlling their destiny. The degree of control gained, in fact, distinguished the high success group from the moderate group (Gerber et al., 1992).

Based upon the above research, a model for career success for individuals who are learning disabled was developed. The model consists of seven factors. Three internal factors helped the successful individual take control, which were then manifested in four external behaviors. The three internal decisions described by Gerber et al. (1992) are strong desire to succeed, goal orientation, and reframing of the LD experience. These lead to external manifestations of persistence, goodness of fit, learned creativity and a social network. In combination, these factors are necessary for a high degree of control. Moreover, internal decisions and external manifestations reinforce one another.

The identification of above success factors for adults helps to establish clear goals for career counseling for students with LD in a Developmental and Comprehensive School Counseling program. Michaels (1997) suggested a program that emphasized the strengths, gifts, and dreams of individuals with LD. Consistent with research findings of Ginsberg et al. (1994) and Reiff et al. (1998), six major program goals are identified:

(1) Accurate self-knowledge about skills, abilities, interests, and goals as well as knowledge of one's disability.
(2) World-of-work knowledge acquired through career exploration, job shadowing, and appropriate work experience.
(3) Self-efficacy enhancement through attributional retraining, anxiety reduction, and reframing.
(4) Self-advocacy skills, including knowledge of civil rights, disclosure issues, accommodations, assistive technologies and compensatory strategies.
(5) Job-search skills.
(6) Development of personal qualities such as persistence, resilience, and the ability to build social support networks (Kerka, 2000).

SUMMARY

Career development is a complex process that takes place over one's life span. It is influenced by psychological, sociological, educational, economic, geographic and other factors. One's career development involves the creation of a career pattern, decision-making style, integration of life roles, values expression, and life-role self-concepts (Herr & Cramer, 1996). The process of career development poses challenges for many individuals, especially those with LD. A significant factor is that career maturity of those with LD appears to lag behind that of non-disabled counterparts. This lag has been identified by various authors as having a negative impact on career adjustment of individuals with LD, on their ability to make astute career choices, on their potential to gain competitive and appropriate employment, and ultimately on their ability to navigate the world of work.

Since career maturity is a developmental process beginning early in life, it may be assumed that the promotion of career maturity requires early intervention strategies. Schools, most specifically school counseling programs, play a significant role in the intervention process. School counseling programs that are Developmental and Comprehensive (K-12) provide both structure and means of delivery for schools to be proactive in promoting and instilling career development and career maturity in all students, including those with LD.

The extent to which students with LD experience success in their transition from high school to important domains of adult living, such as pursuit of vocational or postsecondary education, competitive employment and wages, and independent living, may be correlated with experiences in secondary education. Evidence suggests that strong vocational training programs in high school may reduce drop-out rates. However, the impact of such programs on those entering the work world is not clear. A growing trend is for students with LD to enter community and four year colleges. The "open door" policy of some schools, however, may turn into a revolving door for students with LD. Success in higher education may be related to college services, academic support, testing and learning accommodations, academic advising, and career and personal counseling, as well as the student's knowledge of services and willingness to use them. Yet often students with LD are reluctant or embarrassed to declare their disability, ask for accommodations, or be self-advocates through the ADA for fear of stigmatization or tokenism. Those who do make use of available support services, the ADA, and develop an understanding of the nature of their disability may show greater promise for success in the work world.

While it seems important to help individuals with LD with career development identify areas of weakness to develop a range of strategies for success, emphasis should be placed upon strengths rather than deficiencies. Research evidence clearly states that individuals with LD have lower self-esteem, poorer self-concepts, external locus of control, and lower career maturity than their non-disabled counterparts. It has been suggested that too much emphasis has been placed upon why LD individuals do not succeed rather than what factors and strategies might help them succeed.

Many individuals with LD have made remarkable academic and career achievements by any measure. The single most important principle that has been correlated to that success is the ability to take control of their lives, rather than to be controlled and defined by the learning disability. Successful adults with LD have a strong desire to succeed, are goal-oriented, and reframe their disability in a manner that emphasizes strengths without ignoring weaknesses. Successful counselors understand the nature of LD and help clients focus on strengths and resources to achieve realistic goals. Finally, the promotion of positive career development in all individuals, especially those with LD, can be best achieved when counselors and programs work to foster self-knowledge and self-esteem, clearly defined personal goals, internal locus of control, and strong persistence to achieve.

REFERENCES

Adelman, P. B., & Vogel, S. A. (1990). College graduates with learning disabilities – Employment attainment and career patterns. *Learning Disability Quarterly, 13*, 154–163.

Adelman, P. B., & Vogel, S. A. (1993). Issues in the employment of adults with learning disabilities. *Learning Disability Quarterly, 16*, 219–232.

Altschul, P., & Michaels, C. A. (1994). Access to employment: Building career opportunities for college and graduate students with disabilities. *Journal of Career Planning and Employment, 55*, 50–54.

Bender, W. N. (2004). *Learning disabilities: Characteristics, identification, and teaching strategies.* Boston: Allyn & Bacon.

Benz, M. R., Lindstrum, L., & Youanoff, P. (2000). Improving graduation and employment outcomes of students with disabilities. *Exceptional Children, 66*, 509–529.

Biller, E. F., & Horn, E. E. (1991). A career guidance model for adolescents with learning disabilities. *School Counselor, 38*, 279–286.

Blackorby, J., & Wagner, M. (1997). The employment outcomes of youth with learning disabilities: A review of findings from NLTS. In: P. J. Gerber & D. S. Brown (Eds), *Learning Disabilities and Employment* (pp. 57–74). Austin, TX: Pro-Ed.

Blalock, J. W. (1981). Persistent problems and concerns of young adults with learning disabilities. In: W. Cruickshank & A. Silver (Eds), *Bridges to Tomorrow: The Best of ACLD* (Vol. 2). Syracuse, NY: Syracuse University Press.

Conger, S. D. (1997). Guidance for students with disabilities. *Guidance and Counseling, 12*, 13–19.

Dalke, C., & Schmitt, S. (1987). Meeting the transition needs of college-bound students with learning disabilities. *Journal of Learning Disabilities, 20*, 176–180.

Dickinson, D. L., & Verbeek, R. L. (2002). Wage differences between college graduation with and without learning disabilities. *Journal of Learning Disabilities, 35*, 175–184.

Dowdy, C. A., Carter, J. K., & Smith, T. E. (1990). Differences in transitional needs of high school students with and without learning disabilities. *Journal of Learning Disabilities, 23*, 343–348.

Fourqurean, J. M., Meisgeier, C., Swank, P. R., & Williams, R. E. (1991). Correlates of postsecondary employment outcomes for young adults with learning disabilities. *Journal of Learning Disabilities, 24*, 400–405.

Friehe, M., Aune, B., & Leuenberger, J. (1996). Career service needs of college students with disabilities. *The Career Development Quarterly, 44*, 289–300.

Gerber, P. J. (1997). Life after school: Challenges in the workplace. In: P. J. Gerber & D. S. Brown (Eds), *Learning Disabilities and Employment* (pp. 3–18). Austin, TX: Pro-Ed.

Gerber, P. J., Ginsberg, R., & Reiff, H. B. (1992). Identifying alterable patterns in employment success for highly successful adults with learning disabilities. *Journal of Learning Disabilities, 8*, 475–487.

Ginsberg, R., Gerber, P. J., & Reiff, H. B. (1994). Employment success for adults with learning disabilities. In: P. J. Gerber & H. B. Reiff (Eds), *Learning Disabilities in Adulthood* (pp. 204–213). Stoneham, MA: Butterworth-Heinemann.

Hallahan, D. P., & Kauffman, J. M. (2000). *Exceptional learners: Introduction to special education* (8th ed.). Boston: Allyn & Bacon.

Haring, K. A., Lovett, D. L., & Smith, D. D. (1990). A follow-up study of recent special education graduates of learning disabilities programs. *Journal of Learning Disabilities, 23*, 108–113.

Herr, E. L., & Cramer, S. H. (1996). *Career guidance through the life span.* Boston: Little, Brown.

Hershenson, D. B. (1984). Vocational counseling with LD adults. *Journal of Rehabilitation, 50*, 40–44.

Hitchings, W., & Retish, P. (2000). Career development needs of students with learning disabilities. In: D. A. Luzzo (Ed.), *Career Counseling of College Students* (pp. 217–231). Washington, DC: American Psychological Association.

Hughes, C. A., & Smith, J. O. (1990). Cognitive and academic performance of college students with learning disabilities: A synthesis of the literature. *Learning Disability Quarterly, 13*, 66–79.

Hutchinson, N. L., & Freeman, J. G. (1994). *Pathways.* Toronto, ON: Nelson

Hutchinson, N. L., Freeman, J. G., & Fisher, C. (1993). A two-year cohort study: Career development for youth with learning disabilities. Paper presented at the annual meeting of the American Educational Research Association, Atlanta, GA.

Janiga, S. J., & Costenbader, V. (2002). The transition from high school to postsecondary education for students with learning disabilities: A survey of college service coordinators. *Journal of Learning Disabilities, 35*(5), 462–468.

Johnson, D. R., Stodden, R. A., Emanuel, E. J., Luecking, R., & Mack, M. (2002). Current challenges facing secondary educational and transition services: What research tells us. *Exceptional Children, 68*, 519–553.

Kerka, S. (2002). *Learning disabilities and career development.* ERIC, Practice Application Brief, Nov. 20.

Kling, B. (2001). Assert yourself: Helping students of all ages to develop self-advocacy skills. *Teaching Exceptional Children, 32*, 66–70.

Korterling, L., & Braziel, P. (2000). A look at the expressed career ambitions of youth with learning disabilities. *Journal for Vocational Special Needs Education, 23*, 31–38.

Lehmann, J. P., Davies, T. G., & Lourin, K. M. (2000). Listening to students voices about postsecondary education. *Teaching Exceptional Children, 32*, 60–65.

Levinson, E. M., & Ohler, D. L. (1998). Transition from high school to college for students with learning disabilities: Needs, assessment, and services. *High School Journal, 82*(1), 62.

Lindstrom, L., & Benz, M. R. (2002). Phases of career development: Case studies of young woman with learning disabilities. *Exceptional Children, 68*, 67–83.

Lock, R. W., & Layton, C. A. (2001). Succeeding in postsecondary education through self-advocacy. *Teaching Exceptional Children, 34*, 66–71.

Madans, J. W., Foley, T. E., McGuire, J. M., & Ruban, L. M. (2002). Employment self-disclosure of postsecondary graduates with learning disabilities: Rates and rationales. *Journal of Learning Disabilities, 35*, 364–369.

Mathews, R. M., Whang, R. L., & Fawcett, S. B. (1982). Behavioral assessment of occupational skills of learning disabled adolescents. *Journal of Learning Disability, 15*(1), 38–41.

Michaels, C. A. (1997). Preparation for employment. In: P. J. Gerber & D. S. Brown (Eds), *Learning Disabilities and Employment* (pp. 187–212). Austin, TX: Pro-Ed.

Mull, C., Sitlington, P. L., & Alper, S. (2001). Postsecondary education for students with learning disabilities: A synthesis of the literature. *Exceptional Children, 68*, 97–118.

Murray, C., Goldstein, D. E., & Nourse, S. E. (2000). The postsecondary completion rates of students with learning disabilities. *Learning Disabilities Research and Practice, 15*, 119–127.

Ohler, D. L., Levinson, E. M., & Barker, W. F. (1995). Career maturity in young adults with learning disabilities: What employment counselors should know. *Journal of Employment Counseling, 32,* 64–78.

Ohler, D. L., Levinson, E. M., & Barker, W. F. (1996). Career maturity in college students with learning disabilities. *The Career Development Quarterly, 44,* 279–288.

Price, L. A., & Gerber, P. J. (2001). At second glance: Employers and employees with learning disabilities. *Journal of Learning Disabilities, 34,* 202–211.

Reiff, H. B., Gerber, P. J., & Ginsberg, R. (1998). *Exceeding expectations: Successful adults with learning disabilities.* Austin, TX: Pro-Ed.

Rojewski, J. W. (1993). Theoretical structure of career maturity for rural adolescents with learning disabilities. *Career Development for Exceptional Individuals, 16,* 39–52.

Rojewski, J. W. (1996). Educational and occupational aspirations of high school seniors with learning disabilities. *Exceptional Children, 62*(5), 463–476.

Rojewski, J. W. (1999). Occupational and educational aspirations and attainment of young adults with and without LD two years after high school completion. *Journal of Learning Disabilities, 32*(6), 533–540.

Rosenthal, I. (1985). A career development program for learning disabled college students. *Journal of Counseling and Development, 63,* 308–310.

Rosenthal, I. (1989). Model transition for disabled high school and college students. *Rehabilitation Counseling Bulletin, 33,* 54–66.

Ruhl, K. L., Hughes, C. A., & Gajar, A. H. (1990). Efficacy of the pause procedure for enhancing learning disabled and nondisabled college students' long- and short-term recall of facts presented through lecture. *Learning Disabilities Quarterly, 13,* 55–64.

Sattler, J. M. (2001). *Assessment of children* (4th ed.). San Diego, CA: Sattler.

Scanlon, D., & Mellard, D. F. (2002). Academic and participation profiles of school-age dropouts with and without disabilities. *Exceptional Children, 68,* 239–258.

Smith, J. O. (1992). Falling through the cracks: Rehabilitation services for adults with learning disabilities. *Exceptional Children, 58,* 451–460.

Super, D. E. (1969). *The development of the disabled: An overview.* New York, NY: University Press.

Super, D. E. (1983). Assessment in career guidance: Toward truly developmental counseling. *The Personnel and Guidance Journal, 61,* 555–561.

Super, D. E., & Thompson, A. S. (1979). A six-scale, two-factor measure of vocational maturity. *Vocational Guidance Quarterly, 27,* 6–15.

Thompson, A. R., & Dooley-Dickey, K. (1994). Self-perceived job search skills of college students with disabilities. *Rehabilitation Counseling Bulleting, 37,* 358–370.

Wagner, M., & Blackorby, J. (1996). Transition from high school to work or college: How special education students fare. *The Future of Children: Special Education for Students with Disabilities, 6,* 1–10.

Wagner, M., Blackorby, J., Cameto, R., & Newman, L. (1993). *What makes a difference? Influences on postschool outcomes of youth with disabilities. The Third Comprehensive Report from the National Longitudinal Transition Study of Special Education Students.* Menlo Park, CA: SRI International.

Wolinsky, S., & Whelan, A. (1999). Federal law and the accommodation of students with LD. *Journal of Learning Disabilities, 32,* 286–291.

Zunker, V. G. (2002). *Career counseling: Applied concepts of life planning* (6th ed.). Pacific Grove, CA: Brooks/Cole.

IMPACT OF THE AMERICANS WITH DISABILITIES ACT ON SERVICES FOR PERSONS WITH LEARNING DISABILITIES

Patrick A. Grant, Richael Barger-Anderson
and Patrice A. Fulcher

The 1990 passing of the Americans with Disabilities Act (ADA) (PL101-336) has impacted persons with learning disabilities. The ADA was prompted to challenge the private sector in responding to the needs of persons with disabilities. The ADA, however, has some strategic relevance for persons with learning disabilities. Understandably, it has impacted the workplace in measurable ways (Price & Gerber, 2001). Children and adults who have learning disabilities have benefited in relation to services and accommodations at all educational levels. Not surprisingly, self-identified problems still exists in the provision of services, especially with regard to equal access and program appropriateness. In this chapter, we address the impact of the ADA on services for persons with learning disabilities.

ADA: AN OVERVIEW

The ADA is a civil rights act that "applies to virtually every entity except churches and private clubs" (Smith, 2001, p. 336). It is legislation for persons with disabilities, and its primary purpose is to ensure reasonable accommodations

Current Perspectives on Learning Disabilities
Advances in Special Education, Volume 16, 183–191
© 2004 Published by Elsevier Ltd.
ISSN: 0270-4013/doi:10.1016/S0270-4013(04)16009-1

for persons with disabilities when accessing goods and services. The ADA is comprised of titles I through V:

• Title I addresses discrimination in places of employment;
• Title II addresses government agencies, which include public schools;
• Title III examines public accommodations;
• Title IV addresses telecommunication; and
• Title V addresses Miscellaneous Provisions (Hishinuma & Fremstad, 1997; Shea & Bauer, 1994; Smith, 2001; Yell, 1998).

Congress had reported, at the introduction of the ADA, that discrimination existed in the workplace, housing, public accommodations, education, transportation, communication, recreation, institutionalization, health services, voting and public services by 43 million Americans with disabilities. President George Bush signed the ADA into effect in 1990 with the hopes of diminishing exclusion and discrimination of persons with disabilities in both the private and public sectors (Yell, 1998). As it appears, many physical and health impairments are protected under this law. For instance the ADA protects persons with Acquired Immune Deficiency Syndrome (AIDS) and Human Immunodeficiency Virus (HIV) (Johns, 1990; Kenrick, 1990). Shea and Bauer (1994) indicated that ADA is patterned after Section 504 of the Rehabilitation Act of 1973, which guarantees the civil rights of individuals with disabilities for two decades.

Eligibility considerations based on the ADA must follow the following principles (Yell, 1998):

(1) Definition and the effects of impairment, physical or mental, on functional behavior that limits one or more major life activities.
(2) The impairment must be recorded.
(3) The person must be regarded as having the impairment.

A person with a disability is broadly defined by ADA as *someone* who has a physical or mental impairment (or has a record of such an impairment, or is regarded as having such an impairment) that substantially limits that person's participation in some major life activities (see Shea & Bauer, 1994). Major life activities include such functions as caring for one's self, walking, seeing, hearing, breathing, speaking, learning, working, and executing manual tasks (EEOC & U.S. Department of Justice, 1991 as cited in Hishinuma & Fremstad, 1997). In addition, for a person to be eligible, he/she must be regarded as otherwise qualified (Henderson, 2001). According to Smith (2001), otherwise qualified means that "a person with a disability must be qualified to do something before the presence of a disability can be a factor in discrimination" (p. 338). The ADA, along with Section 504 of the Rehabilitation Act confirm that to be eligible for services a person must be otherwise qualified. An example of otherwise qualified is displayed in the following scenario:

> *A teenager identified with a learning disability, tries out for a position to play the drums in the*
> *high school band. The teenager has never taken drum lessons and actually has never picked up*
> *a set of sticks until the day of try-outs. The teenager did not make the position of high school*
> *band drummer. Under the ADA, this is not considered discrimination. Why does the ADA not*
> *protect this teenager? The answer is simple. The teenager is not otherwise qualified to be a*
> *drummer for the high school band.*

THE ADA AND PERSONS WITH LEARNING DISABILITIES

The ADA provides its own definition of disability. The term is defined as:

> a physical or mental impairment that substantially limits one or more of the major life activities
> of such individual; a record of such an impairment; or being regarded as having such an
> impairment. The phrase physical or mental impairment means: (i) Any physiological disorder
> or condition, cosmetic disfiguration, or anatomical loss affecting one or more of the following
> body systems: neurological; musculoskeletal; special sense organs; respiratory, including
> speech organs; cardiovascular; reproductive; digestive; genitourinary; hemic and lymphatic;
> skin; and endocrine; and (ii) Any mental or psychological disorder such as mental retardation,
> organic brain syndrome, emotional or metal illness, and *specific learning disabilities*. . . . The
> phrase major life activities means functions such as caring for one's self, performing manual
> tasks, walking, seeing, hearing, speaking, breathing, learning, and working (EEOC & U.S.
> Department of Justice, 1991, pp. 16–18 as cited in Hishinuma & Fremstad, 1997).

Apparently, persons identified with specific learning disabilities are covered under the ADA (Hishinuma & Fremstad, 1997). Grant and Grant (2002) affirmed that learning disabilities have been viewed as a perplexing category of exceptionality. Learning disabilities are marked in persons by a discrepancy between intellectual ability and actual school achievement. There are many definitions for the term learning disability. In fact, lack of commonality for defining the term has been cited as the reason for a vast difference in agreement of prevalence (Kirk et al., 2003). As Stanovich (1989) stated, "the decision to base the definitions of a reading disability on a discrepancy with measured IQ is . . . nothing short of astounding. Certainly, one would be hard pressed to find a concept more controversial than intelligence in all psychology" (p. 487). Even though there is a lack of common definition for learning disability, it is agreed upon that students with learning disabilities comprise the largest proportion of students receiving special education services (Kirk et al., 2003). The Federal Register (1999) has established criteria and non-criteria for identification of students with a specific learning disability. The criteria include: (a) presence of academic difficulties; (b) perceptual disabilities;

(c) brain injury; (d) minimal brain dysfunction; (e) dyslexia; and (f) developmental aphasia. The non-criteria include: (a) academic problems due to visual, hearing, or motor disability; (b) mental retardation; (c) emotional disturbance; and (d) environmental, cultural, or economic disadvantage (Murdick et al., 2002).

As indicated, the number of students identified with learning disabilities has grown tremendously since the 1990 passing of the Individuals with Disabilities Education Act (IDEA). Between 1976 and 1977, the first year the federal government reported such data the number tripled (see Heward, 2003). Heward acknowledged that many educators are alarmed by the rising prevalence figures for learning disabilities. He believed the ever increasing numbers of students classified as learning disabled are the result of overrepresentation and misdiagnosis of low-achieving students, which reduces the resources available to serve students who are truly learning disabled. Earlier, Kerka (1998) noted that a possible reason for such high numbers of students being identified as learning disabled is from a misdiagnosis of minority students.

Higher education institutions have been affected by the great influx in the number of enrolled students identified with learning disabilities. Since the passage of the ADA, employers have made efforts to comply with the civil rights legislation in the workplace. However, employers have little knowledge and/or experience with ADA compliance when addressing persons with learning disabilities (Price & Gerber, 2001). The ADA applies to students with learning disabilities enrolled at a college or university. Out of the total number of entering freshmen students identified as having disability, more than 35% had a learning disability (Thomas, 2000). ADA is not as detailed with requirements mandated by law for the college level as with the case of elementary or secondary schools (Shaw et al., 2001). Enrollment in higher education continues to increase and the number of students with disabilities increases. Students with disabilities are becoming aware of their rights for accommodations while enrolled in a college or university (see Thomas, 2000). For a student to receive accommodations for being learning disabled, the student must self-identify his/her disability (Pacifici & McKinney, 1997; Treloar, 1999). This is in contrast to identification of learning disabilities in elementary and secondary schools (see Pacifici & McKinney, 1997).

Many higher institutions have made efforts to comply with the ADA. This is due to wide spread publicity of the civil rights law, recent lawsuits, and an increase in the number of students requesting accommodations. (See Fig. 1 for an account of one prominent lawsuit concerning students with learning disabilities.) A Student Disability Services office, located on campus, helps to accommodate students and provide assistance to professors for providing accommodations in the classroom (Thomas, 2000). According to Treloar (1999) many faculty and staff members lack understanding of the ADA in relation to how it applies to higher education.

Guckenbrger vs. Boston University

Guckenberger vs. Boston University is a lawsuit between Boston University and students with learning disabilities. It is possibly the most prominent case with the end result in favor of the students.

Background information: Boston University (BU) had a very distinguished record for providing accommodations to students with learning disabilities. In fact, many students with learning disabilities traveled a great distance to attend BU for this reason.

In 1995, then Provost Jon Westling openly spoke out about his belief of the existence of learning disabilities. He said people with a learning disability were less th an perfect. H e believed persons with a learning disability would rather ask for help than try to do their own work.

Mr. Jon Westling established new procedures for allowing objectionable accommodations for students with a learning disability and retesting procedures, paid for by the student (up to $1,000), if testing information was not current within the past 3 years of when the new policy came into effect. Also, the Learning Disabilities Student Services office was staffed with unqualified persons.

Lawsuit filed: Students filed a lawsuit against BU. BU would not agree to meet with the students prior to the court date. The court decided that Mr. Westling and his staff had biases against persons with learning disabilities. A waiver was now accepted in place of the retesting procedures and accommodations were reconsidered as being fair, such as course substitutions in the area of foreign languages.

Fig. 1. Guckenberger v. Boston University Case. *Source:* Wolinsky and Whelan (1999). *Journal of Learning Disabilities, 32*(4), 286–296.

Every accommodation that has been requested has not been granted, and some requests have been deemed unreasonable (see Thomas, 2000). It is interestingly becoming apparent that there are some professors who regard the admittance of students of with learning disabilities as unacceptable at the college or university level (see Thompson & Bethea, 1997). They regard accommodations as an extra burden on them as well as an unfair advantage to the non-disabled students. Zuriff (2002), a professor at Wheaton College challenged the differentiation between children who are diagnosed as learning disabled and those who are found to be slow learners, asserting that all children struggling in school deserve assistance. He questioned the tests and assessment strategies that are used to determine the diagnosis of learning disability holding that it is based on false comparisons to individuals with brain damage.

Recently a shift has occurred that emphasizes pedagogy in higher education. This is viewed as having a positive impact on students with learning disabilities at the college level (Shaw et al., 2001). The only pedagogical model that has proven successful at a college level is the University Design for Instruction (UDI). The UDI model is a "systematic method of meeting the needs of diverse learners" (see Shaw et al., 2001, p. 2).

The UDI promotes academics for all students through an emphasis on specific techniques and strategies. When UDI is incorporated, students with learning disabilities receive instructional techniques and methodology that have been proven successful. The following are principles of UDI:

(1) *Equitable use* – Instruction is designed to be useful to and accessible by people with diverse abilities. It provides the same means of use for all students, identical whenever possible, equivalent when not.

(2) *Flexibility in use* – Instruction is designed to accommodate a wide range of individual abilities. It provides choice in methods of use.

(3) *Simple and intuitive instruction* – Instruction is designed in a straightforward and predictable manner, regardless of the student's experience, knowledge language skills, or current concentration level. It eliminates unnecessary complexity.

(4) *Perceptible information* – Instruction is designed so that necessary information is communicated effectively, regardless of ambient conditions or the student's sensory abilities.

(5) *Tolerance for error* – Instruction anticipates variation in individual student learning pace and requisite skills.

(6) *Low physical effort* – Instruction is designed to minimize nonessential physical effort in order to allow maximum attention to learning. [Note: This principle does not apply when physical effort is integral to essential requirements of a course.]

(7) *Size and space for approach and use* – Instruction is designed with consideration for appropriate size and space for approach, reach, manipulations, and use regardless of a student's body size, posture, mobility, and communication needs.

(8) *A community of learners* – Instructional environment promotes interaction and communication among students and between students and faculty.

(9) *Instructional climate* – Instruction is designed to be welcoming and inclusive. High expectations are espoused for all a students.

Community colleges have the highest enrollment of students with disabilities of all higher education institutions. Two accommodations suggested for use on college campuses include creating a receptive environment by the professor in the classroom and using person-sensitive language. These promote respect for individuals and place person before their disabilities (Treloar, 1999). For most people, the reason that they go to college is to find employment in an area of interest after graduation. Even if a student does not further his/her education by going to college, entering the workforce in a respectable position is desired. Employment in the workforce for persons with a learning disability will be examined next.

EMPLOYABILITY PROVISION OF THE ADA

Attention has been frequently drawn toward adults with learning disabilities. Challenges for adults with learning disabilities include education, employment, daily activities, and social aspects. While the emphasis has been with school-aged children, increased awareness of the laws has stimulated programmatic advancements for adults with learning disabilities. Kerka (1998) indicated that "most people do not outgrow learning disabilities" (p. 2). The ADA of 1990 has been in existence for 13 years. The workplace, as required by the ADA, is to provide equal employment opportunities. Price and Gerber (2001) conducted a study that examined employers in relation to the ADA. They found that employers realized that workers with learning disabilities needed jobs but the bottom line is profit.

Clearly, workers with learning disabilities have the right to maximize their fullest potential. As a result they must remain competitive with colleagues. Employees with learning disabilities are susceptible layoffs, especially during downsizing periods. Price and Gerber (2001) found that employers have some interesting beliefs about persons with learning disabilities. They found that employers made: (a) an effort to comply with the ADA; (b) viewed ADA compliance as only physical access to the facilities; (c) thought learning disabilities are a hidden disability; and (d) lacked general of knowledge on how to accommodate needs of employees with learning disabilities. They added that community partnerships are one way to help people with learning disabilities find a job in the workforce. Lastly, Price and Gerber stressed that it is important for employers to fully understand what compliance with the ADA means and that it is much more than just physical accessibility.

PERSPECTIVES

In this chapter, we addressed the impact of the ADA on persons with learning disabilities. Clearly, the purpose of the ADA has been to stop discrimination toward persons with disabilities. Discrimination protection is available in the workplace, public services, and accommodations (Henderson, 2001). When the ADA is combined with other civil rights acts, societal reform is possible. The ADA promotes "empowerment, independence, and full participation of persons with disabilities in American society" including the increasing populations of persons from racial and ethnic minority populations (Middleton et al., 1999, p. 112). The United States needs more efforts to advance the future of persons with learning disabilities. To advance to this new level, there must be available funding, sufficient training and adequate understanding of disabilities (Pacifici & McKinney, 1997). Our future goal should be for equal treatment, not preferential treatment of persons with disabilities (Treloar, 1999).

REFERENCES

Federal Register (1999, March 12). *Rules and regulations §300.7, V64 No. 48: Child with a disability* (pp. 12422). Retrieved February 21, 2003, from http://www.ieadpractices.org/law/downloads/fullregs.pfd.

Grant, P. A., & Grant, P. B. (2002). Working with African American students with specific learning disabilities. In: F. E. Obiakor & B. A. Ford (Eds), *Creating Successful Learning Environments for African American Learners with Exceptionalities* (pp. 67–77). Thousand Oaks, CA: Corwin Press.

Henderson, K. (2001). *Overview of ADA, IDEA, and section 504: Update 2001* (Report No. EDO-EC-01-1). Arlington, VA: Council for Exceptional Children. (ERIC Document Reproduction Service No. ED 452 627.)

Heward, W. L. (2003). *Exceptional children: An introduction to special education* (7th ed.). Upper Saddle River, NJ: Merrill/Prentice-Hall.

Hishinuma, E. S., & Fremstad, J. S. (1997). NCAA college freshman academic requirements: Academic standards or unfair roadblocks for students. *Journal of Learning Disabilities, 30*, 589–607.

Johns, B. (1990). Federal update. *ICEC Quarterly, 39*, 23–29.

Kenrick, D. (1990, July 27). Disabled cheer as Bush signs landmark bill. *Cincinnati Enquirer* (pp. A1 & A16).

Kerka, S. (1998). *Adults with learning disabilities* (Report No. EDO-CE-98-189). Washington, DC: Office of Educational Research and Improvement. (ERIC Document Reproduction Service No. 414 434.)

Kirk, S. A., Gallagher, J. J., & Anastasiow, N. J. (2003). *Educating exceptional children* (10th ed.). Boston: Houghton Mifflin.

Middleton, R. A., Rollins, C. W., & Harley, D. A. (1999). The historical and political context of the civil rights of persons with disabilities: A multicultural perspective for counselors. *Journal of Multicultural Counseling & Development, 27*, 105–119.

Murdick, N., Gartin, B., & Crabtree, T. (2002). *Special education law*. Upper Saddle, NJ: Pearson Education.

Pacifici, T., & McKinney, K. (1997). *Disability support services for community college students* (Report No. EDO-JC-7-08). Los Angeles, CA: ERIC Clearinghouse for Community Colleges. (ERIC Document Reproduction Service No. ED409 972.)

Price, L. A., & Gerber, P. J. (2001). At second glance: Employers and employees with learning disabilities in the Americans with Disabilities Act era. *Journal of Learning Disabilities, 34*, 202–220.

Shaw, S. F., Scott, S. S., & McGuire, J. M. (2001). *Teaching college students with learning disabilities* (Report No. EDO-EC-01-13). Arlington, VA: Council for Exceptional Children. (ERIC Document Reproduction Service No. ED459 548.)

Shea, T. M., & Bauer, A. M. (1994). *Learners with disabilities: A social perspective of special education*. Dubuque, IA: WCB-Brown & Benchmark Publishers.

Smith, T. E. C. (2001). Section 504, the ADA, and public schools. *Remedial & Special Education, 22*, 335–351.

Stanovich, K. E. (1989). Has the learning disabled field lost its intelligence? *Journal of Learning Disabilities, 22*, 448–492.

Thomas, S. B. (2000). College students and disability law. *Journal of Special Education, 33*, 248–266.

Thompson, A. R., & Bethea, L. (1997). Faculty knowledge of disability laws in higher education: A survey. *Rehabilitation Counseling Bulletin, 40*, 166–181.

Treloar, L. L. (1999). Editor's choice: Lessons on disability and the rights of students. *Community College Review, 27*, 30–39.

Wolinsky, S., & Whelan, A. (1999). Federal law and the accommodation of students with LD: The lawyer's look at the BU decision. *Journal of Learning Disabilities, 32*, 286–296.

Yell, M. L. (1998). *The law and special education.* Upper Saddle, NJ: Prentice-Hall.

Zuriff, G. E. (2002). Are learning disabilities a myth? In: M. A. Byrnes (Ed.), *Taking Sides: Clashing Views on Controversial Issues in Special Education* (pp. 276–284). Guilford, CT: McGraw-Hill/Dushkin.

THE IMPACT OF THE NO CHILD LEFT BEHIND ACT

Candace Baker and Beverly Gulley

National trends in education influence practices at the local level in terms of both general and special education. This chapter provides an overview of the recently adopted No Child Left Behind Act, with discussion of the impact of the law and some possible implications for students with disabilities, including learning disabilities.

In January 2002 President George W. Bush signed into law the No Child Left Behind Act (NCLBA). The two major purposes of the Act are to raise student achievement across the board and eliminate the achievement gap between students from different backgrounds. The law requires that states and school districts seriously address schools that are failing and ensure that all students have highly qualified teachers (Center for Education Policy, 2003).

FEDERAL INITIATIVES IN EDUCATION

Somewhat parallel to the NCLBA is the Elementary and Secondary Education Act (ESEA) signed into law by President Lyndon Johnson in 1965. It was intended to provide schools with additional resources and help poor children climb out of poverty by providing them with a better education. Debate about how much ESEA improved the schools persists, but the weight of the evidence seems to suggest that its impact on student learning was modest. Critics suggest that ESEA provided money without accountability. Similarly, critics of NCLBA claim that the law

Current Perspectives on Learning Disabilities
Advances in Special Education, Volume 16, 193–206
Copyright © 2004 by Elsevier Ltd.
All rights of reproduction in any form reserved
ISSN: 0270-4013/doi:10.1016/S0270-4013(04)16010-8

requires strict accountability without adequate resources (Center on Educational Policy, 2003).

The impetus behind NCLBA is the perceived need of many schools to provide an adequate education for students. It is estimated that some four million children attend over 8,000 public schools that are not educating students to meet state academic standards. Fewer than half of pupils pass state tests and, in some cases, less than one-third do so. In some schools, failure has become the norm rather than the exception (Brady, 2003).

The focus of NCLB is on low-performing schools that serve a largely low-income student body. A report issued by the United States Department of Education (1998) addressed low-performing schools as linked to schools in "impoverished communities, where family distress, crime, and violence are prevalent." Aggregate data on student performance supports this assertion, demonstrating that fewer that half the nation's low-income students meet the minimum standard on the National Assessment of Education Progress (NAEP) test in Mathematics, while 43% of twelfth graders do not meet the minimum criteria in Reading. Education reformists and commissions have long called attention to the declining number of high performing schools and the implications for society (Goodlad, 1984; Holmes Group, 1986; National Commission on Excellence in Teaching, 1983; Patriarca & Cegelka, 1992).

ELEMENTS FOR SUCCESSFUL EDUCATION

Not all schools in low-income communities are low performing. Edmonds (1979), an expert on high-performing, high-poverty schools, identified characteristics of effective schools: strong administrative leadership, high expectations for students; orderly and quiet, though not rigid, environment; clear focus on academics; readiness to divert energy and resources to academics; and, frequent monitoring of student progress. Carter (2000) identified seven common traits of successful schools: principals who are free to use resources to run the school; principals who use measurable goals to establish a culture of achievement; master teachers; rigorous and regular testing; achievement as key to discipline; principals who work with parents; and, hard work by faculty and students.

Because some schools in low-income communities have been effective schools, the rationale behind NCLBA is that schools can transform themselves from failure to success. NCLBA assumes that all schools can succeed, that some elements for success are lacking, and that interventions can provide what schools lack. It assumes that all schools can educate all students to high standards, that they have resources and skills to make this transition, and that they have the will to take the steps necessary for success to occur (Brady, 2003).

NCLBA's ELEMENTS FOR SUCCESS

According to Hunter and Bartee (2003) and Rajala (2003), NCLBA is based on four principles designed to increase educational outcomes for schools. The first principle is *accountability*. NCLBA stresses strong accountability for results by requiring all states to set high standards of achievement and create a system of accountability to measure results, especially in reading and math. Each state is required to develop a plan and a definition of proficiency for determining whether schools are making adequate progress in raising student achievement. The second principle is *local control*. NCLBA provides for greater flexibility and local control by cutting federal red tape, reducing the number of federal education programs, and creating larger, more flexible programs that place decision-making at the local level. It provides for school choice and supplemental education services to students in schools that are identified as needing improvement under the terms of the prior law.

The third principle is *highly qualified teachers*. The NCLBA requires all teachers of core academic subjects to be "highly qualified" and also raises the minimum qualifications of paraprofessionals in title I schools. NCLBA also strengthens teacher quality by investing in training and retention of high-quality teachers. The last principle is *research based education practices*. Schools are required to use scientifically based research to inform classroom practices that ensure that every child in public schools reads at or above grade level by third grade.

STEPS TO COMPLIANCE WITH THE NCLBA

Brady (2003) cites seven steps that states are required to follow in complying with the NCLBA.

Step 1 requires that states develop and submit a consolidated state application regarding performance of schools. Graduation rates of all high schools are to be monitored and at least one indicator of elementary school performance must be reported, showing gains on specific measures from year one to year twelve. There are five performance indicators:

(1) By 2013–2014, all students will reach high standards, at a minimum attaining *proficiency* or better in reading/language and mathematics.
(2) All limited English proficient student will become proficient in English and reach high academic standards, at a minimum attaining *proficiency* or better in reading/language arts and mathematics.
(3) By 2005–2006, all students will be taught by *highly qualified* teachers.

(4) All students will be educated in learning environments that are safe, drug free, and conducive to learning.
(5) All students will graduate from high school.

Step 2 requires that states identify for improvement those Title I schools that fail for two consecutive years to make Adequate Yearly Progress (AYP) as the state defines it. Initially, decisions are based on scores on mathematics and reading tests administered at the elementary, middle and high school levels. In 2005, testing is expanded through grades three through eight. In 2007, science is added to the subjects that are tested.

Step 3 requires that schools develop their own improvement plans based on consultation with parents, school and district staff, and outside experts. It also requires that local school districts provide technical assistance to low-performing schools and the option for students in failing schools to transfer to another public school within the school district.

Step 4 requires schools failing to make AYP to offer students the opportunity to obtain extra tutoring from parent-selected and state-approved providers.

Step 5 provides for states to take corrective action to secure desired performance improvement by replacing staff, instituting a new curriculum, significantly decreasing management authority at the school, appointing an outside expert to advise the school, extending the school day or year, or restructuring the school's internal organization.

Step 6 requires school districts failing to meet AYP after a year of corrective action to create plans to restructure schools that include the following options: reopening the school as a charter school; replacing all or most of the staff; out-sourcing operations; turning the school over to the state department of education; or selecting more major restructured school governance models.

Step 7 involves implementing the planned restructuring developed in Step 6 prior to the beginning of the new academic year.

CONCERNS REGARDING NCLBA

Requirements of NCLBA have raised a number of concerns about assessment and accountability by educators. First, many schools may be labeled as in need of improvement, including many that are not really failing. Second, since the rigor of states' content standards, tests, and performance standards vary greatly, states may not be starting on a level playing field, yet the consequences associated with demonstrating AYP are serious. Third, NCLBA allows states to set their own proficiency levels and, thus, unintentionally may provide incentive to lower performance standards. Fourth, NCLBA provides that every school and subgroup be measured from the same starting point, thus permitting some schools and groups the authority not to improve at all.

Additional concerns about testing and accountability are evident. States already have been devising testing and accountability systems that may have to be changed to comply with requirements of the new law; thus, progress and positive movement may be impeded. Secondly, NCLBA requires that states set twelve-year targets for AYP, yet most states are adding new tests or changing existing ones to address changing curriculum and instruction. Requiring twelve-year targets can discourage states from updating and making assessments more rigorous because changes might require resetting AYP targets. NCLBA requires that states quickly analyze and report test data introducing an increased probability of errors. Also, the costs associated with NCLBA extend beyond developing and implementing assessments. There is a need to strengthen testing expertise and capacity as well as establish the capacity for disaggregating and reporting data for indicators, such as graduation and attendance. Finally, technical issues are also evident in so far as school tests are volatile; rural and homogenous schools and districts will not be held accountable for subgroup performance; and, the greater the number of subgroups a school must report, the greater the likelihood that at least one subgroup will be identified as needing improvement.

NCLBA allows for public school choice and supplemental education services, thereby presenting some interesting challenges to schools and districts. Many districts, especially large urban ones, are already experiencing capacity and class size limits. Rural and remotely located districts find it difficult to offer school choice options since there may only be one school or classroom per grade in the district. The law does not guarantee that parents may choose to exercise the right of school choice based on reasons that are different from the intent of the law.

NCLBA uses state certifications and licensures systems as the cornerstone for the definition of highly qualified teacher. Yet, states vary significantly in requirements for certification and licensure. Some states have low cut-off scores, less than rigorous exams, or no exams at all. This will make state standards less useful as a uniform measure of teacher qualifications. In addition, new requirements could make it more difficult to recruit and retain qualified teachers or paraprofessionals, especially for school districts that already struggle with finding and retaining teachers. New certification requirements could discourage prospective teachers from entering the field and drive veteran teachers out of the field. Finding qualified paraprofessionals could prove challenging, since pay is low and the pool of candidates with the required, two-year college degree may be limited.

Finally, NCLBA requires educators to use programs and practices that are based upon the application of rigorous, systematic, and objective, scientific research procedures to obtain reliable and valid knowledge relevant to educational activities and programs. According to Public Law 107–110, NCLBA includes research that uses: (a) systematic, empirical methods; (b) rigorous data analyses; (c) measurements or observational methods that provide reliable and valid data across evaluators and observers, multiple measurements and observations, and replication studies; (d) evaluations that employ experimental or quasi-experimental designs; (e) sufficient detailed and clear reports that permit replication; and (f) peer-review that undergoes rigorous, objective and scientific analysis. Such research may be difficult to obtain and implement.

Because scientifically based research can be interpreted too narrowly and thus limit classroom teaching methods and materials, some states are concerned that the definition is so precise that only a few education programs will meet the criteria for scientifically based research. The Coalition for Evidence Based Policy (2002) has promoted building the knowledge based on effectiveness of educational interventions trough randomized controlled trials.

The success or failure of NCLBA remains to be seen, but in the interim, states are struggling to adhere to its strict requirements. How the law views and treats students with disabilities and the implications of NCLBA for students with disabilities is addressed in the next section.

IMPLICATIONS OF THE NCLBA
FOR STUDENTS WITH DISABILITIES

When considering what NCLBA means for students with disabilities, including learning disabilities, the answer could be "everything" and "nothing." In terms of "nothing," if educators or parents are looking for NCLBA to impact *learning disabilities* as a distinct category, the act states nothing. NCLBA only speaks of students with disabilities as a subgroup to be compared to students without disabilities. There is no part of the law that is applicable to only one group of students. In fact, the law repeatedly states "all students" or "all children."

NCLBA: POSSIBLE MINIMAL IMPACT
ON STUDENTS WITH DISABILITIES

It is assumed that children with disabilities addressed by NCLBA are those children so defined by the Individuals with Disabilities Education Act (IDEA). In the broad picture, students with learning disabilities are treated the same as students with any category of disability who receive services through the IDEA.

Section 602 (3) of IDEA (1990) defines a child with a disability as "a child with mental retardation, hearing impairments and deafness, speech and language impaired, visual impairments and blindness, emotional disturbance, orthopedic impairments, autism, traumatic brain injury, other health impairments, or specific learning disabilities who by reason thereof, needs special education and related services."

Whether a student has a sensory impairment, mental retardation, or a learning disability that requires special education, NCLBA views the student as within the aggregate of "students with a disability." The definition of a student with a disability incorporates the need for specialized instruction within eligibility for IDEA services. It might be preferable for NCLBA to specifically state "a student with an Individualized Education Plan (IEP)." The differentiation of a student with an IEP from a student with a disability has meaning when schools report academic progress for the various subgroups required by NCLBA. Thus, a student with a physical challenge who does not require special education services might be considered a student with a disability, but would not be a student with an IEP. Since NCLBA is aimed at evaluating student progress in response to instruction, it may be important for schools to be able to accurately identify and report which students with disabilities benefited solely from the improved general education curriculum and which continue to need the support of special education as delineated by an IEP. If reported test data showed that students with disabilities were adequately served by an improved general education curriculum and teaching practices, it is logical to conclude that the need for special education, in general, and IEPs, in particular, might be reduced.

NCLBA: POSSIBLE SIGNIFICANT IMPACT FOR STUDENTS WITH DISABILITIES

Having speculated that NCLBA could mean little to students with disabilities, an alternate possibility is that NCLBA may have a significant impact on the education of students with disabilities. The next section discusses how the main pillars of NCLBA impact students with disabilities.

Accountability for Results

The first reference in NCLBA to special education directs states to develop their plans in coordination with other federal acts including the IDEA. In other words, rather than perpetuating two bureaucracies, one devoted to general education and one devoted to special education, efforts should be directed to one system being responsive to *all* students within that system. Under this system, it is clear that students with IEPs are considered general education students first, and that there is one accountability system for all students.

Students with IEPs are expected to achieve the same content standards at the same level of proficiency on the same assessments as students without IEPs. The NCLBA requires State Plans to demonstrate challenging academic content standards that are applied to all schools and children in the state. Again, NCLBA is very clear that "all schools" and "all children" means every student within the state.

Not only does the law address content standards, but also achievement standards. The achievement standards are stated in terms of three levels; basic, proficient, and advanced. When describing the basic level, NCLBA directs states to provide information about the progress of lower-achieving students toward the proficient and advanced levels. The implications of content standards with achievement levels being applied to all students should result in greater access to the general education curriculum for students with IEPs. Students with disabilities will be expected to achieve IEP goals and NCLBA goals aimed at content and proficiency.

States are expected to use valid and reliable assessments that are aligned with content standards and consistently administered to all students. Students with IEPs will receive reasonable accommodations on the state assessments as outlined on their IEP (Rawson, 2003). This is the point where the NCLBA *does* distinguish among students. Students with significant cognitive disabilities will use alternate assessments. (There are guidelines for which students receive alternate assessments, and those assessments are still to be aligned with content standards.) Again, when schools include students with IEPs in the same assessments as students without IEPs, it should result in greater access for students with disabilities to the general education curriculum (Council for Exceptional Children, 2003).

After addressing content standards with accompanying assessments and achievement levels, the states are expected to demonstrate an accountability system to measure AYP toward the levels of proficient and advanced. It is under the umbrella of AYP where there are many unresolved issues concerning students with IEPs. AYP is not only reported as a statewide average, but also disaggregated into averages for subgroups. The subgroupings are: gender, racial/ethnic background, migrant status, disability, low-income and limited English proficiency. If any of the subgroups do not show achievement at the proficient level, the schools will be held accountable. However, as long as the school can demonstrate that the subgroup is decreasing the number of students scoring at the basic level by 10% per year, then AYP is demonstrated.

The AYP attribute of NCLBA constitutes a more stringent system of accountability for students with IEPs than does the IDEA. IDEA holds schools accountable to deliver the services as stated on the IEP, and to state how progress is reported. The legislation and ensuing litigation of IDEA never held schools accountable for whether the students made progress. Therefore, with the IDEA requiring that services be delivered to a student and NCLBA requiring the district to show AYP for its students with IEPs, students with disabilities should receive more appropriate educations than previously delivered by schools. Requiring schools to educate students with IEPs to the proficient level may give greater clarification in determining an appropriate education under IDEA. Because Free Appropriate Public Education (FAPE) is not clearly defined in IDEA, it is one of the most litigated principles of the legislation (Murdick et al., 2002). After 25 years of court rulings in response to litigation under the IDEA, the courts have slowly ruled on a few things that FAPE is not. Perhaps now with the NCLBA requirement of AYP toward proficient levels of academic performance, the courts can finally define what FAPE is.

The NCLBA requires that all families receive an annual report of their child's performance on the state assessments. The law states that these reports will be descriptive and diagnostic. The intent of the report is to show the child's progress and academic needs in terms that families understand. The current legislation may also intend to reduce IDEA paperwork. At the time of this writing, a bill, HR 1350, which eliminates significant changes to IDEA, passed the House. In an attempt to reduce the burden of paperwork of IDEA compliance, HR 1350 proposes that IEP's be reviewed every three years rather than every year as currently prescribed. It could be that the NCLBA requirement for annual assessment and reporting for every student will replace the annual review of the IEP. In essence, the NCLBA will produce an individualized approach to meeting the academic needs of every child and eliminate the perceived need to review the IEP on an annual basis. However, since NCLBA only requires assessment in reading/language arts, math, and science, students with IEP goals in other academic and nonacademic areas may not receive the broader appropriate education to which they were entitled under the IDEA.

Flexibility of Local Control

When considering the second pillar of the NCLBA, flexibility of local control, there appears to be little effect on students with IEPs. NCLBA allows schools the flexibility to designate funds into various categories. However, IDEA funds continue to be identified for special education. NCLBA funds can be used to supplement IDEA, but not to supplant state and local cost of special education.

Parental Choice

Schools that fail to demonstrate AYP will receive remediation in one of three categories: (1) in need of improvement; (2) corrective action; or (3) restructuring. When a school is placed in one of the categories, it must notify parents within that district of the designation. Then parents have a choice regarding whether to continue their child's education within that school or switch to another. An interesting question arises, however, in regard to students with IEPs. If a student with an IEP is in a school that fails to demonstrate AYP for students in general, or within the sub-group of students with IEPs, will that constitute a declaration of not providing "free appropriate public education?" If that is the case, the common remedy for not providing an IDEA identified student with FAPE is compensatory education at the schools expense. Traditionally, the prevailing compensatory education decisions have placed students in private schools.

Research-Based Teaching Methods

The fourth pillar of the NCLBA focuses resources on "what works." The NCLBA assumes that ineffective teaching practices are among the reasons for a student's lack of academic progress. Therefore, NCLBA requires that schools implement strategies that have been demonstrated through scientific research to be effective in achieving positive academic outcomes. Adopting research-based teaching methods could result in a change in the number of referrals to special education.

The focus for effective strategies at this time seems to be limited to reading. Since the preponderance of academic delay for students with IEPs is in reading, the focus on using effective teaching strategies in reading could yield a positive outcome for at-risk students to become proficient readers and thus eliminate the need for IDEA academic intervention services. NCLBA could lead to an increase in scientifically proven reading strategies, such as *Even Start, Early Reading First* and *Reading First* (National Association of State Directors of Special Education, 2002).

The National Association of State Directors of Special Education (2002) describe five essential components of reading instruction that must be identified in the state reading plan: Phonemic Awareness, Phonics, Vocabulary Development, Reading Fluency and Reading Comprehension. Schools will no longer be allowed to rely on a single method of reading instruction such as whole language or phonics. Schools will be required to use proven methods and strategies within the five areas that are effective based on research. With an emphasis on early intervention and proven strategies, perhaps fewer students will be in need of special education services. It is logical to make that hypothesis especially for students whose academic delay lies in reading/language arts.

Some students with learning disabilities have an academic delay in mathematics and not reading/language arts. NCLBA does not emphasize early intervention for math. Thus, students with a math learning disability may continue at the current prevalence rate. Evidence-based strategies for teaching math, however, do exist, and when such strategies are used with students with math learning disabilities, academic progress can occur (Xin & Jitendra, 1999). Schools that use these proven math strategies could lead to better outcomes for students with math learning disabilities.

Highly Qualified Teachers

States are required to ensure that highly qualified teachers instruct students. According to NCLBA, a highly qualified teacher is one who holds a bachelor's degree and passes a rigorous state test. NCLBA specifies that middle and high school teachers must hold a bachelor's degree in the core academic subject that they teach and elementary teachers must have training in math, reading, writing, and other areas of the basic elementary school curriculum. NCLBA specified these educational requirements based on the belief that high numbers of out-of-field teachers in poor, urban school contribute to low student achievement.

Christie (2003) views the requirement for schools to employ only highly qualified teachers as one of the most challenging requirements of the legislation. Also, establishing measurable objectives for meeting the *highly qualified* teacher requirement for all core subject teachers by 2003–2005 may be difficult. Additionally, establishing an annual measurable objective for increasing the percentage of teachers receiving high-quality professional development will need to be defined.

NCLBA labels teachers who provide supplemental services, work in charter school teachers, or obtained state certification via alternative teacher preparation programs as "highly qualified." At the same time, NCLBA labels as "not highly qualified" special education teachers who teach several subjects, but who are not "qualified" in each of the subjects. Also, the law also designates as "not highly qualified" those teachers who were certified as fifth- or sixth-grade teachers, but whose schools were then re-designated middle schools, or vice versa.

Several potential consequences of these designations exist. First, some teachers with little experience and training get to teach children in charter schools and schools partnering for alternative certification programs. This will undermine the actual purpose of NCLBA. Also, teachers who have already proven themselves to be highly qualified must prove again that they are qualified to teach. This requirement worsens the acute shortage of teachers, particularly in special education, as tens of thousands of National Education Association (NEA) members – many of whom have been teaching for years – will be affected.

IDEA articulates the definition of "highly qualified" for special education teachers. The current reauthorization of IDEA that is in the U.S. Senate defines the designation "highly qualified" in a much narrower sense than the original IDEA. Reauthorization of IDEA mirrors NCLBA in that the teacher must have a bachelor's degree and pass a rigorous test. However, if the teacher's caseload is as a consultant or collaborative teacher with a highly qualified teacher, or the teacher is teaching a core academic subject to middle or secondary students who are performing at an elementary level, the special education teacher must follow the requirements for an elementary school teacher in addition to the special education training requirements. If the teacher's caseload includes direct instruction of core academic subjects to middle or secondary students, the teacher must meet requirements for the core subjects being taught.

PRACTICAL IMPLICATIONS OF NCLBA

The implications of NCLBA requirements on special education teacher training are significant. Currently, special education teacher training programs focus on disability characteristics, special education legislation and litigation, assessment, and curriculum adaptation. Colleges and universities will need to redesign programs to focus on academic core subjects. A few programs with dual certification in elementary and special education exist. Because dual programs require a fifth year of education, students will have to pay additional tuition dollars to complete programs. Also, the fifth year delays students' entry into the workforce. Further, holders of dual certification receive similar compensation as other teachers trained in four-year programs. These aspects can be viewed as negative and increase the shortage of special education teachers that already exists.

A number of positive outcomes of NCLBA are possible. It could result in improved opportunities for students with IEPs. Since requirements for consultative teachers are more aligned with traditional special education teacher programs, more students with IEPs may have greater access to the general education curriculum in the general education environment. Currently, traditional special education teacher preparation programs graduate special education teachers that are considered to be highly qualified as consultative teachers. Consultation services include adapting curriculum materials for students with IEPs and working in collaboration with a general education teacher who is highly qualified. NCLBA could provide schools greater opportunities to use methods of inclusion rather than retrain special education teachers in core academic subjects.

The outcomes of NCLBA remain to be seen. However, at any rate, NCLBA creates a major force in education that will impact all students, including those with learning disabilities. On the one hand, the results of NCLBA can be quite positive for children with IEPs by improving educational practices in the general education classroom. At the same time, unintended consequences, such as a dearth of "highly qualified" teachers as defined by the new law, may prove detrimental. Positive outcomes reside in the details of the law and the practical implementation of various aspects contained in it.

REFERENCES

Brady, R. (2003). *Can schools be fixed?* Retrieved February 11, 2003, from http://www.edexcellence. net/library_schools/failingschools.html.

Carter, S. C. (2000). *No excuses: Lesson from 21 high-performing, high-poverty schools*. Washington, DC: Heritage Foundation.

Center for Education Policy (2003). *From the capital to the classroom*. Washington, DC: Author.

Christie, K. (2003). States ain't misbehavin' but the work is hard! *Phi Delta Kappa, 84*(8), 565–571.

Coalition for Evidence Based Policy (2002, November). *Bringing evidence-driven progress to education: A recommended strategy*. Washington, DC: U.S. Department of Education.

Council for Exceptional Children (2003). No Child Left Behind Act of 2001: Reauthorization of the Elementary and Secondary Education Act (A technical assistance resource). Arlington, VA: Author.

Edmonds, R. (1979). Effective schools for the urban poor. *Educational Leadership, 37*, 15–24.

Goodlad, J. I. (1984). *A place called school: Promise for the future*. New York: McGraw-Hill.

Hunter, R. C., & Bartee, R. S. (2003). The achievement gap: Issues of competition, class and race. *Education & Urban Society, 35*(2), 19–23.

Individuals with Disabilities Education Act, P.L. 101-476 (1990).

Murdick, N., Gartin, B., & Crabtree, T. (2002). *Special education law*. Upper Saddle River, NJ: Merrill Prentice-Hall.

National Association of State Directors of Special Education (2002, May). *Reading first programs: An overview*. Alexandria, VA: Author.

National Commission on Excellence in Education (1983). *A nation at risk: The imperative for educational reform*. Washington, DC: U.S. Government Printing Office: Author.

No Child Left Behind Act, P.L. 107-110 (2002).

Patriarca, L. A., & Cegelka, P. T. (1992). The school at the center of educational reform: Simplifications of school-based practices for research. In: T. D. Bunsm, D. Baumgart & L. A. Huany (Eds), *Forum on Emerging Trends in Specific Education* (pp. 80–99). Creely, CO: University of Northern Colorado.

Rajala, J. (2003). Education reform. *THE Journal, 30*(6), 3–8.

Rawson, M. J. (2003). *Special education law* (2nd ed.). Naples, FL: Morgen Publishing.

Tomorrow's teachers: A report of the Holmes Group (1986). East Lansing, MI: Holmes Group.

Turning around low-performing school: a guide for state and local leaders (May, 1998). Washington, DC: United States Department of Education.

Xin, Y., & Jitendra, A. (1999). The effects of instruction in solving mathematical word problems for students with learning problems: A meta-analysis. *The Journal of Special Education, 32*(4), 207–225.

TRENDS IN TEACHER PREPARATION FOR TEACHING STUDENTS WITH LEARNING DISABILITIES

Meg Carroll

INTRODUCTION

The current trends in teacher preparation for educators who will instruct students with learning disabilities reflect larger trends that are influencing teacher preparation in general. Some trends impact the ways in which educators and the public view aptitude and learning, such as the concept of multiple intelligences and the emerging discoveries of the workings of the brain. Some general trends include pre-service teacher testing and screening and specific standards for teacher training programs in efforts to increase educator accountability and classroom performance. Other trends emerge from philosophical and political positions regarding the rights of persons with disabilities to be educated in the least restrictive environment – the general education classroom.

In this vein, the general education classroom has become the preferred setting for the education of students with learning disabilities and other mild disabilities. In the inclusive setting of the general education program, students with disabilities join their peers without disabilities, studying the general education curriculum while receiving special education services through consultation, curriculum modification, resource and team-teaching. Similarly, special education teachers who instruct students with learning disabilities are increasingly expected to perform in the general education classroom in tandem with the general education

Current Perspectives on Learning Disabilities
Advances in Special Education, Volume 16, 207–227
Copyright © 2004 by Elsevier Ltd.
All rights of reproduction in any form reserved
ISSN: 0270-4013/doi:10.1016/S0270-4013(04)16011-X

teacher. Finally, the general education teacher is required to demonstrate a high level of proficiency in directly meeting the needs of children with disabilities within the general education placement as well as a willingness to embrace collaboration with special educators.

In most states and provinces, educational services provided to students with disabilities are called special education. This chapter identifies emergent trends in the preparation of teachers for special education service, including service to students with learning disabilities. Additionally, these trends are considered in terms of their impact upon special education professionals. Three major categories of trends are discussed in this chapter: pre-service preparation of special educators, the professional practice of special education and emerging theories that impact the understanding of learning disability.

Special Educator Preparation Trends

The training of special educators can be viewed as a shared responsibility in educator preparation programs (Garnett & Edelen-Smith, 2002; Gaynor & Little, 1997; Prater, 2002; Prater & Sileo, 2002; Sobel & French, 1998). Movements associated with the formal preparation of special educators include *teacher testing*, an increased emphasis on testing of teachers at various stages of pre- and in-service preparation in one or more areas of special education; *standards-based preparation*, a movement to make special education teacher preparation programs standards-based as opposed to coursework- or syllabus-based; *multicategorical training*, a movement in some states toward competency in multiple disabilities; *upgrading special education as a profession*, a concerted effort by the international professional association for special education to coordinate and increase professional practices for special education teachers; *alternative certification programs* and *professional development schools*, which reflect efforts to meet the national shortage of teachers for students with disabilities.

Special Education Practice Trends in the Schools

Trends affecting special educators in the schools include *improved working conditions*. Improving working conditions is an effort to respond to the national shortage of special educators and the relatively low retention of special educators in the field by providing supports for special educators. *Improving special education services in the general classroom* and *increased mentoring of novice special educators* reflect the trend of increased emphasis on preparing special educators for work with the general education curriculum and encouraging special educators to help students with disabilities participate in general education classes. Part of this trend is the preparation of special educators to support and collaborate with their general education colleagues as special education students spend more time in their neighborhood schools and in general education programming. *Increased mentoring* of novice special educators by experienced special education colleagues assists these teachers in the successful transition to teaching.

Advances in Understanding Learning Disabilities

Advances in theories and research that influence the conceptualization of learning disabilities include *the biological basis of learning disability*. This advance has lead to an increasing number of teacher preparation programs in learning disabilities including information from the growing body of knowledge about neurological function and its known or likely relationship with learning disabilities. A second development that is related to an understanding of learning in general involves the concept of *multiple intelligences*. Hearne and Stone (1995) have "found numerous pieces of evidence suggesting that the multiple intelligence perspective may be a more appropriate view of learning disabilities than the more static view based on a unitary construct of general intelligence" (p. 441). Others stress that its emphasis on the students' strengths may revolutionize academic intervention (Bender, 2002; Campbell, 1994; Gardner, 1993; Hearne & Stone, 1995).

PREPARATION TRENDS: INCREASED EMPHASIS ON TESTING OF TEACHERS

Testing teacher candidates before permitting them to gain licensure or full certification has been a relatively common practice in some states and regions. The city of Chicago, for instance, used the National Teachers' Exam as well as additional testing of its own, including a competency demonstration of piano playing for elementary teachers! Some states have hired consultant groups to construct tests for teacher candidates. Illinois uses tests created by the National Testing Service in New Jersey. Many states, however, employ the Praxis examinations. In fact, 38 states ranging from Alaska to Wisconsin, require some or all of the teachers in the state to qualify with particular Praxis scores or combination of scores (Praxis, 2003).

The Praxis is a set of assessments that has been constructed, statistically validated and reviewed by the Educational Testing Service. Educational institutions use Praxis test data to make decisions about candidates in teacher preparation programs and teacher retention. The Praxis Company offers three assessments. Praxis I is an academic skills assessment and is used by higher education institutions to make decisions about which candidates will be permitted to enter a teacher preparation program. Praxis II includes subject area assessments and is used by state education agencies to make licensing decisions as teacher candidates enter the profession. Praxis III is used during the first year of teaching and is made up of assessments of classroom performance. Praxis III is implemented by local assessors using nationally validated criteria. Individual districts or schools may use the results to make retention decisions and to determine what support novice teachers may need. Some states use Praxis III scores to make decisions about additional levels of certification or moving from provisional or novice status to a more permanent or formal certification (Praxis, 2003).

High stakes tests of teachers are a more common phenomenon in the field of learning disabilities than two decades ago. The accountability movement is most instrumental in bringing about the testing requirement. There is very little data, however, about the relationship between testing teacher candidates and classroom teaching performance, when the tests are paper-and-pencil only. At a cursory level, legislators and parents believe that testing requirements "weed out" persons who would be poor teachers. Testing may also be inadequate for measuring important features of teachers, such as patience and resourcefulness, that are not easy to assess and may be more critical than test performance to the success of learning for students with disabilities.

PREPARATION TRENDS: STANDARDS-BASED SPECIAL EDUCATION TEACHER PREPARATION PROGRAMS

"Currently, every state and province defines for itself who a special educator is and what criteria a professional must meet to be eligible to practice in their jurisdiction. There is more diversity in those criteria than in any other field of education" (Council for Exceptional Children Professional Standards, 2003, p. 1). In order to address these concerns, in 1989, the Council for Exceptional Children (CEC) delegate assembly adopted standards for entry into special education practice. Then CEC took several years to develop a listing of the essential knowledge and skills and published the listing in 1995. The National Council for the Accreditation of Teacher Education (NCATE) adopted and approved CEC's performance-based standards for the preparation and licensure of special educators (see Table 1). There are three categories of standards. The first is the Field Experiences and Clinical

Table 1.   CEC Special Education Content Standards.

Standard	Content
1	Foundations
2	Development and characteristics of learners
3	Individual learning differences
4	Instructional strategies
5	Learning environments and social interactions
6	Language
7	Instructional planning
8	Assessment
9	Professional and ethical practice
10	Collaboration

Practicum Standard. The second set is termed Assessment System Standards and the third is Special Education Content Standards. The number of standards for teacher candidates ranges from several to more than a dozen "indicators" of specific knowledge and performance skills. Teacher preparation faculty must assure that the teacher candidates possess these skills.

Matrices submitted by faculty to the Council for Exceptional Children (often state education agencies as well) for teacher preparation programs must designate in what course the knowledge or performance skill is demonstrated and what experience the faculty use to determine the knowledge or performance skill. For instance, a knowledge indicator required for teachers in the field of learning disabilities is strategies to prepare for and take tests. A faculty member does not have to observe the teacher candidate helping students perform but does need evidence that the teacher candidate knows strategies for helping students prepare for and take tests. A class experience during which this knowledge could be ascertained might be a take-home test in which teacher candidates are asked to list at least three ways to help students with learning disabilities prepare for classroom tests and list at least three ways to assist students in taking tests.

Teacher preparation programs seeking NCATE approval in special education must submit complete reports, called folios, to CEC for evaluation. These folios include the matrices that show each indicator, the course in which the indicator is assessed and what experience the faculty members use to assess that indicator of knowledge or skill. Folios also include supporting evidence and documentation. CEC reviewers use rubrics designed to review the evidence provided in a program report. Each element is determined to be unacceptable or acceptable, in light of a stated target of best practice. In a summary decision, the CEC reviewer makes a recommendation regarding the program's approval for national recognition (Council for Exceptional Children Professional Performance-based Standards, 2003).

PREPARATION TRENDS: MULTICATEGORICAL
TRAINING FOR SPECIAL EDUCATORS

A number of states have offered multicategorical special education licensure. The trend to do so is gaining some momentum. This is based, in part, on the increase in placement of students with exceptionalities in general education programs and classes. If general education teachers must be prepared for all types of exceptionalities, there is some logic in requiring all special educators to be prepared for all types of exceptionalities. Further, there is an argument that students with exceptionalities are more like their general education classmates than they are dissimilar, and that students with exceptionalities are more like each other than they are dissimilar.

Federal and state education agencies as well as local districts use the categories of disabilities to count the number of students receiving special services and to allocate money for the services. Labels, however, may not be particularly helpful to teachers. Many students may benefit from similar adaptations and modifications using strategies that would be effective for a wide range of students, including some general education students who may be struggling with a particular concept or skill (Friend & Bursuck, 2002). Combining students with disabilities may permit more flexible scheduling.

In some models of service delivery, a special educator may be assigned to a grade level and serve any students with exceptionalities at that grade level. In this way, the special educator may gain familiarity with the particular general education curriculum at that grade level and serve students in a variety of roles, such as consultant to their general education teachers or team teacher providing direct services. Working within the general education sector is a relatively new role for special educators who have spent decades providing services for students with exceptionalities in less inclusive settings and commonly having several grade levels of students to teach simultaneously.

CEC recognizes the diversity in different state and province licensure programs and offers a number of options for them (see Table 2 of selected states and their current categorical or noncategorical special education certification or endorsement areas). Each state or province selects the set of standards that most closely aligns with their programs if they adopt CEC standards or accept CEC standards for NCATE accreditation. CEC offers multicategorical standards for both Individualized General Curriculum (usually for teaching students with mild and moderate levels of disabilities) and Individualized Independence Curriculum (designed for teaching students with more severe disabilities).

CEC also offers standards for specific categorical training that include Learning Disabilities, Emotional and Behavioral Disorders, Visually Impaired, Deaf, Gifted, Mental Retardation, and Physical and Health Disabilities. CEC offers an

Table 2. Selected States and Their Special Education Licenses/Certificates.

State	Categories of Special Education Licenses
California	Mild/moderate disabilities Moderate/severe disabilities Visual impairments Deaf and hard-of-hearing Physical and health impairments Early childhood special education
Colorado	Moderate needs Severe needs cognitive Severe needs affective Severe needs vision Severe needs hearing Severe needs communication Profound needs Early childhood special education
Florida	Exceptional student education Hearing impaired Speech-language impaired Visually impaired Endorsements: autism, gifted, orientation and mobility, Prekindergarten, severe or profound disabilities
Georgia	Generalist (educational disabilities) Hearing impaired Visually impaired Specialization area endorsements Consulting teacher
Illinois	Learning behavior specialist I (multicategorical) Visually impaired Hearing impaired Early childhood special education
New York	Blind/visual impairment Deaf/hard of hearing Mild-moderate disabilities Severe-profound/multiple disabilities
Utah	Special education Special education birth-age 5
Vermont	Consulting teacher/learning specialist Teacher of the handicapped

age-specific set of standards for Early Childhood Special Education. Finally, CEC offers standards for Paraeducators.

PREPARATION TRENDS: EFFORTS TO "PROFESSIONALIZE" SPECIAL EDUCATION TEACHERS

The concerted effort to coordinate and "professionalize" special education teachers is being undertaken by the International CEC. This non-profit organization takes as its worldwide mission the improvement of educational outcomes for individuals with exceptionalities. CEC carries out its mission in support of special education professionals and others who work with and for individuals with exceptionalities. CEC is part of an international organization, International CEC, and is, by far, the largest and most comprehensive of special education organizations, supporting not just the education of students with disabilities, but those students with gifts and talents as well. CEC has established a code of ethics that it asks members to uphold and advance. It has also adopted standards for professional practice (Council for Exceptional Children Professional Standards, 2003).

CEC has also developed its own certificate in order to have a "standard" or universal category of special education certification across all states and provinces. This certificate is called Professionally Recognized Special Educator (PRSE). Individual special education teachers, special education administrators, and educational diagnosticians may elect to pursue PRSE status. From 1997 through December 31, 2002, CEC offered a "granted" certificate. Applicants were required to meet criteria based on the applicant's education, teaching experience, and meeting state or provincial licensure standards. These "granted" certificates all expire in 2009. From 2002 on, only "regular" certificates will be issued. Those educators who had previously achieved "granted" status have until the expiration date of 2009 to meet the requirements for the "regular" certificate. Those with "granted" status may use that time to develop skills or knowledge that must be demonstrated through mastery; they must also keep their certificates current by meeting PRSE continuing education requirements (Council for Exceptional Children Performance-based Standards, 2003).

"Regular" certificates may be earned through assessment, which CEC is now working to develop with other agencies that offer required assessments in education. The purpose of this collaboration is to assure that these published assessments are aligned with CEC standards. Once CEC is satisfied on that point, the available assessments may be used to qualify for the regular PRSE certificate. "Special educators who pass the assessment of The National Board for Professional

Teaching Standards (NBPTS) or other CEC-approved assessments of advanced or exemplary practice will be able to submit such evidence in lieu of the basic assessment (National Board for Professional Teaching Standards, 2003, p. 2).

Regular PRSE certificates must be renewed every five years. CEC is now developing a description of appropriate ways to meet this requirement. It is anticipated that the requirements would be in the range of 35 hours per year and would include attending university courses and professional workshops, reading professional literature, and other kinds of continuing education and renewal (National Board for Professional Teaching Standards, 2003).

CEC reports a number of benefits that accrue to special educators who acquire PRSE certification. Each PRSE educator is listed in one of CEC's publications and in a directory of Professionally Recognized Special Educators. Each PRSE educator also receives a press release to distribute to local news agencies and gains the right to add PRSE after his or her name in public forums (including business cards and letters). Finally, the employer of the PRSE special educator receives a letter noting that the employee has earned PRSE status.

PREPARATION TRENDS: ALTERNATIVE CERTIFICATION PROGRAMS

Driven by the shortage of special educators nationwide (Cegelka & Alvarado, 2000; Fishbaugh et al., 1999), a number of agencies, foundations and state boards of education have developed alternative certification programs. In a national survey, Buck (1995) found that 38 states had alternative certification programs and 62% of respondents reported that these programs addressed the needs of students with disabilities. Alternative certification programs tend to be much more diverse than traditional teacher preparation programs and considerably more creative in the way that requirements may be met. Edelen-Smith and Sileo (1996) reported that an alternative certification special education program attracted more mature, life-experienced persons than traditional programs and recruited more minority students and males as well.

Alternative certification programs may target particular groups of persons as recruits. For example, the FACE program in Chicago was originally designed to recruit returning Peace Corps volunteers. Used to low pay, already in the habit of volunteering and, in almost all cases having acted as teachers in their host countries (even if it was teaching how to build a bridge or grow crops), returning Peace Corps volunteers might find teaching in tough urban environments consistent with their altruism. Ongoing training is also part of the design. The FACE teachers are trained on the job by mentors in the schools and by faculty from the universities that are part of the consortium. Other programs recruit persons who may have always wanted to teach when they were younger, but who went into a different field and now would like to train for that "first love." Retiring military personnel (who, after 20 years of service, may be eligible for retirement and still quite young) have been targeted by other teacher preparation programs.

The screening procedures for alternative certification programs vary widely, from form completion to observation, artifact evaluation and multiple interviews (Benner & Judge, 2000). Many of the alternative certification routes are designed for persons who already hold bachelor's degrees, are making some kind of career or personal change choice, and only need specific training to teach. In some cases, psychological testing or personality typing is done; in one case, interns completed the Myers Briggs Type Indicator (MBTI) and the results were used to determine personality features that would be useful in special education teacher training (Meisgeier & Richardson, 1996).

Once teacher candidates are chosen, training may occur in nontraditional ways. Modified curricula and modular instruction may be used (Conderman et al., 1999) and distance learning may be employed (Fishbaugh et al., 1999). Teacher candidates receive critical on-the-job training and support (Weichel, 1999) and are awarded special education certification at the end of the programs in many cases (Conderman et al., 1999). Some programs award a master's degree in special education, such as the FACE program in Chicago and a Johns Hopkins program in Maryland (Rosenberg & Rock, 1994). Collaboration among all the institutions involved in the alternative certification programs seems to be a critical element of non-traditional training of special educators.

PREPARATION TRENDS: PROFESSIONAL DEVELOPMENT SCHOOLS

Another trend, supported by the National Council for the Accreditation of Teacher Education (NCATE) (1997), is the use of professional development schools. Professional development schools are extended programs of teacher training. Used quite frequently in other countries, particularly Japan, teacher candidates work for several semesters in schools with which higher education institutions have formal agreements. These programs tend to be collaborative and are connected to the real, daily work of teachers. Additionally these programs offer a sustained and intensive experience for teacher candidates. The *professional development* in professional development schools benefits in-service and pre-service teachers alike (Darling-Hammond, 1998; Holmes Group, 1990; Merchant, 2002; Muchmore et al., 2002; Odland, 2002).

The use of professional development schools is not universal and most of the data is in the form of evaluation responses of participants, not student achievement results (Abdal-Haqq, 1998). The benefits are most likely to be garnered from long-term relationships; the best data will come after many years of operation (Brown & Thomas, 1999).

Although the use of professional development schools is a trend in special education as well as general education, there has been some hesitancy to use professional development school models for special educators partly because teacher candidates might not be able to gain experience with students with the disability for which they have been training (Yssel & Merbler, 2002). As special educator teacher shortages increase and perhaps as teachers philosophically see students with various disabilities as more similar than different (Friend & Cook, 2000), this hesitancy may be reduced. Important considerations also seem to be parity in investment and commitment to professional development schools for universities and their K-12 school partners and the role of personal values in the partnerships (Christensen, 1996).

PRACTICE TRENDS: EFFORTS TO IMPROVE THE WORKING CONDITIONS OF SPECIAL EDUCATORS

One of the contributing factors to the current shortage of teachers in special education is the relatively high turnover rate of newer faculty in the field (Stempien & Loeb, 2002). Novice special educators reported that the single significant reason that they were considering leaving the field was frustration. These teachers noted that they did not have a sense of accomplishment, that they perceived paper work to take more of their time than teaching children, that they often felt isolated with their students, and, in some cases, that they did not feel that they were really teaching when they assisted in general education classrooms (Billingsley, 1993; Stempien & Loeb, 2002).

These concerns are not unique to novice special educators. One way to address the concerns, shared by novice and veteran special educators, is to improve specific working conditions. Stempien and Loeb (2002) recommended the following:

(1) Reduce or avoid stress by giving novices, in particular, a reasonable workload, including built-in time to prepare individualized education programs (IEP's).
(2) Recognize the need that novices have for special attention – this includes induction into the school environment, finding resources, knowing where to turn for information and supplies.

(3) Foster collegial relationships – many teachers report a sense of isolation and a lack of certainty about efficacy.

(4) Foster creativity and challenge – it seems especially important in special education to present difficult situations merely as challenges that creativity can be used to resolve instead of must-fix make-or-break problems.

PRACTICE TRENDS: COLLABORATION WITH THE GENERAL EDUCATION CURRICULUM AND EDUCATORS

Inclusion represents the philosophy that students with disabilities should be fully integrated into general school environments and that education should focus on their abilities rather than their disabilities (Friend & Bursuck, 2002). Inclusion is increasingly the way in which special education services are delivered, especially for students with mild disabilities, such as learning disabilities. Thus, students with learning disabilities learn in the general education classroom with the help of a special educator or paraprofessional, or they may use simplified materials and alternative assignments.

The federal reauthorization of the original "civil rights act" for students with disabilities (Public Law 94–142) maintains a title from a 1990 version: Individual with Disabilities Education Act. This 1997 reauthorized version included amendments that, among other things, insured access to the general education curriculum and required standardized testing of students with disabilities on the same measures as their non-disabled peers (Marchand, 2003). Thus, in the standards for teacher certification from the CEC, there are several mandated indicators for teacher candidate knowledge and skill in the areas of general education curriculum and instruction. Other indicators have to do with assuring that special educators know how to modify and adapt materials and content from the general education curriculum to accommodate students with disabilities (Council for Exceptional Children Professional Standards, 2003).

No longer will there be large numbers of separate classrooms and separate curricula for students with disabilities. Not only must special educators be familiar with the general education curriculum but they must also demonstrate collaboration skills for work with general educators and other professional and paraprofessionals in a variety of settings. Friend and Cook (2000) have delineated key factors to the success of collaboration among school personnel:

(1) Voluntary – it is possible to require school personnel to work in close physical environments but the decision to share information and responsibilities is a voluntary one.

(2) Parity – while persons in collaborative relationships may play different roles, the contributions of all participants should be valued and an effort made to maintain reasonable work sharing.

(3) Shared goal – collaboration requires a shared goal and additional communication of that goal as implementation toward it proceeds.

(4) Shared responsibility for key decisions – stakeholders assess what needs to be done and then mutually decide how the work will be distributed.

(5) Shared accountability for outcomes – teachers who share responsibility for children also share in the outcomes of their work.

(6) Shared resources – this may be one of the most important aspects of collaboration, in part because of the "two heads are better than one" concept and in part because the isolation of the teaching role is mitigated.

(7) Emergent – collaboration is not a stagnant experience; it is one of ongoing work, negotiation, sharing, and helping.

Consistent with state standards and standards in individual fields, the Interstate New Teacher Assessment and Support Consortium (INTASC) adopted ten standards for teacher performance. The tenth standard relates specifically to the importance of collaboration: The teacher fosters relationships with school colleagues, parents, and agencies in the larger community to support students' learning and well-being (INTASC, 2003).

This collaboration must be based on a strong knowledge about individual differences, reflected in the third INTASC principle that teachers understand how students differ in their approaches to learning and the teacher creates instructional opportunities that are adapted to diverse learners. Do university faculty possess the information implied in the third INTASC standard? Interestingly, the Holmes Group (1990) found that teacher candidates did not necessarily find collaboration between general educators and special educators modeled for them by faculty in higher education settings.

This was echoed in the research findings of Ryndak et al. (1999) who studied advertisements for assistant professors in special education. Ryndak et al. identified five trends in the field of special education: general-education curriculum and instruction; inclusion; collaboration between university faculty and school personnel, collaboration among special and general-education faculty; and a unified teacher-education program. However, the authors determined that even the advertisements for faculty to fill assistant professorships in special education did not emphasize these trends in their requirements. Despite the fact that the preparation of teacher candidates is in the hands of special education faculty; the Ryndak et al. research indicated a lack of congruence between advertisements and trends. Will there be congruence between trends in the field and the ability of teacher candidates to perform consistent with those trends?

PRACTICE TRENDS: FORMAL AND
SUSTAINED MENTORING PROGRAMS

Professional development schools are only one of the ways for new teachers to be mentored as they train for and begin a career as teachers. The importance of mentoring in some form is underscored by a number of research studies. White and Mason (2001) conducted an investigation of mentoring practices. They cite an increase in teacher retention if new teachers are mentored (Colbert & Wolff, 1992; Kahan, 2002; Odell & Ferraro, 1992). Colbert and Wolff (1992) also noted that mentored teachers had better student engagement and increased use of research practices. Houston et al. (1990) reported that teachers who rated their mentors as effective were more confident, experienced greater job satisfaction, and expected to stay in teaching longer than new teachers who were not mentored or those who rated their mentors as not effective. Shipper-Cordaro (1995) noted benefits to mentors such as being recognized as a valued, knowledgeable and loyal member of the school or district organization. CEC further asserted that mentoring may help new teachers become acculturated to the school climate and reduce their stress.

White and Mason (2001) determined that effective mentoring programs followed particular guidelines and they recommend the following six guidelines for the mentoring program they developed: (1) objectives of the program must be clear to and agreed upon by all participants, including district and building level administrators; (2) information about roles, policies, expectations, and outcomes are readily available and shared; (3) the mentor program is planned and fully funded; (4) all first year teachers participate; (5) mentoring for first year teachers may be coordinated with other mentoring programs; and (6) the mentoring program is for assistance and support and is not related to formal evaluations, certifications, or reemployment. As with all human endeavors, significant sources of social support are required to help teachers successfully transition from pre-service to in-service status (Murray-Harvey, 2001).

ADVANCES IN UNDERSTANDING:
NEW NOTIONS OF INTELLIGENCE

The federal definition of learning disabilities is:

Specific learning disability means a disorder in one or more of the basic psychological processes involved in understanding or in using language, spoken or written, which may manifest itself in an imperfect ability to listen, think, speak, read, write, spell or to do mathematical calculations. The term includes such conditions as perceptual handicaps, brain injury, minimal brain dysfunction, dyslexia, and developmental aphasia. The term does not include children who have learning problems which are primarily the result of visual, hearing, or motor handicaps, of mental retardation, or emotional disturbance, or of environmental, cultural, or economic disadvantage (U.S. Office of Education, 1977).

This definition implies that whatever difficulties students with learning disabilities have regarding acquisition of basic skills or grasping academic content, these difficulties cannot be due to low intellect. Assessing intelligence, therefore, has been an element of learning disabilities diagnostic testing. The federal definition does not cite *how* states should go about determining that students' learning difficulties are not caused by retardation. So, many schools require a numeric discrepancy that results from a comparison of ability test scores and achievement test scores. Usually the discrepancy is based upon a comparison of scores from standardized academic achievement tests and a standardized intelligence test score. Schools may then use formulas to determine whether the discrepancy is large enough to qualify for services for learning disabilities or use tables of values that indicate an adequate discrepancy (Division of Learning Disabilities, 2003).

Intelligence is not a tangible item and this may account for the variability in thinking about it. Intelligence is a construct or theoretical abstraction, a concept that humans have developed to try to consider the native ability or capacity to learn. While it cannot be seen, researchers and educators deduce that it exists based on what can be observed in human behavior (Garguilo, 2003). Beirne-Smith et al. (1998) purported that researchers are "attempting to explain one of the most complex and elusive components of human functioning" (p. 106).

Most teacher preparation programs do not train teacher candidates to administer intelligence tests, however, information about intelligence is a staple of teacher training, so that teacher candidates can be informed consumers of test data in case studies. Reviewing intelligence tests and learning about discrepancies between intelligence and achievement is particularly relevant for educators working with students with learning disabilities (Siegel, 2003; Siegel & Himel, 1998).

The concept of intelligence is not universally defined and there have been shifts in how the term is explained in teacher preparation programs. There are a number of researchers who hold that intellect is, in fact, not a single entity, but a collection of abilities that operate together in combined and recombined ways to deal with incoming information. The controversy has surfaced for almost a century with Spearman (1927) asserting that intelligence is a global aspect of human beings, referred to as the g-factor. Others (Guilford, 1985; Thorndike, 1927) described intelligence as a multitude of factors. There is discussion about whether intelligence is fixed. There is debate as to whether intelligence indexes, reported with variability to allow for situational factors such as illness or test-taking conditions, are sufficiently accurate measures of student aptitude. Most researchers consider two models of intelligence: that there exists a central factor that represents intelligence or that there is a cluster of cognitive abilities that comprise intelligence (Beirne-Smith et al., 1998).

No wonder, then, that there are so many ideas about what intelligence is and how best to assess it. Despite the fact that typing the word *"intelligences"* (deliberately the plural) on most computers elicits an error message, Gardner (1983) has asserted that intelligence is not a single thing nor is it a collection of factors but instead a collection of types of intelligences. This theory, though not empirically validated to date, enjoys acceptance by many educators. Further, the theory of *multiple intelligences* (Gardner, 1993) is widely disseminated by teacher educators (Rubado, 2002).

Gardner proposed at least seven intelligences, including verbal/linguistic, logical/mathematical, intrapersonal/introspective, musical/rhythmic, bodily/kinesthetic, interpersonal/social, naturalistic/perception of the world, and visual/spatial. (He added an eighth, with continuing research on a ninth intelligence.) Gardner asserted that each of these intelligences has its own site in the brain, its own timetable for development, its own patterns of development, and its own trajectory for decline and loss (Gardner, 1983).

Faculty typically provide students with a variety of theories about intelligence and, in the last decade or more, Gardner's theory has been included (see Bender, 2004). Because the standard assessments of intelligence remain the Stanford-Binet and the Wechsler Intelligence Scales, however, case study results of intellectual functioning that teachers are likely to encounter at a staffing are based on instruments that do not incorporate the concept of multiple intelligences. The use of the multiple intelligences theory has been aimed more at diversifying approaches to instruction and at informal teacher-made assessments than at altering the method of assessing intelligence (Beirne-Smith et al., 1998).

The discussion of emerging conceptualizations of intelligence relates to teacher candidates as they address the ninth INTASC principle: the teacher is a reflective practitioner who continually evaluates the effects of personal choices and actions on others (students, parents, and other professionals in the learning community) and who actively seeks out opportunities to grow professionally. Additionally, definitions of learning disability may become challenged if the concept of multiple intelligences reveals that many children labeled learning disabled have untapped intelligences that the school environment has failed to cultivate.

ADVANCES IN UNDERSTANDING: NEUROLOGICAL INFORMATION ABOUT STUDENTS WITH LEARNING DISABILITIES

In the early phases of research on learning disabilities, sometimes even called the "medical phase" or "clinical phase" in the early 1920s, labels such as mild mental retardation, minimal brain dysfunction, dyslexia, perceptual impairment, slow learner, and neurological impairment described children having similar difficulties in school performance (Division on Learning Disabilities, 2003). Medical doctors conducted research in clinics and private school and laboratory settings (see Bender, 2004). However, the results of those studies did not prove neurological damage in all cases and this phase of the field ended around 1940.

During the 1940s, with the unfortunate opportunity to study thousands of persons with brain damage from war experiences and new medical techniques as well as streamlined record keeping, research documented the location of brain injuries and degrees of impaired activities (see Bender, 2004). By 1950, attention turned once again to persons who had trouble acquiring similar skills. If soldiers once had a skill and lost it through brain injury to a certain region of the brain, could damage in the same region from birth or later produce an inability or great difficulty in acquiring the same skill in the first place?

The term "learning disability" came into use officially in 1963 when Samuel Kirk employed it at a presentation to a group of concerned parents (he and Barbara Bateman had used the term in print a year earlier). A lingering suspicion of a neurological basis for difficulties in perception, linguistic effectiveness, and learning was present. At the same time, the pressing need for practical classroom-based solutions to the learning difficulties of students with learning disabilities was acute. The need for immediate applications to assist students with learning difficulties is, at times, at odds with the desire to answer the question of why the difficulties with learning exist in the first place (Bender, 2004).

Historically, the field of special education has been strongly influenced by the field of medicine. Medical information may be important in the diagnosis of some students with learning disabilities, as evidence of the effects of alcohol, smoking and other fetal developmental insults to the brain and central nervous system is collected (Bender, 2004). While neuropsychological assessment has been developed, it is still not a common educational practice to use these tools for the diagnosis of learning disabilities (Bender, 2004). Also, a number of treatments and educational methods that have a medical component are generated (Moats & Lyons, 1993). A basic knowledge of the brain and the central nervous system is required to interpret and respond to these treatments and methods (Bender, 2004).

Increasingly, texts and faculty members consider neurology as part of the discussion of learning disabilities. Neurology and information about the implications of its functions has been "translated" for nonmedical consumption (Caine & Caine, 1994; Sylwester, 1995). Neurological function is taught as a basis for understanding the difficulties students with learning disabilities experience. Neurological responses to medications and the medications themselves are listed or described in an increasing number of textbooks. The neurological basis of learning and of learning disabilities is included as part of a well-rounded view of learning disabilities.

SUMMARY AND CONCLUSIONS

Education for children with learning disabilities is rooted in special education. Teacher preparation for educating educators who will instruct students with disabilities begins with candidate screening and teacher training programs. Effective work by special educators in the schools flourishes with appropriate supports for special educators. Additionally, the philosophies that guide special educators' preparation and practice are impacted by new developments that advance the understanding of intelligence and learning.

This chapter has identified and defined trends in teacher preparation, practice and advances in understanding that impact the education of students with learning disabilities. These trends reflect a movement away from disability-specific teacher preparation and practice, and a movement toward increased collaboration between special and general educators. These trends promote increased facility of the general educator to instruct children with learning disabilities, as well as higher expectations that that the special educator demonstrate expertise in the general education curriculum. Trends that support the profession of special education as well as consider the impact of the philosophy of inclusion on teacher preparation and practice were presented.

REFERENCES

Abdal-Haqq, I. (1998). *Professional development schools: Weighing the evidence*. Thousand Oaks, CA: Corwin Press.
Beirne-Smith, M., Ittenbach, R., & Patton, J. (1998). *Mental retardation* (5th ed.). Upper Saddle River, NJ: Prentice-Hall.
Bender, W. N. (2002). *Differentiating instruction or students with learning disabilities: Best practices for general and special education*. Thousand Oaks, CA: Corwin Press.

Bender, W. N. (2004). *Learning disabilities: Characteristics, identification, and teaching strategies.* Boston: Allyn & Bacon.

Benner, S. M., & Judge, S. L. (2000). Teacher preparation for inclusive settings: A talent development model. *Teacher Education Quarterly, 27*(3), 23–38.

Billingsley, B. S. (1993). Teacher retention and attribution in special and general education: A critical review of the literature. *Journal of Special Education, 27*(2), 137–144.

Brown, E. T., & Thomas, J. A. (1999). Expecting the best, producing success. *Peabody Journal of Education, 74*(3), 224–235.

Buck, G. H. (1995). Alternative certification programs: A national survey. *Teacher Education and Special Education, 18*(1), 39–48.

Caine, R. N., & Caine, G. (1994). *Making connections: Teaching and the human brain.* Parsippany, NJ: Pearson Learning.

Campbell, B. (1994). *The multiple intelligence handbook: Lesson plans and more.* Stanwood, WA: Campbell & Associates.

Cegelka, P. A., & Alvarado, J. L. (2000). A best practices model for preparation of rural special education teachers. *Rural Special Education Quarterly, 19*(3–4), 15–29.

Christensen, L. (1996). Anatomy of six public school-university partnerships. *Teacher Education & Special Education, 19*(2), 169–179.

Colbert, J. A., & Wolff, D. E. (1992). Surviving in urban schools: A collaborative model for a beginning teacher support system. *Journal of Teacher Education, 43*(3), 193–199.

Conderman, G., Stephens, J. T., & Hazelkorn, M. (1999). A "select" method to certify special education teacher. *Kappa Delta Pi Record, 36*(1), 16–18.

Council for Exceptional Children: Performance-based standards. Accessed on March 29, 2003. http://www.cec.sped.org/ps/nw_perf_based_stds.html.

Council for Exceptional Children professional standards. Accessed on March 29, 2003. http://www.cec.sped.org/ps/.

Darling-Hammond, L. (1998). Strengthening the teaching profession: Teacher learning that supports student learning. *Educational Leadership, 55*(5), 6–11.

Division on Learning Disabilities (2003). *Teaching LD.* Accessed on March 29, 2003. http://www.teachingld.org/.

Edelen-Smith, P., & Sileo, T. W. (1996). The alternative basic certification program in special education: In search of quantity and quality in special education. *Teacher Education and Special Education, 19*(4), 313–330.

Fishbaugh, M. S. E., Christensen, L., & Burdge, J. (1999). Keeping qualified special educators under the big sky. *Rural Special Education Quarterly, 18*(3–4), 29–35.

Friend, M., & Bursuck, W. D. (2002). *Including students with special needs: A practical guide for classroom teachers.* Boston: Allyn & Bacon.

Friend, M., & Cook, L. (2000). *Interactions: Collaboration skills for school professionals* (3rd ed.). White Plains, NY: Longman.

Gardner, H. (1983). *Frames of mind: The theory of multiple intelligences.* New York: Basic Books.

Gardner, H. (1993). *Multiple intelligences: The theory in practice.* New York: Basic Books.

Garguilo, R. M. (2003). *Special education in contemporary: An introduction to exceptionality.* Belmont, CA: Wadsworth/Thomson Learning.

Garnett, J. S., & Edelen-Smith, P. J. (2002). The nature of the people: Renewing teacher education as a shared responsibility within colleges and schools of education. *Remedial and Special Education, 23*(6), 335–348.

Gaynor, J. F., & Little, M. E. (1997). The expanding role of the LEA's in special education teacher preparation: The view from a local school district. *Teacher Education & Special Education, 20*(4), 281–300.

Guilford, J. P. (1985). The structure-of-intellect model. In: B. B. Wolman (Ed.), *Handbook of Intelligence: Theories, Measurements, and Applications* (pp. 225–266). New York: Wiley.

Hearne, D., & Stone, S. (1995). Multiple intelligences and underachievement: Lessons from individuals with learning disabilities. *Journal of Learning Disabilities, 28*, 439–448.

Holmes Group (1990). *Tomorrow's schools: Principles for the design of professional development schools*. East Lansing, MI: Author.

Houston, W. R., McDavid, T., & Marshall, F. (1990). *A study of the induction of 300 first-year teachers and their mentors, 1989–1990*. Texas Education Agency, Houston Independent School District & University of Houston. (ERIC Document Reproduction Services No. 338558.)

Interstate New Teacher Assessment and Support Consortium (2003). *Model standards for beginning teacher licensing and development: A resource for state dialogue*. Accessed March 29, 2003. http://www.nebo.edu/e_portfolio/docs/INTASC.doc.

Kahan, D. (2002). Development and evaluation of a screening instrument for cooperating teachers. *The Teacher Educator, 38*(1), 63–77.

Marchand, P. (2003). *The Individuals with Disabilities Education Act (IDEA) Amendments of 1997*. Accessed on March 29, 2003. http://thearc.org/ga/qa.html.

Meisgeier, C. H., & Richardson, R. C. (1996). Personality types of interns in alternative teacher certification programs. *Educational Forum, 60*(4), 350–360.

Merchant, G. J. (2002). Professional development schools and indicators of student achievement. *The Teacher Educator, 38*(2), 112–125.

Moats, L. C., & Lyons, G. R. (1993). Learning disabilities in the United States: Advocacy, science and the future of the field. *Journal of Learning Disabilities, 26*, 282–294.

Muchmore, J. A., Marx, G. E., & Cromwell, R. A. (2002). Beyond a rite of passage: Initiating an alternative master's degree program for in-service teachers. *The Teacher Educator, 38*(1), 16–33.

Murray-Harvey, R. (2001). How teacher education students cope with practicum concerns. *The Teacher Educator, 37*(2), 117–132.

National Board for Professional Teaching Standards. Accessed on March 29, 2003. http://www.nbpts.org/standards/index.cfm.

National Council for the Accreditation of Teacher Education (1997). *Draft standards for identifying and supporting quality professional development schools*. Washington, DC: Author.

Odell, S. J., & Ferraro, D. P. (1992). Teacher mentoring and teacher retention. *Journal of Teacher Education, 43*(3), 200–204.

Odland, J. (2002). Professional development schools: Partnerships that work. *Childhood Education, 78*, 160–162.

Prater, M. A. (2002). Introduction to the special issue: School-university partnerships in special education preparation. *Remedial and Special Education, 23*(6), 323–324.

Prater, M. A., & Sileo, T. W. (2002). School-university partnerships in special education field experiences: A national descriptive study. *Remedial and Special Education, 23*(6), 325–334.

Praxis series: Professional Assessments for beginning teachers (2003). Accessed on March 29, 2003. http://www.ets.org/praxis/.

Rosenberg, M. S., & Rock, E. E. (1994). Alternative certification in special education: Efficacy of a collaborative, field-based teacher preparation program. *Teacher Education & Special Education, 17*(3), 141–153.

Rubado, K. (2002). Empowering students through multiple intelligences. *Reclaiming Children and Youth, 10*(4), 233.

Ryndak, D. L., Webb, K., & Clark, D. (1999). Faculty advertisements: A road map for future faculty. *Teacher Education & Special Education, 22*(1), 25–40.

Shipper-Cordaro, P. (1995, Winter). Mentoring: Components of success. *The Mentoring Connection,* Quarterly Newsletter of the International Mentoring Association.

Siegel, L. S. (2003). IQ discrepancy definition and the diagnosis of learning disabilities: Introduction to the special issue. *Journal of Learning Disabilities, 36*(1), 2–3.

Siegel, L. S., & Himel, N. (1998). Socioeconomic status, age, and the classification of dyslexics and poor readers: The dangers of using IQ scores in the definition of reading disabilities. *Dyslexia, 4,* 90–104.

Sobel, D., & French, N. (1998). A partnership to promote teacher preparation for inclusive, urban schools: Four voices. *Teaching & Teacher Education, 14*(8), 793–806.

Spearman, C. E. (1927). *The abilities of man.* New York: Macmillan.

Stempien, L. R., & Loeb, R. C. (2002). Differences in job satisfaction between general education and special education teachers: Implications for retention. *Remedial and Special Education, 23*(5), 258–267.

Sylwester, R. (1995). *A celebration of neurons.* Alexandria, VA: Association for Supervision and Curriculum Development.

Thorndike, E. L. (1927). *The measurement of intelligence.* New York: Columbia University, Teacher's College Press.

U.S. Office of Education (1977). Assistance to states for education of handicapped children: Procedures for evaluating specific learning disabilities. *Federal Register, 42,* 65082–65085.

Weichel, W. (1999). Preparing teachers though alternative-certification programs. *Kappa Delta Pi Record, 36*(1), 19–22.

White, M., & Mason, C. (2001). The mentoring induction process: What new teachers need from mentors. *Teaching Exceptional Children, 33*(6), 81.

Yssel, N., & Merbler, J. B. (2002). Professional development schools and special education: A promising partnership? *The Teacher Educator, 38*(2), 141–150.

SUPPORT SERVICES FOR COLLEGE STUDENTS WITH LEARNING DISABILITIES

Sunday O. Obi

Postsecondary developmental programs designed to assist the under prepared college applicant have been in existence for much longer than is usually acknowledged. Divisions or departments currently labeled as "developmental studies" or learning assistance" by institutions of higher education operate for the same basic purposes as services that were once known as "college preparatory." The presence and problems of under-prepared students were recognized in some of the most prestigious institutions of higher learning as early as the 1860s (Tomlinson, 1989).

Since 1978, postsecondary institutions have experienced a significant increase in the number of students with disabilities (Henderson, 1999). In that year, less than 3% of entering first-time, full-time students reported having a disability. In 1988, the number was 7% and grew to more than 9% in 1998. Henderson also reported that students with learning disabilities went from 1.2% of entering first-time, full-time students in 1988 to 3.5% in 1998. In raw numbers, this means that in 1998, out of a total first-time enrollment of 1.6 million, 154,500 had disabilities and 58,000 of those were learning disabled. This increase in enrollment has been attributed to at least four factors. First, services and support now exist at the postsecondary level for students who are otherwise qualified based on Section 504 of the Vocational Rehabilitation Act of 1973 (PL 93-112), The Education of All Handicapped Children Act of 1975 (PL 94-142) and its amendments and the Americans with Disabilities Act (ADA) of 1990 (PL 101-336). Second, students with disabilities like many high school students, have many aspirations of entering

Current Perspectives on Learning Disabilities
Advances in Special Education, Volume 16, 229–245
© 2004 Published by Elsevier Ltd.
ISSN: 0270-4013/doi:10.1016/S0270-4013(04)16012-1

professions or occupations that require postsecondary education (Brown et al., 1992; Henderson, 1999). Third, many students with disabilities are receiving better academic preparation in high school (Bender, 2004). Fourth, the number of students with disabilities continuing their education may be due to the enhanced educational requirements for emerging jobs as the national economy shifted from a manufacturing base to a services and technology base (Acne & Kroger, 1997).

Apparently, the increase in students with learning disabilities attending college is undoubtedly due to legislation prohibiting discrimination against persons with disabilities (Murray et al., 2000). At one time, college was out of the question for many students with learning disabilities. Beginning in the mid-1970s, however, federal law prohibited institutions of higher education from discriminating against students with disabilities. After the passage of Section 504, colleges and universities did not suddenly open their doors to students with disabilities. Over time, as the courts helped to define the parameters of the law and public opinion about persons with disabilities improved, many colleges and universities have become more comfortable with the idea of admitting and accommodating students with disabilities, including learning disabilities. Many colleges/universities now have full-time faculty or staff persons who direct programs for students with learning disabilities. In fact, some institutions of higher education have gained reputations as good places for students with learning disabilities to attend because of the level of support offered (Bender, 2004). The overall purpose of this chapter is to examine the broader array of issues and problems that impact on developmental programs for college-bound students with learning disabilities. It also aims at conceptualizing effective techniques to reverse problems or difficulties, confronting these students.

ISSUES IMPACTING SUPPORTIVE SERVICES FOR COLLEGE-BOUND STUDENTS WITH LEARNING DISABILITIES

The transition from school to work or to postsecondary training is a critical period for all students. For students with learning disabilities who have the potential to pursue higher education, colleges and universities offer an age-appropriate, integrated environment in which they can expand personal, social, and academic abilities leading to an expansion of career goals and employment options. The transition, however, of high school students with LD to higher education settings has been made difficult by inadequacies in the preparation received in secondary schools. Still secondary schools face serious difficulties in developing effective instructional programs for college-bound high school students with LD (Halpern & Benz, 1987; Mangrum & Strichart, 1983). It appears that many students with LD find themselves unprepared at college entry in a number of areas including inadequate knowledge of subject content, underachieving in academic skills, poor organizational skills (e.g. time management and study skills), poor test-taking skills, lack of assertiveness, and low self-esteem (Cordoni, 1982; Dalke & Schmitt, 1987; Mull et al., 2001; Vogel, 1982).

If the student with leaning disability is to be adequately prepared for post-secondary education, then secondary education programs must reflect those skills and competencies that are important for coping with academic and social demands found in a college setting. The content of the secondary program must provide learners with learning disabilities with the skills necessary for access to and success in college programs (Halpern & Benz, 1987; Janigo & Castenbader, 2002; Seidenberg, 1986). The effective mainstreaming of secondary students with LD into regular college preparatory programs requires that both regular and special educators contribute to the process. Therefore, the extent to which each group provides students with preparatory skills needed to meet the demands of college setting is important.

The process of transitioning high school students with LD into postsecondary settings stresses the need to prepare them for the college environment. However, there appears to be discrepancies between high school and college faculty regarding different experiential bases or philosophies with respect to the college preparatory of students (Seidenberg, 1986). Only recently have adolescents and young adults begun to receive a fair share of special education services (Bender, 2004; Halpern & Benz, 1987; Patton & Polloway, 1993; Schloss et al., 1990). Despite this recent trend toward increasing services for high school students, students with LD continue to experience extensive academic and social difficulties (Bender, 2004; Maheady et al., 1988). As Wagner (1990) noted, the most probable factors contributing to course failures by these students include absences totaling more than 8 days and disciplinary problems. School policies and limitations in special services may also increase the probability of their failure; for example, the majority of these students seem to be graded on the same standards as their non-disabled classmates and they generally are not provided with tutoring services or other assistance outside of their special education classes. Moreover, a majority of regular education teachers tend to receive little support in instructing these students. Wagner (1990) observed that "encouraging greater instruction of students with disabilities in regular education classes, without serious attention to the instruction that goes on in these classes, would seem simply to encourage greater rates of academic failure" (p. 28). The consequences of failing course are serious, particularly those courses needed for graduation. Students who fail to accumulate sufficient numbers of required credits to pass 9th grade frequently drop out of high school before graduation (Thornton & Zigmond, 1986). Although passing 9th grade does not guarantee successful completion of high school or transitioning into postsecondary, failing at this grade level increases the likelihood of dropping out. By leaving school early, they may miss educational experiences most important for their transition to adulthood (Wagner, 1989).

Students with disabilities are, in general, significantly less likely than non-disabled students to graduate from high school, get any postsecondary education, find employment, or become engaged in any productive activity after high school (Wagner, 1989). These outcomes assume greater importance because successful post school transition appears strongly related to success in school (Rieth & Polsgrove, 1994). It is clear that programs for students with LD characteristically focus on teaching academics with a goal of mainstreaming these students. For example, Edgar (1987) and Sigmond (1990) observed that the bleak results yielded by this approach warrant a reappraisal of the secondary special curriculum. Edgar argued that if the ultimate goal of special education is to prepare students with mild disabilities to be productive and independent citizens, there must be a radical modification of the curriculum away from academics toward developing vocational, functional, and independent living skills. Short of a complete restructuring of the current special education curriculum, it seems clear that research model demonstration programs are required to develop and evaluate effective alternative educational curricula to meet long-term needs of this population.

COLLEGE AND UNIVERSITY POLICIES AND PROCEDURES ON STUDENTS WITH LEARNING DISABILITIES

Colleges and universities administrators understand the benefits of educating a diverse student body. Students with LD represent a significant segment of this group. Because of the wide variance in postsecondary institutions in such terms as size and mission, there is little consistency in the way that institutions provide services to these students. As these students pursue not only undergraduate education but also graduate and professional education (Henderson, 1995), it has become increasingly critical for institutions to review both their mission and philosophies as they work toward an integrated model of service provision.

Section 504 of the Vocational Rehabilitation Act of 1973 (PL 93-112) and the American with Disabilities Act (ADA) (PL 101-336) have articulated the rights of individuals with LD in higher education. The laws mandate that postsecondary institutions provide equal access to programs and services for these students.

Given their interpretation of such legislation, individual colleges and universities are at various stages in the development and integration of policies and procedures for providing accommodations to students with disabilities (Bourke et al., 2000). The National Joint Commission on Learning Disabilities (NJCLD) (1999) defined learning disabilities as *A . . . a* heterogeneous group of disorders manifested by significant difficulties in the acquisition and use of speaking, reading, writing, reasoning, or mathematical abilities. These disorders are intrinsic to the individual, presumed to be due to central nervous system dysfunction, and may occur across the life span . . . (p. 65). Successful individuals with LD tend to be goal-oriented, determined, persistent, and creative (Reiff et al., 1993). Persons with these characteristics are often assets to the university community. Many students with LD are aware of their disabilities before matriculation. Some students, such as nontraditional and returning students, are frequently not diagnosed with learning disabilities until after their admission to college. Once diagnosed, it is the student's responsibility to disclose his/her learning disability and the extent to which it affects academic access (Lynch & Gussel, 1996). A student's eligibility for services and the particular type of service he/she needs must be based on appropriate documentation (Brackett & McPhearson, 1996). With appropriate accommodations, it is more likely that students with LD will experience a successful college career. Witte et al. (1998), in their study, found that students with LD were competitive academically with their peers and graduated with grade point averages not significantly below the control group. This study also found that students with LD on average took only one semester longer to graduate.

Presently, institutions are establishing learner outcomes for all programs. While students with LD should be expected to meet the institutions academic standards, they should be given the opportunity to fulfill learner outcomes in alternative ways. The process by which these students demonstrate mastery of academic standards may vary from that of the larger student body, but the outcomes can and should remain the same. Accommodating these students need not jeopardize the academic standards of the institution. While the ADA requires institutions to make academic adjustments to provide equal access, they do not require postsecondary institutions to make changes to essential elements of the curricula and therefore do not compromise curricular standards (Scott, 1994). The courts and the Office of Civil Rights (OCR) have been clear that postsecondary institutions can and should establish policies that identify and maintain those essential components of the college curriculum (Guckenberger et al. V. Trustees of Boston University, et al., 974 F. supp. 106 [D. Ma, 1997]; Ranch Santiago Community College [CA], 3NDLR & Para 52 [OCR, Region 1X, 1992]; Bennett College [NC] OCR case no. 04–95–2065 [Region IV, 1995]). A team approach to reviewing the institution's policies for evaluating its essential programmatic elements results in a balanced and integrated plan for both academic integrity and educational access. Faculty and staff from various programs can work to outline essential program components in relation to the institutions mission. Collaboration among administrators, faculty members, and disability service professionals should ensure that academic standards are delineated and maintained. Although the team approach to policy design may involve a number of administrative offices, it is highly recommended that services for students with disabilities including those for students with LD be housed within the administrative structure that promotes a strong academic focus and shared faculty responsibility for providing accommodations (Shaw, 1999; Siegel, 1999). For some campuses that office reports directly to the President or Provost; for others disability issues may be under the purview of the academic or student affairs offices (NJCLD, 1999).

For policy issues, it is essential to have written policies that ensure that students with LD receive the same high-quality education as their peers. These policies should address the issues of admission, documentation of a learning disability, accommodations, and curriculum modifications. It is important that students be made aware of the existence of an appeal process, which is set forth in writing. Students should have easy access to all written policies and procedures including the appeal process. Such documents should be made available in a variety of formats, in all appropriate campus literature, and through available technology, such as a web site, which all students can access (NJCLD, 1999) In terms of admission, colleges and universities vary in their admission requirements and policies; some have open admissions, while others have rigid entry requirements. Most students with LD meet the standard admission criteria and will not be readily identifiable during the admission process. However, some students may appeal the standard entry requirements because of the effects of their disability on their academic performance or test scores. Within the appeal process for admission available to all students, a mechanism is needed to consider the impact of a student's learning disability on his/her learning. It is recommended that the admission appeal process for students with learning disabilities involve a team approach to decision-making. It is imperative that the team consists of institutional representatives who are knowledgeable about learning disabilities (NJCLD, 1999).

In the area of documentation, whether a college or university accepts a student's documentation as adequate or requires additional information before providing services, accommodation decisions should be addressed on an individual basis. The campus learning disability professional, in conjunction with the student, should evaluate the effect of the student's disability in relation to the curriculum and academic standards. During this process, faculty and other campus representatives may be consulted to review the academic environment and its relationship to the student (NJCLD, 1999).

A learning disability is not static; its effects may change in relation to a number of student, environmental, and curricular factors. Such factors as the student's abilities, the classroom setting, methods of instruction, or task demand may entail the need to provide differing academic adjustments. These accommodations requested by students, must be made on a case-by-case basis to ensure the integrity of the academic program and the educational experience. Requests for accommodations must be responded to in a timely fashion. The decision-making process for academic adjustments may involve the faculty member, the student, and the learning disabilities professional. Identifying and selecting appropriate accommodations require an analysis of the task, the student's disability, course objectives, and faculty input. Examples of accommodations may include, but are not limited to: (a) alternative test formats; (b) extended time; (c) alternative; (d) access to oral and written material; and (e) course substitutions. There are a number of new technologies and software options available that foster access to academic materials, such as text-to-speech, speech synthesizers, visual outliners, reading programs, textbooks on tape, print enlargers, visual tracking, phonetic spell checkers, and other emerging technologies. It is critical that technology on campus be reviewed and made accessible to students with disabilities (Riley, 1997).

Regarding curriculum adjustments, the federal laws and subsequent court decisions make it clear that colleges are not expected to make changes in the curriculum that compromise essential components of a program. In certain well-documented cases, a student may be unable to meet all of the requirements of a degree program. For example, a student seeking a bachelor's degree in nursing must complete all required courses in the program. However, if such a student had a history of poor performance in the acquisition of a second language that was directly linked to a learning disability, that student might then petition for substitution of a different requirement in place of the foreign language requirement (see Shaw, 1999). Before course substitutions are considered, an evaluation of the course's purposes and outcomes should be conducted. Alternatives to course substitutions might include alternative testing, alternative evaluation of perfor- mance, and course audits. Because both the integrity of the academic program and the educational experience of the student are at stake, policy of this magnitude should be established and implemented through shared decision making. A team including the faculty member, disability service provider, student, and a learning disability specialist constitutes a balanced forum for decision-making (NJCLD, 1999). Acceptable course substitutions to be considered by college personnel include culturally oriented courses, anthropology courses, or sign language in place of foreign language courses; logic, philosophy, or computer science courses as an alternative for math requirement. The team making this decision should consider the individual's disability in relation to the student's chosen academic program (Tucker, 1996). It should be noted that proportionately very few students with LD petition for course substitution (Sparks et al., 1996).

PROBLEMS ASSOCIATED WITH POSTSECONDARY PROGRAMMING

America's special education system was intended to give disabled kids an edge. But it is cheating many . . . and costing the rest of us billions (Shapiro, 1993, p. 46). The National Association of School Boards of Education (NASBE) (1992) Special Education Study Group had called for "a fundamental shift in the delivery of education . . . to a new way to organize special and general education . . . name an inclusive system of education THAT STRIVES TO PRODUCE BETTER OUTCOMES FOR ALL STUDENTS." Schools are ultimately about enhancing the quality of life of people; they are also about creating better communities. This movement strives to create schools that are truly inclusive, where learning that occurs in accommodating and supporting students with disabilities contributes to the creating a new culture in colleges and universities. Ultimately, this movement creates communities in which diversity is honored, learning is active and applied, and supports are provided to accommodate the unique needs of students. This vision is both feasible and necessary! To foster this inclusion movement, it is helpful to consider the historical evolution of the relationship between students with LD and America's higher education system. Understandably, in response to the needs of the under prepared students, programs classified as "college preparatory" since the mid-1800s have served many of the same goals as those programs that have more recently been labeled, "academic development," "learning assistance," or "developmental studies." The change in the labeling of preparatory programs is, to some extent, associated with the change in student populations. Whereas socioeconomic status, instead of ability, was once the primary determinant of attendance at a college or university, some students are now admitted to institutions of higher education through developmental programs.

As a result of the growing diversity among enrollees at postsecondary institutions of learning, a number of developmental program models have emerged. Some of these models are comprehensive and some are specialized. There are at least four different types of program categories: college campus tutorial/remedial, college outreach programs, campus assistance centers, and off-campus instruction. The specific types of intervention involve the teaching/learning process, counseling, peer support, and supplemental use of media and the arts to develop student's articulation of basic skills and the application of those skills to various content areas in the college curriculum. Of the numerous developmental programs across the nation, several can be identified as exemplars in terms of their success. However, many programs, including those considered successful, have encountered a variety of problems. The continuous burdens that the programs face include problems of funding, staff recruitment and retention, admission and placement standards, minority student enrollment, the relativity of curriculum, the quality of tests, and perceptions of the program. There are other problems that affect implementation of developmental programs. Many of these problems are contingent on each other such that one tends to exacerbate the other and, thereby, thwart the effective delivery of services to possibly larger numbers of students. Any of these problems or a combination of them can also be identified in programs that are considered successful (Tomlinson, 1989).

In recent years, services to students with learning disabilities in postsecondary settings have improved; however, many problems still exist that inhibit the delivery of these services, such as funding. Although legislation now entitles all American youths to financial assistance for postsecondary education if they fall within the designated limit on household income, the unreliable funding of some developmental programs leads to a path of tenuous existence. In many instances, impressive sums of money are designated for developmental programs at the system-wide level, but the allocation of such funds to the various schools within the system does not necessarily coincide with the particular needs of each institution. Where funds are said to be distributed equally, some recipient institutions must make more intensive use of faculty, staff, equipment, and facilities in order to meet the special demands of its disadvantaged students (Tomlinson, 1989). The most common problem related to funding has been threats of cancellation of grant funding.

It is common knowledge that more students with LD are accessing postsecondary education. This trend is expected to grow! Basic services offered at the career development centers and disabled student services offices need to be studied. Students must become better at self-advocating and more willing to self-disclose so that they receive the available services they need. Colleges must realize the need to provide better career development services for the increasing number of students with LD on their campuses.

Recruitment of program staff continues to be a problem for most colleges and universities due to staff turnover. Instructors for many programs are hired as non-tenure track and/or temporary faculty and, thus, job insecurity is heightened, competent individuals are reluctant to pursue such positions, and incentives for scholarly contributions in curriculum development, research, or service are scarce. Poor staff moral and faculty burnout also exacerbate the problem of recruitment and retention of individuals who are needed for the successful delivery of developmental services (Scott & Gregg, 2000). Salaries that are not competitive, cut backs in travel reimbursement, few opportunities for upward mobility within universities, and a shift toward more stringent tenure and promotional requirements have also created obstacles to the successful operation of developmental programs.

Standards vary within systems at various institutional levels such that there is no consistent indicator of what is held to be the threshold of preparedness or under-preparedness. Within an institutional level (University, four-year college, two-year college); minimum admission criteria now vary across categories of entering freshmen. Students are also accepted with minimal entrance scores and then deemed by faculty as too deficient to be taught effectively. Where as systems allow each institution to determine its own admission standards by a combination of high school grade point average and SAT or American College Test scores that is said to predict success or failure, there is cause to consider whether the process is adequate – whether all who are accepted or rejected are accurately predicted for success or failure (Tomlinson, 1989). Although many developmental programs were instituted, as a part of the movement toward desegregation, there is often a pervasive misconception that affirmative action is the sole purpose of such programs. At most institutions where desegregation has been an issue, minority students within developmental programs are a small percentage of the program's enrollment. Another misconception is that the developmental program exists solely for the purpose of serving those who are under-prepared as a result of disadvantages. At many institutions, the student population of developmental programs includes individuals from affluent and middle-class homes. In some instances, foreign students speaking English as a second language have been enrolled in developmental programs because there are no other services to assist them in overcoming language barriers. Despite such an enrollment mix, many developmental programs continue to suffer the stigma of being perceived primarily as a vehicle for affirmative action – particularly for desegregation. This misconception was born of an age of accountability in which, to a considerable extent, desegregation orders have periodically driven developmental program policies and procedures as well as institutional policies system-wide.

At the same time that various institutions are attempting to serve the diversified learning needs of increasing numbers of individuals who do not meet regular admissions criteria but who wish to pursue the benefits of higher education, various factions within the public sector have questioned the efficacy, relevance, feasibility, and academic status of such programs within their respective institutions and among the larger educational community (Tomlinson, 1989).

It is not enough to merely place students with LD in supportive developmental programs without providing appropriate training, materials, and support to them and to their professors. To do so certainly calls for their failures! As Wagner (1990) observed, "encouraging greater instruction of students with disabilities in regular education classes, without serious attention to the instruction that goes on in these classes, would seem simply to encourage greater rates of academic failure" (p. 28). Also, if students with LD are to be effectively assisted in supportive program, issues and problems surrounding these programs must be addressed.

INNOVATIVE STRATEGIES FOR THE FUTURE

It is obvious that enhancing postsecondary support services to benefit students with LD requires a process of system change, as opposed to isolated programs and invalidated instructional practices often common with programming for these students. There is a pressing need to help colleges and universities meet the needs of these students. A useful process for improving postsecondary education is by reviewing the various concerns of researchers, scholars, and advocates who are calling for changes in the way two and four-year colleges and universities provide supportive services. In recent years, many questions have emerged during the development of services for students with learning disabilities: What documentation is necessary to determine eligibility for which services? What are the institution's responsibilities to modify a curriculum? What constitutes true access to education? Kroeger and Schuck (1993) gave specific directives for creating a responsive environment and called for: (a) organizing and structuring services; (b) further defining access to higher education; (c) clarifying available sources and allocations of funding services; and (d) consistently evaluating services and models for collaborating with faculty. Following are recommendations for building a responsive campus community to provide appropriate services to students with LD:

(1) Review the Structure of the Institution
  • Ensure that written college and university policy statements regarding services for students with LD are consistent with the mission of the institution.
  • Review all campus literature for statements of equal access and the procedures students with LD must follow to request services.
  • Consider housing the office for disability services in academic affairs or a similar administrative office for effective reporting and support.
(2) Establish Policies
  • Ensure confidentiality of student information.
  • Develop written policies and procedures, including the appeal processes, regarding student with LD in the areas of admission, documentation, academic accommodations and curriculum adjustments.
  • Make policies and procedures available to the entire campus community via student handbooks, catalogs, and course schedules in alternative formats.

(3) Promote Awareness
  • Establish mechanism for dissemination of information about learning disabilities to students, administration, faculty, and service professionals.
  • Disseminate information to the campus community about available services.
  • Familiarize faculty, staff, administration, and students with laws governing accommodations for students with learning disabilities.
  • Clearly designate the individuals who make the decision regarding accommodation so that intra faculty or staff disputes are minimized.
(4) Collaborate
  • Build campus expertise through collaboration and consultation.
  • Establish a team of service providers and faculty members for decision-making in regard to admission, documentation, academic adjustments and program accommodations for students with LD.
  • Remain current regarding disability issues.
  • Provide cost-effective, reasonable accommodations for students with LD.

Because of their frequent experiences with failure, many students with learning disabilities do not aspire to education beyond high school. The emphasis should be on preparing students to make the right choices of colleges as well as on delineating what accommodations they will need in their programs. Choosing a college for any student is difficult. Reputation, academic rigor, location, types of majors offered, extra curricular activities, and costs are just a few of the many variables that parents and students consider in selecting a college. In the case of students with LD, the choice can be even more difficult. In addition to the above factors, students and their parents will want to consider the level of support offered. For example, special accommodations must be available for students with LD when they take the Scholastic Aptitude Test (SAT) and the American College Test (ACT). Following are several questions that can serve as guidelines for choosing a college (see Michaels, 1987):

(1) Does the college provide services? To address this question, institutions should provide:
  • A full-time or part-time coordinator of services for students with LD.
  • Preliminary diagnostic services in order to determine student abilities to work at a college level.
  • Pre-admission advisement.
  • Short-term and long-term student counseling.
  • Study skills course work.
  • Remedial and basic skills classes.

- Feedback systems from professors to coordinators of services for learning disabled students.
- Termination services (counseling, testing, etc.) for those learning disabled students who leave college.

(2) Does the college furnish services? To address this question, institutions should provide:
- Access to required course syllabi.
- Access to tutors, readers, and note takers.
- Computers for student use.
- Taped textbooks and recorded lectures.

(3) Does the college allow services? To address this question, institutions should provide:
- Modified college admission procedures.
- Visits to college classrooms in advance of enrolling in the college.
- Untimed exams.
- Varied testing options.
- Advanced acquisition of required reading assignments.

(4) Does the college supply services? To address this question, institutions should provide:
- Full-time or part-time educators to assist with the needs of the learning disabled population.
- Guidance in structuring the student workday.
- Student groups that facilitate making friends.
- Access to early registration procedures.

(5) Does the college give services? To address this question, the institution should provide:
- Assistance with the class scheduling.
- Listings of outside services and support groups in the college community for use by students with LD.

As indicated above, Section 504 of the Vocational Rehabilitation Act of 1973 requires that colleges make reasonable accommodations for students with LD. These accommodations are of three general types:

(1) The way in which specific courses are taught; giving extra time on exams, allowing students to take exams in a distraction-free room, allowing students to take exams in a different format (e.g. substituting an oral exam for a written one).

(2) Modifications in program requirements; waiving or substituting certain requirements (e.g. foreign languages, allowing the student to take lighter academic loads each semester).

(3) Providing auxiliary aids; providing tape recordings of textbooks, access to a Kurzweil Reading Machine (a computer that scans text and converts it into an auditory output), and recruiting and assigning note takers for lectures.

Although there are no simple solutions to meeting the educational needs of college-bound students with LD, research and experience show that the educator has a significant impact on the success of college-bound students LD. To facilitate continuing academic success for these students, colleges and universities need to have an understanding and awareness of the classroom changes that can make a difference. Colleges and universities need to institute strong policies and procedures aimed at helping to incorporate these changes into both their everyday teaching plans as well as their classroom management techniques. One of the classroom changes that can greatly benefit college-bound students with LD is infusion of study skills into the teaching of content material.

Study skills are a very broad term that encompasses a multitude of skills that enhance the effectiveness and efficiency of learning. They are often considered to be mainly instructional strategies such as note-taking skills, memory techniques, or test-taking procedures. Just as important to learning, however, are organizational strategies, time management skills, and self-awareness skills (see Janigo & Castenbader, 2002). The purpose of study skills must be to teach students how to learn. The development of skills that are transferable to all academic areas makes the teaching of study skills indispensable in education (Schumaker & Deshler, 1988).

Many college students use strategies to compensate for their learning disability in college work. The following list indicates the types of strategies that are most frequently mentioned. Should educators and specialists have to assist a student with LD in selecting a college program, these strategies can be used as rough indicators of the quality of the college program for the student. Bender (2004) noted that the college learning-disabilities clinic can:

(1) Arrange alternative times and modes of presentation.
(2) Arrange to tape-record lectures.
(3) Obtain copies of class notes from others for study.
(4) Arrange assistance in time planning for big projects during the semester and for smaller weekly assignments.
(5) Schedule an appropriate load of courses or a lighter load.
(6) Offer assistance in completing homework and daily assignments.
(7) Arrange for the use of highlighted books, or taped books.
(8) Offer no cost tutoring assistance on a daily, biweekly, or weekly basis.
(9) Arrange for use of word-processing/editing programs and computer time.

(10) Identify college faculty who are willing to assist students with LD in their classes.

(11) Instruct the student in using learning strategies that promote meta-cognitive understanding of the material to be learned.

CONCLUSION

For many students with LD, participation in postsecondary education is appropriate. However, to achieve this goal, comprehensive transition planning is essential. The primary objective of this planning is to help students select access and succeed in a postsecondary education program. This chapter has presented issues and problems surrounding the delivery of support services, learning strategies, accommodations and modifications, and exemplary programs designed to enhance the full participation of college-bound students with learning disabilities. Legal mandates ensure that equal opportunity is provided to all individuals with LD. Fortunately, increased knowledge of legal rights will help administrators, teachers, parents, and advocates ensure that students with LD receive appropriate accommodations and curricular modifications that are not expensive or time-consuming. For many students with LD, provision of appropriate accommodations is the only way they will ever achieve equal education opportunity. In the coming years, educators must direct their attention on college-bound students with LD and postsecondary support services if the problems they face are to be reduced. Also, as legal rights and protections are implemented and realized fully, college-bound students with LD will have equal access and appropriate opportunities to maximize their academic potential. In other words, legislators must realize that special education will continue to exist. This existence will be solidified when educators come to the realization that all students deserve educational opportunities equal to those made available to students without disabilities.

REFERENCES

Acne, B., & Kroger, S. A. (1997). Career development of college students with disabilities: An interactional approach to defining the issues. *Journal of College Student Development, 38*(4), 344–356.

Bender, W. N. (2004). *Learning disabilities: Characteristics, identification, and teaching strategies* (5th ed.). Boston: Allyn & Bacon.

Bourke, A. B., Strenhorn, K. C., & Silver, P. (2000). Faculty members' provision of instructional accommodations with LD. *Journal of Learning Disabilities, 330*, 26–32.

Brackett, J., & McPhearson, A. (1996). Learning comparison of discrepancy-based diagnosis models. In: N. Gregg, C. Hoy & A. Gay (Eds), *Adults with Learning Disabilities: Theoretical and Practical Perspectives* (pp. 68–840). New York: Guilford Press.

Brown, D., Gerber, P., & Dowdy, C. (1992). *Pathways to employment for people with learning disabilities: A national strategy from the delegates to the pathways to employment for people with learning disabilities.* Washington, DC: President's Committee on Employment of People with Disabilities.

Cordoni, B. (1982). The learning-disabled college student. *Journal of Learning Disabilities, 15,* 599–603.

Dalke, C., & Schmitt, S. (1987). Meeting the transition needs of college bound students withal learning disabilities. *Journal of Learning Disabilities, 20,* 176–180.

Edgar, E. (1987). Secondary programs in special education: Are many of them justifiable? *Exceptional Children, 53,* 555–561.

Halpern, A. S., & Benz, M. R. (1987). A statewide examination of secondary special education for students with mild disabilities: Implications for the high school curriculum. *Exceptional Children, 52,* 122–129.

Henderson, C. (1995). College freshman with disabilities. A statistical profile. Washington, DC: Health Resource Center. *Journal of Learning Disabilities, 29,* 23–30.

Henderson, C. (1999). *College freshman with disabilities: A biennial statistical profile.* Washington, DC: American Council on Education, HEATH Resource Center.

Janigo, S. J., & Castenbader, V. (2002). The transition from high school to postsecondary education for students with learning disabilities: A survey of college coordinators. *Journal of Learning Disabilities, 35,* 462–468.

Kroeger, S. A., & Schuck, J. (1993). *Responding to disabilities issues in student affairs.* San Francisco: Josey-Bass.

Lynch, R. T., & Gussel, L. (1996, March/April). Disclosure and self-advocacy regarding disability-related needs: Strategies to maximize integration in postsecondary education. *Journal of Counseling and Development, 74,* 352–357.

Maheady, L., Sacca, M. K., & Harper, G. F. (1988). Class wide peer tutoring with mildly handicapped high school students. *Exceptional Children, 55*(1), 52–59.

Mangrum, C. T., & Strichart, S. S. (1983). College possibilities for the learning disabled. *Learning Disabilities Quarterly, 5,* 57–68.

Michaels, R. J. (1987). Evaluating the college of choice. *Academic Therapy, 22,* 485–488.

Mull, C., Sitlington, P. L., & Alper, S. (2001). Postsecondary educators for students with learning disabilities: A synthesis of the literature. *Exceptional Children, 68,* 97–118.

Murray, C., Goldstein, D. F., & Nourse, S. E. (2000). The postsecondary school attendance and completion rates of high school graduates with learning disabilities. *Learning Disabilities and Practice, 15,* 11–127.

NJCLD (1999). *Secondary to postsecondary education transition planning for students with learning disabilities.* Austin, TX: Pro-ed.

Patton, J. R., & Polloway, E. A. (1993). Learning disabilities: The challenges of adulthood. *Journal of Learning Disabilities, 25,* 410–415.

Reiff, H. B., Gerber, P. J., & Ginsberg, R. (1993). Definitions of learning disabilities from adults with learning disabilities: The insiders' perspectives. *Learning Disability Quarterly, 16,* 114–125.

Rieth, H. J., & Polsgrove, L. (1994). Curriculum and instructional issues in teaching secondary students with learning disabilities. *Learning Disabilities Research & Practice, 9,* 118–126.

Riley, R. (Ed.) (1997, September 7). *Letter to educators from the secretary of education.* Washington, DC: U.S. Dept. of Education.

Schloss, P. J., Smith, M. A., & Schloss, C. N. (1990). *Instructional methods for students with adolescents with learning and behavior problems.* Boston: Allyn & Bacon.

Schumaker, J. B., & Deshler, D. (1988). Implementing the regular education initiative in secondary schools: A different ball game. *Journal of Learning Disabilities, 21,* 36–42.

Scott, S. (1994). Determining reasonable academic adjustments for college students with learning disabilities. *Journal of Learning Disabilities, 27,* 403–412.

Scott, S., & Gregg, N. (2000). Meeting the evolving educational needs of faculty in providing access for college students with LD. *Journal of Learning Disabilities, 33,* 158–167.

Seidenberg, P. L. (1986). The high school-college connection: A transition model to expand higher educational opportunities for learning disabled students. In: A. Gardner (Ed.), *Reflections on Transition.* New York: City University of New York, Center For Advanced Study in Education.

Shapiro, J. (1993, December 13). Separate and unequal. *U.S. News and World Report.*

Shaw, R. A. (1999). The case for course substitutions as a reasonable accommodation for students with foreign language learning disability. *Journal of Learning Disabilities, 32,* 320–328.

Siegel, L. S. (1999). Issues in the definition and diagnosis of learning disabilities. A perspective on Guckenberger v. Boston University. *Journal of Learning Disability, 32,* 304–319.

Sigmond, N. (1990). Rethinking secondary school programs for students with learning disabilities. *Focus on Exceptional Children, 23,* 1–14.

Sparks, R., Phillips, L., & Ganschow, L. (1996). Students classified as learning disabled and the college foreign language requirement. In: J. Liskin-Gasparro (Ed.), *Patterns and Policies: The Changing Demographics of Foreign Language Instruction.* Boston: Heinle & Heinle.

Thornton, H. S., & Zigmond, N. (1986). Follow-up post-secondary age LD graduates and dropouts. *LD Research, 1,* 50–55.

Tomlinson, L. (1989). *Postsecondary developmental programs.* Washington, DC: School of Education, George Washington University.

Tucker, P. B. (1996). Application of the Americans with disabilities act (ADA) on section 504 to colleges and universities: An overview and discussion of special issues relating to students. *Journal of College and University Law, 23*(1), 1–41.

Vogel, S. (1982). On developing learning disabilities college programs. *Journal of Learning Disabilities, 15,* 518–528.

Wagner, M. (1989, March). The transitions experiences of youth with disabilities: A report from the national longitudinal transition study. Paper presented at the International Convention of the Division of Research, Council for Exceptional Children, San Francisco, CA.

Wagner, M. (1990, April). The school programs and school performance of secondary students classified as learning disabled: Findings from the national longitudinal transition study of special education students. Paper presented at the National Convention of Division G, American Educational Research Association, Boston, MA.

Witte, R., Phillips, L., & Kakala, M. (1998). Job satisfaction of college graduates with learning disabilities. *Journal of Learning Disabilities, 31,* 259–265.

WINGS ACADEMY: A NEW CHARTER SCHOOL FOR STUDENTS WHO LEARN DIFFERENTLY

Dani La Porte and Nicola Leather

WINGS ACADEMY FOR STUDENTS WITH LEARNING DIFFERENCES

Wings Academy is a charter school[1] in Milwaukee, Wisconsin that opened in August of 2002. It is located in the basement of an enormous, beautifully decorated and well maintained convent which houses several social service agencies, retired School Sisters who live there and another charter school. This school was envisioned and created by the authors (Co-Directors), two special education teachers (one is also a parent of a child with Asperger's Syndrome) who believed the local districts were not providing an appropriate education for students with special education needs, and those with a label of "learning disabled" in particular. Prior to meeting, the Co-Directors had thoughts of creating their own Utopian school in which all students were taught with appropriate methodologies. By the time they had met, they both knew what their school would look like. Eventually, they combined their ideas and opened a school three years later. In this chapter, they describe the rationale for this school and programmatic realities that they have adapted to achieve their vision.

Current Perspectives on Learning Disabilities
Advances in Special Education, Volume 16, 247–264
Copyright © 2004 by Elsevier Ltd.
All rights of reproduction in any form reserved
ISSN: 0270-4013/doi:10.1016/S0270-4013(04)16013-3

MISSION AND VISION STATEMENTS

The goal of Wings is to provide a strong, structured curriculum using simultaneous multisensory teaching techniques and art-based instruction designed to focus on the needs of *individuals who learn differently* in order to allow them equal access to the print-based and social world around them. Wings believes all people can learn if provided with a learning environment specific to their learning style.

Wings will provide a small school learning environment for *all* students, *but in particular*, those with learning *differences* whose educational needs cannot be met within the regular education setting. This will be accomplished through:

- A safe and effective learning environment.
- Small classes.
- A focus on strong math, language and reading instruction.
- Direct instruction.
- Art-based instruction.
- Structured, sequential approach to learning.
- Application to real-life skills designed to meet the specific needs of our students.
- Self-discipline through the martial arts (Martial Arts for Peace).
- Technology in the classroom to facilitate learning.
- Instruction and practice using social skills appropriately.

It is generally well-known that those with learning disabilities (LD) have a high rate of unemployment and that the prison population is overwhelmed with those who have LD (Lindamood et al., 1997). In order to avoid this all too frequent result of an ineffective education, students at Wings learn to be self-sufficient in school, at home, and in the community. By so doing, they become productive, involved citizens who are concerned about the world around them.

PROGRAM OVERVIEW

Wings Academy is a school that is designed to serve 50 non-traditional students in grades 6 through 10 during the first year (growing to 120 students, grades K-12 within 6 years) who have experienced school failure due to problems learning to read, spell, write, perform mathematical concepts and organize themselves. Admission is not limited to students with identified disabilities. Potential Wings students may have been identified as having a learning disability or have a history of school failure (i.e. at-risk students). Many students may have experienced extreme difficulties in school which have resulted in passive, aggressive, or attention seeking behaviors. Their teachers often report that they do not know what to do with them because of these behavioral and motivational concerns. Many students get to middle or high school without the ability to read past a third grade level, which has added to their growing frustration with the school setting. Their parents often report that these students are bright and can figure out how to put things together or do other tasks that do not have a language component. These students, the "many needless casualties . . . from contemporary educational systems" (Gardner, 1991, p. 12), are the students the Wings Academy program reach and teach.

Wings Academy intends to meet the needs of all students, but in particular, those who have not learned how to read, spell, write or perform mathematical operations. Wings is an alternative for students whose educational needs have not been met through traditional methods of education. Its program utilizes the exemplary and unique educational model practiced at the Lab School of Washington, D.C. (the Lab School) and explicit reading and spelling instruction. The Lab School was founded and designed by Dr. Sally Smith in 1967 for intelligent children with LD. Smith was concerned about the same issues identified by Wings' Co-Directors: *a traditional approach to educating students with severe LD does not work and the least restrictive environment is not necessarily the regular education setting. Some students simply need intense and different educational practices.* Logically, instruction is provided in very small groups for literacy and math instruction. Reading and language arts instruction feature instruction of explicit phonemic awareness (decoding and spelling), expressive and receptive language, written expression, comprehension and handwriting. Math features a sequential, multisensory, hands-on project-based approach. Social studies and science are presented in an arts and project-based academic club format. Through these clubs, students learn content facts but also transfer knowledge from skills to application through arts-based experiences and the use of the five "Habits of Mind" as used at New York's Central Park East Secondary School and described by Meier (1995) in *The Power of Their Ideas* (p. 50). The goal of this approach avoids simplistic or exceedingly difficult questions and finds the, "medium questions that take you somewhere" (Bruner, 1977, p. 40).

Wings recognizes that there are differences in how people "learn, represent and utilize knowledge . . . [and plans to] challenge an educational system that assumes everyone can learn the same materials in the same way" (Gardner, 1991, p. 12). Learning differences manifest themselves differently and as a result, students are not taught with identical practices. "It is our job to find out how [each student] learns and then teach him how he learns" (Smith, 1995, p. 151). Wings students are provided daily opportunities to show their strengths in academics without relying solely on written language. Students are assessed at the beginning of the school year to determine their current functioning in academic areas. All instruction is in small groups which address current abilities of students and their developmental readiness. Sequential, simultaneous, multisensory instruction is used to teach and reinforce literacy concepts in small groups and throughout the day. Students participate in arts-based academic project clubs which reinforce sequence and organization through the use of the content curriculum (Kendall & Marzano, 1997). These experiences represent the "many different ways of acquiring and representing knowledge" (Gardner, 1991, p. 14). Eisner (1994) commented that these "other views of mind, knowledge and intelligence" are too often absent in curriculum, resulting in unequal opportunities for students, "whose aptitudes reside in areas that are neither attended to or adequately assessed" (p. 363). Much attention is given to these "other views of mind" and lesson activities are designed to mesh with the content area curriculum. Instructional strategies of Wings emphasize sequential, multisensory and arts and project-based methods. If a child is not acquiring skills and concepts they need to continue learning, the teaching team will collaborate with the parents and child (if appropriate) to find an approach that is successful. The student is not blamed for failure to learn. Wings believes all students, if provided appropriate learning experiences, can learn!

Wings classes ideally range in size from 5 to 10 students, depending upon teaching practices and discourse involved. This allows teachers and students to create a learning environment that provides individual attention and modifications for each child. The smaller environment and ability to create a safe, supportive, success-oriented classroom culture encourages students to take risks within that setting that they would not otherwise consider, such as reading aloud or asking for help. In an example of the effective use of the arts in education combined with risk-taking, Greeley (2000) used drama in her classroom to provide a "safe" form of risk taking and to build community. She found that through this exploration, "real growth and learning occurred" (p. 115). The Wings faculty demands a lot of intensive work and participation from students. As a result, two guided 15 minute breaks are allotted each day (one in the morning and one in the afternoon). At these times, students practice relaxation techniques they have learned in Martial Arts for Peace and have a healthy snack. It is Wings' intention that these energy renewing breaks help ease any tension, frustration, and exhaustion that may have developed. The school's culture reflects the classroom culture. Students show respect for each other and their accomplishments through celebrations, performances, and displays of completed products. Students need to feel safe in school, not just physically, but emotionally. Disrespect and ridicule are not tolerated. A small environment in addition to the educational practices described in a later section allows this climate to be established.

The Wings program addresses educational needs of students with learning differences, who due to educational settings and experiences they have had, have not yet learned or retained the basic skills needed to function in a literate society.

Many of these students also lack necessary social skills. Just as reading is not a natural skill, interpreting and learning appropriate social skills are also not natural skills. They often overreact to conflicts and escalate interpersonal and intrapersonal problems. Finally, some students struggle with recalling and implementing math facts and processes, these are the essential skills the curriculum address.

The Wings faculty believe the ultimate goal of schooling is to learn to learn, acquire and utilize knowledge. Yet, every student has different aspirations for her future and what she will accomplish with this education. Wings appropriately addresses students' needs to make sure they not only learn to read, spell, write, and think mathematically, but also to have the necessary social skills to achieve success and reach their full potential. Wings personalizes instruction to enable learners to maximize their abilities so that those who wish to go on to college, vocational training or directly into the workforce are prepared to do so. Students who attend Wings learn how to read, spell and write. They learn to interpret and communicate socially. Students enjoy the education process. The staff of Wings do not believe they can change the influence of two-thirds of the day the child is not in school, but can strive to make the remaining third give each child the belief in herself and the courage to succeed in school and life.

ASSESSMENT AT WINGS ACADEMY

The goal of assessment at Wings is to provide the teacher, student, and parent with frequent feedback about student progress. This assessment is an important factor in the success of the program because teaching practices are immediately adjusted to needs and styles of each learner. Multiple forms of assessment are used in order to show students and parents the achievement the student has made. Pre, mid-year and end of year assessments which include attitude surveys, achievement and cognitive assessments, student goals, portfolios and teacher narratives are used to compare individual student growth. Students also receive daily feedback about their progress. Parents receive progress reports and are invited to parent-teacher-student meetings three times per year (every eight to ten weeks). Portfolios are reviewed at this time, progress is assessed and strategies are refined if needed.

Eisner (1994) advocated for multiple forms of assessment in order to "embrace the entirety of what counts educationally," which numerical data alone cannot do (p. 192). Wings teaches and assesses the whole child. At minimum, it fully expects its students, students who have made very little demonstrable progress for many years, to demonstrate a year's growth in reading and math skills the first year they are with the program. However, Wings expects progress to be even greater for most students; this is documented with a standardized assessment such as the

Woodcock-Johnson III and individualized assessments such as curriculum based measurement and reading inventories.

PARENTAL INVOLVEMENT

Parents are encouraged to speak with the Co-Directors prior to enrolling their child. At this time, the Wings program and expectations for students, parents and staff are clearly explained. Parents of students with and without special education needs are encouraged to attend annual and interim IEP, Individualized Education Plan (or Individualized Student Plan for students without special educational needs) meetings (held three times per year) and are encouraged to attend board and other school-related meetings. Parents are asked to participate in school activities such as sharing a skill and teaching it to students, supervise a computer lab (or other non-instruction class), school operations, chaperone field trips and other roles as the needs arise. They are asked to read to (or with) their child and review sight-words every night. Wings likes to see parents visiting and participating in activities on a frequent and regular basis. The faculty at Wings Academy recognize the unique perspectives parents have of their child and create an environment conducive to working together for the well-being of all.

EMPLOYMENT REQUIREMENTS

It is the desire of the Wings' founders that the entire staff will hold degrees and State Department of Public Instruction licenses in any category of special education (or a non-categorical certification), speech and language, occupational therapy, physical therapy, social work, regular education or related fields. Potential staff who have an extensive background in a certain area (i.e. a set designer, computer technician or artist) but without a degree in education or related field may fill teaching positions while obtaining an emergency or provisional license. Finally, all staff will meet the local district's background check requirements.

PROGRAMS AND THEORIES THAT GUIDE
WINGS ACADEMY

Wings has innovative ideas, programs, and theories that assist the planning of the school. The administrators feel strongly about all of these components and insisted the faculty learn how to implement each one. Interestingly, while there are many good programs "out there," neither of the administrators want a pre-packaged program. They want to create a new model that includes the components they believe their target population requires. Following is a brief description of the program orientation of Wings Academy:

- *Integrated Arts and Academic Clubs* (the Lab School Approach): Students use the arts as a vehicle for learning and acquiring basic skills and content knowledge (Smith, 2001). Arts are used to make concepts more concrete or to build upon what is already understood.
- *Orton-Gillingham and Lindamood-Bell* – These are sequential, simultaneous, multisensory instructional methods which have been described by the National Institutes of Child Health and Human Development as "the best strategy for preventing and correcting reading difficulties" (Adams, 1997, p. 3).
- *Martial Arts for Peace* – This is a non-violent program which incorporates the use of sequential movement through Karate along with peaceful conflict resolution techniques. The social lessons are reinforced and modeled as needed throughout the school day.
- *Developmentally appropriate instruction* – Activities used to help students conceptualize a topic at a concrete level (or wherever that student is functioning, as described by Piaget's stages of learning) so that further learning may be built upon it (Bybee & Sund, 1982, p. 37). (*This is a feature of the Lab School method.*)
- *Multiple intelligences* – In *The Unschooled Mind*, Gardner (1991) stated that, "Students who have perfectly adequate intuitive understandings often exhibit great difficulty in mastering the lessons of school. It is these students who exhibit learning problems" (p. 10). Teaching through the multiple intelligences (which reinforces the Lab School method) is the basis for daily teaching practices.
- *Alternative calendar* – Wings employs an alternative school year calendar in order to account for significant loss of acquired learning and prolonged recoupment. This will require interim educational opportunities.
- *Fitness for Life* – We believe in the "healthy body/healthy mind" axiom. Healthy eating, which will include breakfast and lunch programs as well as morning and afternoon snacks, will be promoted throughout the day. Consumption of chips and soda at school will not be allowed. Along with Martial Arts for Peace, aerobic exercise will be a daily part of the physical fitness curriculum.
- *Community* – Wings will be a grass-roots organization for linking agencies, parents, children and adults with learning disabilities and teachers concerned with learning disabilities in Southeasten Wisconsin. At some point in the future, Wings would like to offer evening courses for adults with learning disabilities.
- *Small School size* – Many studies have been conducted that point to the effectiveness of small classroom size, small schools and even small districts, especially

for inner-city youths. This also applies to students with significant academic and social needs. The only way Wings believes these students' multiple needs can appropriately be addressed is with small class sizes and a small school environment (Bickel & Howley, 2000).

Wings Academy's educational program is partially modeled around the methods used at the Lab School (the Lab School Method). The theory that guides the Lab School Method originated in the 18th century with educators who felt that prevailing methods of teaching were not effective. Traditional education was a passive form of acquiring knowledge, where the teacher was the disseminator of information and the students were to listen, read, write and compute. Several educators saw that this method was ineffectual. This revolution in educational philosophy was led by Johann Heinrich Pestalozzi, who created a school in Switzerland and Friedrich Froebel, the founder of kindergarten (De Pencier, 1967). Both educators firmly believed that a child learned by doing. Through Pestalozzi's school, Froebel's kindergarten and others who created similar programs, the focus was on the children as active participants in their education. The level of true learning and gains their students made provided the proof needed to demonstrate the effectiveness of these methods (p. 14). John Dewey put these ideas into practice at The Dewey School in Chicago (De Pencier, 1967). Dewey felt that education was too often taught from the adult perspective and in a manner that was not beneficial for most students. The Dewey School was set up to be a laboratory to put Dewey's theories of learning into practice. As De Pencier pointed out, the school was highly successful in educating students (p. 18).

The theory of Jean Piaget was an additional guiding factor in the creation of the Lab School Method (Smith, 1990). Piaget identified four stages of development. From birth to one and a half, children are in the sensory motor stage where they organize their world through movement and sensation. The next stage of development which occurs between the ages of one and a half to seven, is known as the preoperational stage. The child at this stage uses symbolic representations to solve problems and is unable to take another person's point of view. The third phase, the concrete operational stage, occurs between the ages of seven and eleven. Here, the child learns through concrete experiences and generally cannot learn abstract material unless it is presented in a concrete manner. The final phase, the period of formal operations, occurs from approximately age 11 through adulthood. If this phase is attained, it is at this point that the child begins to learn abstract concepts without concrete examples and can make deductions (Good & Brophy, 1990). These stages are usually met by children within certain ages, but some children may be at one stage longer than other children of the same age. Wings expects to enroll many students who have had difficulty moving beyond the concrete stage (and some who may still be in the preoperational stage). To learn new concepts, these students must be taught in a way in which they are able to make concrete associations that directly relate to their lives. Smith (1995) indicated that, "Because learning disabled children are so concrete, they need to be introduced to abstract ideas through their bodies and objects and pictures" (p. 158). By providing concrete experiences within a structure that allows students to use their background knowledge, they can learn new concepts. By doing this, Wings provides students with strategies to start new tasks, gather and store new information and solve problems.

The Lab School Method has embraced the theories of Dewey and Piaget to create a way to effectively educate students with severe learning disabilities. This method is referred to as the Art and Academic Club Method or Lab School Method. Through this practice, the arts are a major part of the students' day. They are used to provide students with age appropriate yet concrete ways to solve problems and learn. Listed below are some of the art forms used and the skills that are learned from each genre (see Smith, 1990):

Art Forms	Skills
Woodwork	Applied math, physics, organizational skills
Collage	Planning, part-whole separation
Printmaking	Reading readiness (left-right orientation, pattern recognition)
Music	Reading readiness (linking sound and symbol) Math readiness (rhythm, counting)
Puppetry	Language Arts, social skills, visual-motor skills
Drama	Language Arts (inferences, analogies), social skills
Film Making	Organizational skills, cause-effect relationships, attention to detail, following a main theme
Dance	Following Directions, sequencing, orientation in time and space, rhythm, self-confidence (p. 79).

Another portion of the day is spent in academic clubs. In clubs, abstract concepts are taught through concrete material using play and the arts. For example, Smith (1990) described the Industrialists' Club in the statement below:

> The older elementary school children become the robber barons who were also inventors, politicians and businessmen. They identify with such historic figures as DuPont, Carnegie and Rockefeller. They study the methods these greats used to accumulate their wealth and the legacy they left behind. Through role playing, they not only learn history, geography and civics, but begin to debate moral and ethical issues and are exposed to the rudiments of economics (p. 80).

In addition to the Integrated Arts and Academic Club method, direct, explicit instruction in reading, spelling, writing and math are taught within a small group setting. Depending upon the needs of the student, they will learn reading and spelling through the Orton-Gillingham or Lindamood-Bell methods. Wings is currently reviewing various math programs (i.e. Cloud Nine®, and "Mathematics: A Way of Thinking"). Due to the variance of individual needs, more than one program is used at Wings. Most math classes use manipulatives and hands-on projects to reinforce basic skills and to make the curriculum relevant to students. This is another unique feature of Wings. Many schools or districts adapt one program that must be adhered to. At Wings, the needs of each child guide teachers in the selection of appropriate curriculum and pedagogy. [Note: Contact Wings Academy for other programmatic details.]

FINDINGS SINCE WINGS' ESTABLISHMENT

When one conducts research, writes, discusses, and promotes her dream for many years, it is hard to believe that the dream has come to fruition. While as co-directors, we knew this was going to be a difficult process, the difficulties we have encountered have been greater than we expected; we sometimes have to remind ourselves that we left our secure, financially comfortable jobs with great benefits willingly. We knew this was not going to be an absolutely Utopian school in practice, but hoped there would be fewer challenges than what we have encountered. We also thought that the first year of a new school is always the most difficult. In this section, we discuss some of our challenges and successes.

Wings Academy is marketed to students who have struggled to learn in traditional settings, despite being of average or better intelligence. We opted for opening to students in the secondary level (grades 6–10) because when we polled potential parents from local parent advocate organizations and parents of children with dyslexia, we found the greatest interest was within this grade range. Today, 51 students are enrolled at Wings Academy (our goal was 50 students). At least 30 students have identified special education needs, most have labels of LD and a handful have speech, cognitive or emotional disabilities (about three students have dual diagnoses, as well). Since we are a public school, we are not allowed to "screen" students to ensure compatibility with the program. Fortunately, most students "fit" the educational needs we are designed to serve. Our first lesson with this population was that students who have experienced many accumulated years of school failure were not going to be grateful and suddenly compliant because they had teachers who were eager to help them learn via appropriate methods. We did not expect this aspect to be easy, but we sure did not expect the abusive defiance engaged by some students.

Our second lesson was that most students were not accustomed to being expected to participate in class or to be held accountable to high standards. As a result, they planned to do what they have learned to do to survive: *avoidance by any means necessary*. We have had to build relationships with students who have learned not to trust teachers, or education in general, before we could fully implement the teaching approaches we planned to use. Fortunately, the parents or primary caregivers of most of our students have been very supportive of our efforts to work with their children, even when they have challenged every philosophical belief the school was founded upon. For example, we do not believe in suspending students. However, some behaviors have been so inappropriate (i.e. calling one of the female teachers with a buzz-cut a, "Bald-headed mother-f – – – "), a weapons violation and small amounts of drugs, that we have been left with few options. We would prefer to be positive; but, on occasion, we have had to implement after school and Saturday detentions in addition to suspensions and other punishments for unacceptable behavior. To counter this negative behavior, good decision making and classroom participation is acknowledged privately or publicly, depending upon the student and the event. Most students long for this positive reinforcement about their academic and social abilities. Many have rarely experienced this. Students do receive positive feedback about their performance, such as notes and phone calls to their home. Future plans to reinforce positive behavior and participation include frequent incentive activities such as bowling, a movie, skiing or other outings and events. We have frequent contacts with parents and are able to openly share concerns and successes. Parents like to hear that their child is succeeding – not just when they are not. Parents have complained that in past school experiences, they have only been called for the "bad stuff." At Wings, parent contacts for the good and the bad are frequent. For example, teachers have nearly two hours of planning time each day, which, on most days, gives plenty of time to call.

Originally, we planned to have groups no larger than 5 students for literacy-based classes. Unfortunately, our budget did not allow for this. We have been able to keep these, and all other classes, to a maximum of 15 students. Most academic classes have between 8 and 10 students – not the 30 to 40 students to which they were accustomed. Despite the vastly improved student teacher ratio, we have found that some students need even smaller groups. For example, some students truly require one-to-one reading instruction in order to have a chance at achieving a functional literacy level or better (better is our preferred outcome). We are not able to provide this level of instruction to these students and they continue to struggle with classroom activities centered on written language. Without one-to-one instruction, some of these children will not learn to read. Other problems we have encountered have centered around the organization of the school day and week. Wednesdays were intended to be days in which programs such as Capieora, African drumming, drama, sculpture and other activities that are not a part of the daily curriculum were offered. We found these days to interfere with the flow of the rest of the week and were discontinued. However, we wanted to offer additional experiences for students. To accomplish this, African drumming is provided on Wednesday afternoons to the group studying Africa and Capieora is offered to two of the Tae Kwon Do classes. We hope to add after school activities, such as drawing, student council, and bell choir will to supplement the regular program in the future.

The school day originally was scheduled to include two breaks. The first was in the morning for about fifteen minutes. A local bagel company agreed to donate left-over bagels on a daily basis. This morning break has remained, but instead of being held in a common area, the break is now held in individual classrooms due to inappropriate name-calling and other poor behaviors. Students look forward to this break and remind us when it is time for them to be served. The afternoon break is simply a bathroom and water break instead of a snack as originally intended. While we can not financially offer food right now, it would be interesting to compare achievement and incident referrals during the afternoon period (this is a two-hour class of combined social studies, science, English and the arts) before and after a snack is added.

We had planned a twelve week session of staff development that included learning and practicing the new techniques we employ; discussions about characteristics and strategies for working with students with learning differences and attention deficit disorder; classroom management; the philosophy and practice of Tae Kwon Do; the creation of a safe and supportive classroom and school environment; and instruction in our expectations for unit and lesson plan organization and delivery. We were able to cover some basic information about working with our intended population, however there were often many absences because a few people could not leave their current place of employment until three weeks before the opening of the school. We continued to proceed, but only with half of the staff. The two members who have had difficulty with meeting our expectations were two of the three who were not able to attend the sessions. The plan was to brief them in the few weeks before school was to begin, along with the additional training we had organized.

Due to circumstances beyond our control, the two weeks prior to our opening was consumed with collecting furniture and physically organizing the school. We had hoped to move into our space about seven weeks before school opened. When we planned the staff development sessions this seemed like plenty of time to organize and work on staff development. However, the owners of the property were having new heating and air conditioning installed. The contractors were supposed to have finished installation in our leased space before our planned first date of occupancy. They finished two weeks before students were to arrive. Our back-up plan was to work on the topics we did not cover during our staff meetings in the school year (we formally meet twice a week for 30 minutes and once weekly for 60–90 minutes). Now that we are in session, most of these meetings have had to center around immediate concerns about students, state mandated testing and other issues that needed to be addressed. While staff development is crucial, other commitments (e.g. how to operate the administrative functions of a school and meet the bureaucratic obligations to our charter authorizer and state department of instruction) have had urgent attention.

The faculty of Wings Academy is fantastic! We have been able to "hand-pick" our teachers. Those selected have been people we believe have the inner strength and ability to work with our students and each other. We need people who: (a) are able to work as a team; (b) who recognize things that need to be done; and (c) can "jump in" and complete what needs doing. The Wings staff consists of two regular education teachers, two special education teachers and three people with emergency licenses who have applied to teacher education programs. Of these three, one has a Master's degree in curriculum and instruction; another has a Master's degree in Fine Art; and the third is completing his Master's degree in philosophy. Their range of experiences helps inform their teaching practice in unique ways and brings additional expertise and knowledge to the team. In addition, three faculty members have learning differences themselves. The faculty, however, is lacking in ethnic diversity. Fortunately, two of our consultants, a few board members and many of our family volunteers help fill this disparity between staff and students.

The ability of the staff to work as a team is very important, but the ability to manage one's classroom is equally vital. There have been difficulties in this area that have been and will continue to be addressed in staff meetings and on an individual basis. Students who attend Wings Academy demand a great deal of attention and structure. We would like to provide attention for acceptable behaviors and academic successes, not just to redirect students. Classroom organization is essential to promoting student success. These were areas we hoped to address prior to the beginning of the school year. Instead, we have had to address them as problems have occurred instead of pro-actively, as we would prefer. In order to help foster the safe climate we want students to sense here, which includes feeling they can succeed, teachers must be very organized and structured when teaching. It has been very evident that consistent teacher behaviors and routines have not yet been established at the time of this writing. As a result, teachers are now required to turn in an outline of their unit (for one to eight weeks) and daily lesson plans for the week every Monday. They must have an "attention getter" established for students to work on when they arrive in class, such as a problem on the chalkboard to work on while the teacher takes attendance and students get settled. Their units must include goals, objectives, major themes/concepts, people and events, a lesson sequence, and means of incorporating the arts at least three times a week and various forms of assessment. Lessons must include goals and objectives, an introduction, modeling, guided practice, individual practice, assessment and reflection. Not long ago, Incentive Publications (1995) incorporated Gardner's (1983) theory of multiple intelligences with Bloom's taxonomy (1954). In this work, educational objectives and goals were listed to re-emphasize the importance of student centered activities, such as those employed at Wings Academy. The use of this list as a reference and guide for developing lessons has been stressed. It is part of the responsibility of teachers to make sure they provide the structure to help students feel safe (academically, physically, and emotionally) and to uphold the mission and vision of the school. The use of more traditional teaching methods is to be the exception. Unit outlines and lesson plans, and subsequently classroom instruction, need to reflect the unique characteristics of the Wings Academy program.

Tae Kwon Do and academic clubs have proven to be the more difficult subjects to teach and manage. Some students do not want to participate in Tae Kwon Do and others are too active in this setting. For example, a few students practice kicking each other at inappropriate times. Students are about to begin wearing doboks, Tae Kwon Do uniforms, which may improve the classroom climate and decrease inappropriate behaviors. Students will be tested to earn stars to sew on their uniforms to show the incremental steps they have earned between earning belts. The combination of the uniforms and belt level may help improve the atmosphere and participation in the dojong (Tae Kwon Do room). Younger students seem to present the biggest challenge with regards to impulsive, potentially dangerous actions. High school students either participate or flat-out refuse – they may change their mind when they realize they will not be getting a physical education credit if they do not participate.

The academic clubs (integrated science, social studies, English and the arts) have been difficult for some teachers to structure. Some of this is due to the extremely challenging behaviors some students present and the mixture of person-alities within each room. There are many advantages to being a small school, but one disadvantage is that we cannot move a student from one class to another. There is no other appropriate (academically or socially) class to which to move them. This is especially true with club because students are, for the most part, grouped by grade level for this class. Other difficulties have included the varied levels of background knowledge of the students in club. Students get bored listening to something they "think" they know about or when it is overly complicated to them at that time. Teachers who have a consistent routine and organized lessons have been more successful with this period. It should be noted that these teachers also have younger students who tend to be less defiant and behaviorally challenging than some of the older students (all the more reason for these teachers to be well organized!).

Students have been making good progress in reading, spelling/language arts and math. These classes are by nature more easily structured and routine than the others may be. Each teacher uses Orton-Gillingham or Lindamood Bell© methods in reading and spelling/language arts, but personalizes them. It has been remarkable to watch students learn concepts they should have learned years ago, apply them, and become independent readers and more accurate at spelling. What a self-esteem boost! Some may argue that students could get books on tape or use spell check instead of spending time explicitly learning these skills. Those things, and we make this clear to students, are "crutches." Finally, the math program is well-structured and individually paced. There is a lot of repetition and review as well as practice with practical applications.

While there have been an unexpected number of challenges in these first two months of school, a lot of individual growth has been observed and reported anecdotally. The most noticeable is in regards to one of our high school boys, Mike.[2] His father, a single father of several adopted boys, asked to meet with us before the school year started. He prepared each of the teachers a folder about how to work with students with ADHD (attention deficit hyperactive disorder), which manifests in two of his children. Mike also has difficulty controlling his anger. Given this, he shared how to best work with three of his children he was enrolling at Wings. Not only did this prepare us for these students' individual idiosyncrasies, it probably planted a bias for (or possibly against) them. We do not believe it colored any of our attitudes negatively towards Mike. If anything, it gave us the ability to better understand his needs and personal nuances when there were incidents or potential problems in which he was involved. Mike started the year very well. He presented himself as a mature, responsible student right away. Then he skipped school with two others who had already been pegged as "trouble makers" by students on the third day of school. Unlike the other two students, he returned when his father was able to reach him on his cell phone. He admitted his error and genuinely apologized. This type of incident has not happened since that first week. The only other serious incident he has been involved with was instigated by girls his age who were intentionally trying to get him angry, and succeeded. We are all very impressed with his ability to behave appropriately given the difficulties a few other students present to him. He has even acknowledged he does better in school (i.e. able to make good, responsible social and academic decisions) when he is not around one of his friends. His growth in ability to monitor and control his angry outbursts, in addition to his mature classroom presence as a positive school leader, have continued to be demonstrated and have increased in intensity as the weeks have passed.

CONCLUSION

In this chapter, we have described Wings Academy, an innovative program for students who learn differently. As Co-Directors, we have struggled with student behaviors and staff preparation. For anyone who may be in the process of designing a school, we would recommend that they not work in another capacity (we did not have the finances available to leave our teaching positions) and to begin staff development well in advance of the first two months of schools. Staff needs to be prepared for working with challenging students, new pedagogies, and lesson design. Even experienced teachers benefit from a review of practices and strategies for working with all students, but especially those with highly demanding behaviors and academic needs. As discussed, we had planned to address these areas, but this had to be tabled just to get the school physically ready for students. School planners also need to be realistic in what can reasonably be accomplished in any given time frame. We would have liked to have made home visits to all who enrolled prior to the school year. We hoped to test all students for basic academic levels and to learn their strengths before the school year began, but were only able to test about one-third of the students. We had staff development sessions prepared, but were unable to complete this to our satisfaction. It is important that you prioritize what needs to happen and scale back some plans if circumstances in the amount of time or money available change or in an unexpected event occurs.

It is equally critical to learn the working habits of your potential staff. We really enjoy all of the teachers we have hired, but some intuitively know when they need to assist in some way. Others need to have the expectations for working in a school environment clearly set out. They need to realize that their day does not end when the students go home. There is work that needs to be done for the benefit of the entire organization.

Despite our obstacles, Wings Academy soars! That may become our motto!! There have been numerous challenges to overcome as a new school, but many successes at many different levels have already been seen in this first phase of existence. So much has happened, yet there is still much to implement and practices that need to continue to develop. Our parents are very supportive and eager to assist us. Students, based on noted improvement in participation and improvement in applying concepts, are doing well in reading, language arts and math, but there is a lot of inconsistency within the arts-based academic clubs. Many students enjoy the Martial Arts for Peace (MAP) program, but students continue to establish a brutal pecking order, despite our attempts to combat this problem which the MAP program is intended to address. Bully-awareness, non-violent means of expressing anger, and appropriate social skills are being taught and classroom structure addressed, but it will take a long time for students and staff to change and regularly practice or implement new strategies for effectively managing these behaviors. Two of the tenets of Tae Kwon Do are "indomitable spirit" and "perseverance." Our students and staff have these characteristics. These strengths, along with many other complimentary attitudes, will carry all of us through the years as Wings Academy becomes the school we envision for our children who learn differently.

NOTES

1. Charter schools are public schools that are held to higher accountability standards in return for some flexibility in school management, curriculum and organization. The local school district authorized the charter but the staff of Wings Academy are not employed by this district.
2. Name changed to protect student's privacy.

REFERENCES

Adams, M. J. (1997). About the NICHD program of research on reading development and disorders (p. 3). www.interdys.org/article4.stm, Note: Interdys.org is now (keyword) Ldonline.

Bickel, R., & Howley, C. (2000). The influence of scale on school performance: A multilevel extension of the Matthew principle. *Education Policy Analysis Archives*, 8(22). http://olam.ed.asu.edu/epaa/v8n22/.

Bloom, B. S. (Ed.) (1954). *Taxonomy of educational objectives: The classification educational goals: Handbook I, cognitive domain*. New York: Longmans.

Bruner, J. (1977). *The process of education*. Cambridge, MA: Harvard University Press.

Bybee, R. W., & Sund, R. B. (1982). *Piaget for educators*. Prospect Heights, IL: Waveland Press.

De Pencier, I. B. (1967). *The history of the laboratory schools: The University of Chicago 1896–1965*. Chicago: Quadrangle Books.

Eisner, E. (1994). *The educational imagination: On the design and evaluation of school programs*. Upper Saddle River, NJ: Prentice-Hall.

Gardner, H. (1983). *Frames of mind*. New York: Basic Books.

Gardner, H. (1991). *The unschooled mind: How children think and how schools should teach*. New York: Basic Books.

Good, T. L., & Brophy, J. E. (Eds) (1990). *Educational psychology: A realistic approach*. New York: Longman.

Greeley, K. (2000). *Why fly that way? Linking community and academic achievement*. New York: Teachers College Press.

Incentive Publishers, Inc. (1995). *Multiple intelligences: Bloom's taxonomy of action verbs and student outcomes*. Nashville, TN: Author.

Kendall, J. S., & Marzano, R. J. (1997). *Content knowledge: A compendium of standards and benchmarks for K-12 education*. Aurora, CO: Mid-Continent Regional Educational Laboratory.

Lindamood, P., Bell, N., & Lindamood, P. (1997). Sensory-cognitive factors in the controversy over reading instruction. *The Journal of Developmental and Learning Disorders*, 1(1), 147.

Meier, D. (1995). *The power of their ideas*. Boston: Beacon Press.

Smith, S. (1990). Concrete is not just for buildings: An experiential approach to teaching children with learning disabilities. *Learning Disabilities: A Multidisciplinary Journal, 1*(3), 77.

Smith, S. (1995). *No easy answers: The learning disabled child at home and school*. New York: Bantam Books.

Smith, S. (2001). *The power of the arts: Creative strategies for teaching exceptional learners*. Baltimore, MD: Brookes.

SUBJECT INDEX